Bulls
Balls
Bicycles
&
Actors

BULLS
BALLS
BICYCLES
&
ACTORS

by
CHARLES BICKFORD

PAUL S. ERIKSSON, INC.
New York

To my best friends
Clancy, Cricket, Sugar, Spice and Shane
All registered with the A.K.C.

PREFACE

No man of letters, I. and when an acquaintance of mine, a knowledgeable gent, surprised me with the suggestion that I write the story of my life, my reaction was decidedly in the negative; it being my opinion that excepting a very few political or intellectual personalities who may have something of real importance to express, the writer of an autobiography must either be motivated by extreme ego or by the compulsion to capture a fast buck.

"Egotistical I may be," I answered, "but not to that extent. And although I am not averse to latching on to a fast buck now and then, the compulsion is not that strong."

He argued the point. "Your true story," he said, "is interesting, newsworthy and provocative. It would be an inspiration to millions of people who have supported you over the years. You owe it to them to write this book."

"Nuts," I replied.

"As an artist you are known throughout the world," he continued, "and yet the public knows nothing of you as a person excepting what they may have gleaned from the few facts and many fictions released by motion picture publicity departments. Your public is entitled to know something of the real you. You are an unusually colorful and exciting character—personable, dynamic, sensitive, intelligent, generous, courageous, arrogant, cantankerous, talented and successful."

By this time I was unashamedly weeping. My acquaintance, as you may have gathered, is a most eloquent fellow.

I did manage, however, to recover sufficiently to hold to my negative position. Through my sobs I declared my ignorance of even the elementary principles of semantics, morphology or syntax. I confessed that I know nothing of the system of marks and signs used to separate sentences, independent clauses, parenthetical phrases and so forth.

"In brief," I said, "I am not a writer. And if I were, it so happens that I am one of those eccentric characters who believe they are entitled to a degree of privacy in their personal lives. The answer is no."

Let it be said that my acquaintance did not make his pile by accepting "No" for an answer. He persisted.

"All right," he said, "Preserve your precious privacy. Forget the words 'memoirs' and 'autobiography.' Call it the story of your fifty years in show business. Yours has been an extraordinary career and the story has a fascinating potential. Write it. I'll publish it."

And thereby hangs the tale.

                                          Charles Bickford

Hollywood, California

Bulls
BALLS
BICYCLES
&
ACTORS

NEW YEAR'S eve, 1890. The horse and buggy age; the era of kerosene lamps, primitive heating and unpaved roads. The Bickford family lived in an old frame house on Story Street, in Cambridge, Massachusetts. Harvard college was a stone's throw away and but a few blocks distant stood the blacksmith shop which was the inspiration for Longfellow's "The Village Smithy."

On the morning of December thirty-first it had started to snow and by nightfall the storm had developed into a real ripsnorter of a blizzard. By nine o'clock the Bickford children, Ruth, aged eight, Tom, aged six, John, aged four, and William, aged two, were snug in their beds.

Downstairs in the kitchen, hugging the big range for warmth, sat my father, Loretus, my mother, Mary Ellen, and my maternal grandfather, Captain Tom Woods, skipper of his own two-masted schooner, *Diedre*.

They were waiting for me.

My mother suddenly gasped and said, "I think it's time, Loret. You had better call Doctor Ordway." My father jumped for the wall telephone only to discover that it was dead.

The storm was at its height. The lines were down, the roads were knee deep in snow and the doctor lived four miles across town. My father donned his rubber boots, ear muffs, blanket coat and muffler and plunged into the storm.

Captain Tom helped my mother to bed, stoked the fire, placed buckets of water on the stove and then kept vigil by my mother's side, doing his best to ease and comfort her during the increasingly frequent moments of agony induced by my rapidly mounting impatience.

Three hours passed. The bells began to toll. The old

year of 1890 was about to go out as the new year, and I, came in with a whoop and a holler.

Kicking and scratching, and aided by the fumbling hands of my grandfather, Captain Tom Woods, I made my entrance upon the world stage at exactly one minute past twelve on the morning of January first, eighteen-hundred and ninety-one, anticipating the return of my father and Doctor Ordway who, a few seconds later, rushed into the room.

Doctor Ordway took over as the intrepid Captain Tom, to his later chagrin, quietly fainted.

Appropriate enough, I suppose, that I should have come in on the wings of a blizzard; I've been blowing up a storm ever since.

My earliest recollections begin at the age of five. The family then numbered nine. My sister Esther had arrived in '93 and Dorothy in '95. I remember being thoroughly annoyed because the grownups lavished most of their attention upon those two insignificant little creatures. And when I was instructed to love and protect them because they were my lovely little baby sisters, it was just too much.

I had been blessed with a strong body and robust health and with my snub nose, blue eyes and red-blonde hair, I greatly resembled grandfather Tom. In his own words, I was "the spitting image of him." He lived in East Boston but spent a lot of time at our house and I adored him. I never tired of listening to his stories of the sea and of far places. I began to develop a most colorful vocabulary and would frequently startle my mother with sudden bursts of strange oaths. I had determined that I, too, would be a sea captain. I tried to imitate his way of speaking, and his manner of walking. The results linger to this day.

After I was enrolled at school it became increasingly evident that I was like Captain Tom in more ways than one. I was a rover. I became an habitual truant because of my compulsion to travel. A popular means of transportation was the horse-drawn hack which was usually equipped with a trunk rack at the rear. This was my delight. I would crawl onto one of those racks and ride to the end of the line, wherever it might lead.

At the age of six I had even acquired a police record. It became routine for the police of adjacent cities such as Boston, Somerville, Medford, Everett or Malden to call my parents and deliver the laconic message, "The character is here again. Come and get it."

A newspaper reporter happened to be present one day when I was brought into a Boston precinct station. He wrote a story about me, tagging me with the sobriquet, "Sunshine of Cambridge," evidently because of my hair, which up to this time was worn in long golden-red curls.

The day after the story appeared, a young monster, older and bigger than I and burdened with the erroneous impression that I was some sort of sissy, waylaid me in the school yard and taunted me with such epithets as "Mamma's boy," "Little Lord Fauntleroy," and other endearing names.

I emerged from the fight with sundry bruises, a bloody nose and a cut lip. I was also the winner, having been hauled away from my weeping and recumbent foe by the school janitor and a policeman.

My mother was out when I got home from school, whereupon I found a pair of shears and amputated every curl, close to my head. Later that afternoon when my mother beheld me, to say that she flipped would be an understatement. The situation was aggravated by the arrival of my teacher, bearing charges by the parents of my erst while opponent that I had perpetrated an unprovoked attack upon their offspring and was guilty, according to them, of assault and battery, mayhem and attempted murder.

To my disillusionment and chagrin, my mother, influenced no doubt by my appearance—the swollen nose, bruised face and hacked-off hair gave me a wonderfully villainous look—assumed that I was guilty. After assuring the teacher that proper disciplinary measures would be taken, she locked me in the woodshed where I was to remain, in duress vile, until my father should arrive home from business, at which time my punishment would be decided.

My poor mother didn't know it, of course, but she had lost her baby boy. The apron strings were cut with the closing of that woodshed door. Never again would she be my all-wise guardian angel.

I must have been in solitary about an hour, during which time I had made up my mind to run away to sea. Then, as my mother had left the house, my brother Bill, two years my senior, came to console me. He discovered that the key was still in the lock but was reluctant to set me free until I told him of my plan to run away and be a sea captain like Grandfather Tom.

This idea intrigued him. In fact, he thought it such a hell of a great thing to do that he decided to go with me. There was one hitch, though. He thought that because he was the oldest, he should be the captain, and wouldn't unlock the door until I compromised by agreeing that we would take turns at being captain.

Then I laid low in the shed while Bill raided the kitchen for provisions. He returned with some crackers, a hunk of cheese and some doughnuts wrapped in a towel, and twenty cents which he'd found on the kitchen table.

We slipped stealthily through the back yard, climbed the fence and were on our way to a life of adventure on the seven seas. Reaching Harvard Square, we climbed aboard the trunk rack of a two-horse hack, which, as luck would have it, was bound for Boston.

It was after dark when we alighted from the carriage in the neighborhood of Boylston and Tremont Streets, in Boston. From there, we made our way on foot to Atlantic Avenue and the docks. It was now late at night. We were tired, sleepy, and confused.

There we were, at the very edge of the Atlantic Ocean. And although there were any number of ships in the harbor, we didn't quite know what to do. Every time we approached a pier entrance some sinister looking character would swear at us and chase us away.

Squatting behind garbage cans in an alley, we ate our provisions and discussed the situation. I came up with the answer—Grandfather Tom. His ship was in port, tied up at a dock in East Boston. We'd sign up with his crew. And after much wandering and inquiring, we found the East Boston Ferry slip and boarded a ferry boat.

It was then after midnight and back home, in Cambridge, our parents were frantic with worry. My father was roaming the streets, searching. My mother was at the police station bombarding the harassed officers with requests for reports and with hysterical suggestions.

Bill and I, after a long and exhausting search, found the pier in East Boston where the *Diedre* was berthed. Boarding her, we were confronted by a boozy watchman who chased us off. When we finally got through to him that we were Captain Woods' grandsons come to join the crew, he allowed us to come aboard and, after listening to our story, put us to bed in grandfather's cabin, where we promptly went to sleep.

He then slipped ashore and at the nearest telephone called Grandfather Tom who told him to keep a close eye on us until he got there. Grandfather then called our parents, informed them of the situation, telling them that he would bring us home.

Which he did. Much to my disappointment and disillusionment. Even grandfather Tom didn't understand. It all seemed to add up to the fact that a kid just could not put his trust in grownups. Any grownups.

And so I was brought back to face charges brought by the stupid parents of the kid I had beaten. What griped me was that my own parents seemed to believe the lying little bastard's story. I clammed up and even when brought before the school principal, I refused to deny nor admit the charges. After some vague talk about possible suspension, the matter was dropped.

But the repercussions lingered on. Every tough kid in the neighborhood seemed impelled to take a crack at me. At the beginning these encounters were rather scary but before long I began to look forward to them. The reason being, I suppose, that I almost always managed to emerge the victor. I was licked once, I'll admit, but by a much older and heavier boy.

When grandpa Tom heard about that defeat he took me in hand and taught me how to handle myself in a rough and tumble fight. "Forget about rules," he said. "There aren't any rules in an alley fight and if you try to fight clean, you'll end up on a slab. The world is full of vicious people, young and old, and whenever one of them shows any signs of coming at you, slug the son-of-a-bitch and sink him. You can always argue later, if you have to."

Sound advice. And I was an apt pupil. I was never beaten again and as time passed, so formidable grew my reputation that it was a tough kid indeed who went out of his way to pick a scrap with me.

Meanwhile, I had acquired two pals. One was a kindred spirit of my own age named Johnnie O'Brien. Johnnie's father was dead and his mother supported herself and Johnnie by dress-making. The other was a dog. His name was Tige, and he was a genuine, dyed-in-the-wool, all-American dog. Old, unbeautiful and positively not house-broken; he was no prize, but he was my first dog and I loved him.

Tige had come into my life one day when I found him, bone-thin, swarming with fleas and desperately searching for someone to accept the love and devotion he was brimming with.

I took him home and, knowing my father would refuse to let me keep him, sneaked him into the house. We had back stairs so it was no problem to smuggle him up to my room in the attic.

We had baked ham for dinner that night. After dinner I swiped a big piece of what was left. Judging from the way Tige gulped it, together with a huge slab of corn bread, it was the first meal he had enjoyed in a long time.

Later that night, when everyone else was sleeping, I sneaked him out to kick a tree in the back yard. Then, after fixing him a bed in the corner of my room, I went to sleep, confident that everything was ship-shape for the night. But I had not reckoned with old Tige's fleas. He was constantly on the scratch and each time he

scratched, he beat a tattoo on the floor with his elbow. As
my father's room was directly below mine it was not too
surprising that by four a.m. the repetitious tattoo had
penetrated his consciousness and prompted him to investigate.

Meanwhile, poor Tige, unused to the rich fattiness of
baked ham, had suffered an acute attack of diarrhea.
Thus it was that when my father, who had neglected to
put on his slippers, entered my room, he stepped directly
onto, and into, an unsavory mess that had been deposited
in a most strategic location.

Poor father. Poor Tige. And poor me.

My father, ordinarily a very well balanced man, hit
the rafters. His rage was heroic. He loosed oaths I'm sure
even grandpa Tom had never heard of and, of course,
woke everyone in the house. Soon the entire family was
gathered in my little room. Father, instead of gaining the
sympathy which he so ardently desired, found himself an
object of mirth. Never had I seen or heard my mother
laugh so heartily. And so contagious was her laugh, and
so comical did my father look—standing first on one foot
and then on the other, all the while cursing at the top of
his voice—that they all followed suit. And the louder
they laughed, the louder he yelled, and the madder he
got. And the madder he grew, the more hysterical they
got. And the more hysterical they got, the more difficult
it was for me to keep from laughing too.

Then Tige got into the act. At first, he had been frightened by all these people but suddenly deciding that the
whole thing was some sort of a game, he began to crouch
and leap around my father, barking an invitation to the
chase. His ridiculous antics tickled my father's funny
bone and he suddenly began to laugh.

It wasn't until then that I let go. My mistake. When my father saw me laugh he remembered that he was very angry with me, and with Tige. My reckoning was postponed until morning but Tige was banished immediately. Because of the coldness of the night, however, my mother interceded and Tige was permitted to spend the rest of the night in the basement.

The next day, after a rough session, my father relented and decreed that I could keep Tige.

Johnnie O'Brien shared my fondness for Tige and the three of us became inseparable. We had many things in common. For instance, we loved a good scrap. Tige was getting on in age; he wasn't too steady on his legs and his teeth were blunting up. But he had heart and if attacked would fight anything from a Chihuahua to an elephant. Johnnie was short and chunky; his build suggested that he'd been quarried. Slow to anger, he punched like a mule kicks and woe to any poor slob that tangled with him. Neither quarrelsome nor vicious, we never sought trouble, although I must admit that we never sidestepped when we saw it coming.

The three of us were born rovers and equally averse to confinement of any sort. Particularly repugnant to Johnnie and me was the restriction necessitated by attendance at classes, the result being that we set a record for truancy that I doubt has ever been equaled.

We developed a system. Mornings we would leave our respective homes with school books under our arms and meet at some pre-determined spot. From there, season and weather dictated our course. We'd go swimming, hiking, skating, or to work. We had a deal with a black-smith whose shop was located across town. During school hours we'd ride horses to and from the owners' barns. For this we received a dime a mount. When it came time for school to be out, we'd quit work and go home.

We had no report card problem. Johnnie had pinched a package of virgin report cards from a teacher's desk. We became expert forgers and our mothers were ever pleased by our unvarying high marks. Amazingly, we got away with it for an entire semester and well into a second before the inevitable dénouement.

It came on a Saturday morning. Johnnie and I were in the basement of my house where my brother Bill and I had set up a gymnasium of sorts. Our equipment consisted of boxing gloves, flying rings and a trapeze. As added attractions, Bill raised Belgian hares there and my specialty in the zoological line was white mice.

On that particular morning, Johnnie and I were watching in wide-eyed fascination as a litter of white mice was born into the world. Tige had been with us but as his interest seemed to be limited to the notion that the tiny newcomers were but potential tidbits, we had relegated him to the back yard.

My mother suddenly called from upstairs and asked me to hurry down to the drug store and pick up a prescription she had ordered filled. After admonishing Johnnie to intervene in case the mother mouse developed cannibalistic tendencies, I started for the drug store, situated on the far side of the main street, a block and a half away. A trolley-car line operated along the main street and as I crossed the tracks, a car was approaching. It was coming fast but as it was far enough away to give me time and to spare for safety, my awareness of it was purely automatic.

Then, as I was entering the store, I heard the frantic

clanging of the gong and turned just in time to catch a fleeting glimpse of Tige. The little guy had jumped the fence and followed me. And as I watched, the car bore down on him and he disappeared.

Yelling in anguish, I rushed forward, hoping against hope that he had escaped the wheels. But it was forlorn hope. The car, which had slowed almost to a stop, picked up speed and continued on its way, disclosing the decapitated remains of my poor little friend.

Sobbing hysterically, I moved what was left of him to the side of the road. Then, still crying, I took off for home, running at top speed. I slipped into the basement by way of the bulkhead entrance at the back of the house, scaring the bejesus out of Johnnie by my wild appearance. I was smeared with Tige's blood and was still sobbing. As he'd never seen me cry before, he realized that something tremendous had happened and bombarded me with questions as I grabbed up my repeating air rifle and dashed out again.

Johnnie followed closely as I ran all the way back to the scene of the accident and the only answer he got to his queries was, "I'm going to kill the son-of-a-bitch."

I knew that the trolley car was part of a shuttle service and that the end of the line was but ten blocks away. At that point, the two man crew, consisting of the motorman and a conductor, would reverse the trolley pole and start on the return trip. And when the car reached the spot where Tige had died, I'd be there, waiting.

We reached the scene with minutes to spare and when Johnnie saw Tige and realized what had happened, he cried too. When I explained that the motorman hadn't even stopped the car, he nearly went berserk.

Then we saw the car coming. Moving out to the middle of the tracks, we stood shoulder to shoulder, grimly determined that Tige's killer would not see the light of another day.

In those days the street cars had open platforms; thus the motormen, when performing their duties, were not only exposed to the elements but, as in this instance, to the vengeance of grief-maddened little boys.

As the trolley approached, the motorman stomped on his gong, just as he had when he had seen Tige before him. The conductor came forward and stood in the doorway watching as the motorman, realizing that we had no intention of getting out of the way, frantically turned the big brass handle that controlled the braking apparatus.

The car came to a jolting stop about ten feet from us and as it did, I pulled the trigger. A little black spot appeared in the center of the man's forehead and he slumped back into the arms of the bewildered conductor. I was sure I had killed him. And I was glad.

A crowd seemed to materialize from thin air. Someone snatched the rifle from my hands; then Johnnie and I were grabbed and held.

Mr. Robie, the druggist, came running from his store and took command of the situation. He had the injured man carried into his store for first aid treatment, phoned for an ambulance, notified the police, and brought Johnnie and me away from the crowd to the shelter of his office.

In due time the motorman was taken to a hospital. Johnnie and I were loaded into the Black Maria and carted off to the police station. Our parents were notified and we were held until a report came from the hospital that the victim was not seriously injured. The frontal bone had been dented but not cracked, nor penetrated.

He was suffering mostly from shock and a severe head-ache.

Johnnie was absolved of any guilt in the matter and I was released in the custody of my parents pending a hearing which was held three days later.

As the hearing got underway, it was brought home to me that if one cherished his privacy, he must never fall afoul of the law. All of my most cherished secrets, and Johnnie's, were disclosed as a veritable army of witnesses paraded to the stand. Among others there were the school principal, teachers, a truant officer, a schoolboard member, parents of kids I had allegedly beaten up, the blacksmith Johnnie and I had worked for, policemen, and the motorman and conductor.

All of our heinous crimes were revealed, including Johnnie's theft of the report cards, our forgeries and our truancies. I began to feel that the whole world was out to blast us as unregenerate delinquents.

The feeling began to change though, when my father's attorney, who was representing me, commenced his cross-examination of some of these witnesses. He made monkeys of most of them and reduced the unfortunate motorman to minced meat. He forced him to admit his awareness of running over the dog and to confess fleeing the scene of the accident in the hope that it had gone unobserved.

It was after this testimony that the judge took over, and what a blistering he gave that poor devil. He also blasted me, explaining the evil consequences of attempting to take the law into my hands, but cited extenuating circumstances—my age, the grief occasioned by the death of my dog and the anger induced by the callous indifference of the motorman. Then, after admonishing my father to put a stop to my truancy, he dismissed the proceedings.

The real ruckus began that night at my home. Grandpa Tom was there; also my mother's brother, my uncle Ambrose. After dinner, my brothers and sisters were banished to their rooms and I was put on the grill. Truthful as always, I admitted to everything that had come to light at the hearing—and more. It was not a confession; it was a simple statement of facts. And although I was sorry for nothing I had done, I was not defiant. I did my best to explain my aversion to school. Because it was a place I was forced to go, I hated it. I couldn't stand being shut in. I yearned to be in the open, to swim in the river, walk in the fields, to go places.

My mother was fairly sympathetic but reminded me that in a few years I would be a grown man and that I must start now to educate myself so that I would be prepared to shoulder my responsibilities as a proper member of society.

The others backed her strongly. Grandpa Tom, who I think had complete understanding of me, said, "Your mother is telling you right, Charlie. You must have a proper education. Otherwise you'll wind up a bum, or find yourself swinging a pick for the rest of your life at fifty cents an hour."

I really couldn't see anything too frighening in the prospect of being a bum. And fifty cents an hour sounded pretty good to me. But to save further argument I went along with the pitch and promised to do my best to stop playing hooky.

So far, so good. Everyone was pleased. Everybody but me, that is. I wasn't enjoying this little session one little bit and the worst was yet to come. I felt that my mother wouldn't let me off the hook until I expressed proper regret for my murderous attack on the motorman. And I knew that no pressure could squeeze the tiniest iota of repentance from me. At that time my only regret was that the air rifle had not been a real gun. It was going to take a lot of convincing to change my attitude. And mother was clearly out to supply that conviction.

If I have termed the judge's rather sympathetic diatribe a blast, mother's denunciation must be recorded as a holocaust. She cited no extenuating circumstances. Age, grief and anger were but incidental to the glaring fact that I had committed an assault with intent to kill.

After doing her utmost to impress me with the enormity of my crime, she pleaded with me to admit the error of my ways and to repent. But the best she could get out of me was my oft repeated statement that I had tried to kill the son-of-a-bitch and that I'd do it again.

Poor mother. It must have been a trying experience for her to be forced to the conclusion that her angel child had a vicious streak in him. It all tied in, she said, with my proclivity for fighting.

Finally, provoked by my unregenerate attitude, she even turned on grandpa Tom. "It's easy to see where he gets it," she said. She blamed his influence for my foul language which she declared was unfit even for the forecastle of a ship. She castigated him for having given me boxing lessons which were responsible for my becoming a monstrous young bully. It was largely his fault, she said, that I had gotten out of hand, that I was going from bad to worse and that in all likelihood I would eventually be expelled from school and sent to a reformatory. She said she'd rather see me dead than have that happen.

Both my father and uncle Ambrose tried to intervene

but my grandfather stopped them. "Let her alone," he
said. "It's good for her to get it out of her system. She's a
bit hysterical now but she'll think better of it later."

But mother was really on the prod. "I mean every
word I'm saying, father," she said. "You're ruining that
boy and it's got to stop."

Grandpa was furious. "Now you're going too far,
Mary," he said. "If you'd use half the brains you were
born with, you'd realize it's you that's doing the ruining.
You and your Goddamned ridiculous curls. You should
know by this time that you'll never make a tame cat out
of this boy. He's got the makings of a real two-balled
man—the kind that'll stand on his own two legs and fight
the world for what he wants."

"That's just the trouble," mother snapped. "He's nine
years old and he's fighting the world already. What's
going to become of him ten years from now? He's trying
to pattern himself after you, father. Can't you see that?"

"And what the Hell is wrong with that?"

"Everything. You were born out of your age, father.
You should have been a buccaneer—a pirate. You're
giving him the wrong outlook on life and if it goes on
something dreadful will happen to him. It's got to stop.
Otherwise I'll have to ask you to stay away from my
home."

For one dreadful moment I thought Grandpa Tom
was going to cry. I don't think I could have stood that.
He stared at her incredulously, then turned to me and I
saw that his eyes were kind of misty. He just stood there
looking at me, and although he said nothing, I knew he
was blessing me. Finally he reached out and gave me a
little pat on the head. Then he was gone.

I'm the one who cried. Then my mother put her arms
around me and she cried too.

A few days later we learned that grandpa had gathered his crew together and sailed. We didn't see him again for nearly three years. We all missed him, me most of all. And although mother never let on, what he had said to her about me had its effect. She reversed her attitude towards me, seeming to have more understanding of her maverick son. Her tactics of gentle persuasion worked to the extent that I did my damndest to be what they used to call "a good boy."

The remaining years of grade school were uneventful. I had, of course, acquired a measure of celebrity. To my elders I was probably the boy most likely to end up in the electric chair. To my contemporaries and the younger kids I was a hero of sorts. Johnnie also. We continued to be close pals and although we at times reverted to our truant tendencies, we managed to concentrate on our studies to the extent that in due time we graduated and entered high school.

My brother John had enrolled at Massachusetts Institute of Technology and was working part time for an engineering firm which was engaged in a bridge project near Boston. I visited him on the job a few times and became fired with the ambition of becoming a construction engineer. I decided that after finishing high school I, too, would enroll at M.I.T.

By this time grandpa Tom had sold his ship and retired from the sea. Mother and he had resolved their differences and he was again a welcome and frequent visitor at our home. It was to him that I first confided my new objective. And although he was frankly disappointed that I was not to follow in his footsteps, he backed me up a hundred percent.

"It's not what you do but what you really want to do

that's important," he said, "and if you're honestly determined to be a construction engineer, that's what you
should be." Furthermore, he insisted that he be allowed
to finance the course.

My parents were delighted by these events and for the
next three years I buckled down to my studies. It really
began to look as though my feet were set firmly on the
path that leads to foursquare respectability.

During my senior year in high school Grandfather
Tom died. As I had loved him very much, it was understandable that I should mourn his passing but, strangely
enough, my ambition died with him. Whatever the reason, I lost interest in my studies and, after a few weeks of
desultory attendance at classes, I dropped out of school.

Johnnie O'Brien, true pal that he was, went stupid at
the same time. We took to roaming the Boston water-
front where we occasionally got jobs hustling freight on
the docks.

We acquired a taste for drinking; it was not unusual
for us to kill a full quart of rye whiskey in a day.

The slum districts held a peculiar fascination for us. I
can't tell what we were seeking. Surely not romance. I
presume we were flexing our muscles, developing a few
callouses and getting our first peep into the world of violence and vice.

One cold blustery day we passed a labor recruiting
office where they were signing men to work in a lumber
camp. The pay was thirty a month and found. The camp
was situated in northern Maine and the crew was to leave
that night via the Boston and Maine Railroad.

The idea of spending a winter in the North Woods
appealed to me, but Johnnie couldn't see any percentage
in the deal. Even if he favored the idea, he explained, he

couldn't go for it because his mother was ill and needed him at home.

He did his best to talk me out of it. "Look at them," he said, indicating the men who swarmed about the place. "They're the crummiest bunch of bums I ever saw. It must be a pretty lousy set up if they're reduced to hiring that kind of scum. Forget it."

But I had the urge and signed on. The train was scheduled to leave the North Station at seven p.m., leaving plenty of time for me to purchase heavy clothing and boots before knocking off a few farewell drinks with Johnnie.

My last act before boarding the train was to phone my mother and tell her my plans. As I expected she would, she did her best to dissuade me. My poor, dear mother. To her dying day she thought of me as her baby boy and I'm afraid I caused her more worry than the rest of the family combined.

She was the more alarmed by this lumber-camp caper because she'd become aware of my drinking habits, and her imagination pictured the dire things that could happen to me if I got out of line in an isolated camp full of tough lumberjacks. Not that I blamed her. It alarms me, now that I think of it. But she bowed to the inevitable and after receiving my promise that I'd take good care of myself, she gave me her blessing.

I had a brief feeling of nostalgic loneliness as I hung up. After all, I was only a kid. But it was displaced by an exultant sense of adventure as I reached the gate and joined the motley crew of derelicts and tough mugs— some of them reeling drunk—which were being herded through by a burly "Canuck" foreman.

We boarded a battered old day coach, the fetid atmos-

phere of which was indescribable. The stench of unwashed humanity, excrement, cheap whiskey and vomit,
mingled with an ammoniacal miasma emanating from
the filthy lavatory, turned my stomach and forced me to
spend most of the long, sleepless night on the open rear
platform of the train. I nearly came down with pneumonia but at least I could breathe out there.

In the morning at Bangor, Maine, we changed trains
and even though I was tired, cold and hungry, I was still
imbued with a haunting, secret excitement.

After an all day ride through the ruggedly beautiful
Maine landscape, we were disembarked at a siding near
the Canadian border. The ground was knee deep in snow
and the temperature well below zero as we were loaded
onto horse-drawn pungs and driven six miles through the
woods to the camp.

We were fed an enormous meal, consisting of beef
stew, boiled potatoes, corn bread and coffee, after which
we were assigned to work gangs, then shown to our quarters which consisted of two large, log bunk houses. Word
was passed that we'd be turned out at five a.m. for breakfast.

I turned in and despite the raucous din, fell almost
immediately into a sound sleep.

It was pitch dark and quiet when I woke to the startled
awareness that I was no longer alone. All I could tell was
that he was huge and stank like a goat.

The guy was as strong as a bear and when I struggled
to get out of the bunk he pinned me down and clasped a
filthy hand over my mouth. I sank my teeth into it whereupon he yelled like a Comanche and started to slug me. I
fought back as well as I could but lying on my back in
the narrow bunk with the big brute now sitting astride

me, I was fairly helpless and yelled for help as he let me have it with both fists.

Everybody in the place woke up and gathered around. Someone lighted a lamp and in the dim light I recognized my assailant as a man who had been pointed out to me on the train as a tough guy and bully.

Nobody made a move to help me and I knew that I might be maimed for life, or possibly killed by this drink-maddened animal.

Strictly on my own, I thought of my grandfather and some of the tricks he had taught me. I tore hanks of hair from his head, gouged at his eyes with my thumbs, tore at his face with my nails until finally, with the aid of a well-placed knee in his groin, I got away from his clutch and out of the bunk.

Then, for the next ten minutes I was engaged in the toughest fight of my life. When the end came I was cut, bruised, breathless and exhausted.

But, as the fellow says, "You should have seen the other guy." I had cold-cocked him and stretched out on the floor he looked like something that had been caught prowling around a den of wild cats.

The men showered congratulations on me but I would have none of it, calling them a bunch of God-damned cowardly bastards and ordering them to stay the hell away from me.

Then, grabbing up my blankets, I went out to a three-sided structure that sheltered the hay supply, where I spent the rest of the night.

I awoke to find myself a personage. There were forty men in that camp and I was the sole topic of conversation. I was a "scrapper"—I could "hit like a mule kicks"—I "sure knew how to handle my dukes." In fact so formidable had been the reputation of the man I had whipped that there was no doubt I was Paul Bunyan returned to the North Woods.

Scuttlebutt had it that superintendent, Joe Bigelow, was the toughest boss in the industry. When you worked for Bigelow, you delivered, or else. He allowed nothing to interfere with getting out the logs. So I guess I walked pretty small after I got the word to report to him in his office.

I was amazed to find him a little guy, about five foot eight, thin, wiry, dark, and wearing a big mustache. But what a big little guy he was—quiet, well-spoken, and fairly oozing authority. The first second I looked at him I had the feeling that everything was going to be all right.

"Good morning, champ," he said. "Sit down. Tell me about yourself."

I did just that. Such was the confidence he inspired that in a few minutes he knew just as much of my background as I did.

It wasn't until I had spilled everything that he started asking questions; he wanted to hear more about my grandfather, the reason for my dropping out of school, and my future plans after this job finished in April. Finally he came to the subject of the fight. He wanted to know if the man had accosted me during the trip from Boston, if I had had any argument or discussion with him during or after supper.

He was vastly amused that I still hadn't the slightest inkling as to why I had been attacked and said it was high time I learned a few facts of life. The man's name was Carl Swenson, a veteran lumber jack, famed in the camps for his prowess as a fighter and notorious as a homosexual.

I found this hard to believe. I had heard of this perversion but pictured a pansy as something puny, fastidious and feminine. I could hardly reconcile this image with the brawny, tough and vicious Swenson.

Bigelow spelled it out for me, explaining that homosexuality was prevalent among tough men who were isolated from feminine society for long periods of time—sailors, for instance, and convicts. "You can scratch many a tough guy and draw mother's milk," he said. Swenson, he explained, had selected me to be his chicken and when I had resisted, he had attempted to beat me into submission.

He laughed at my embarrassment on learning that I'd been fighting to protect my virtue.

I was not amused. "Why," I asked, "if you know about him, do you hire a character like that?"

A man's morals, he explained, were his own concern and that all he asked was that a man do the work he was paid to do. "Swenson," he said, "is one hell of a good lumberjack and in these days they're hard to come by."

"And just what do you expect me to do if the bastard attacks me again?" I asked.

"Beat the hell out of him, just as you did last night. All I ask is that you don't kill him. I need him to work. But I'll guarantee he won't bother you again. He'll walk soft around you from now on. So will the other Jaspers in this camp. Which brings me to the point of this conversation. I like the cut of your jib. You're a smart kid and you can handle yourself. Beating up Swenson has given you enormous prestige and I've got a hunch you can keep the men in line. How would you like to be my assistant?"

"I'd love it."

As of that day, my pay was raised to sixty dollars a

month and I found myself boss of forty men. Bigelow had a cot moved into his office which became my sleeping quarters. I loved the job and the men appeared to like me for I evidently performed very well.

There were no more passes made at me, nor were there any fights. That is, with me. Among the men there were many quarrels and my practice was to let them fight it out. Some of them were injured; a few badly. Fortunately, no one was killed.

By the middle of December there had been a couple of heavy snow falls and the camp was snowed in, meaning that until April we were in complete isolation. I thrived in the frosty air and the working hours were a glory to me.

Not so the leisure hours. At the start I spent many after dinner hours chewing the fat with Joe Bigelow, thoroughly enjoying the conversation and his bourbon whiskey, of which he had a goodly stock. But early in January Joe had a bad fall and wrenched his back. He suffered a great deal and took to hitting the sack around nine o'clock. This left me with a surfeit of time on my hands.

I tried the early-to-bed business but soon gave it up as I was seldom able to get to sleep until after midnight.

Mostly I mingled with the men in the bunk houses, sat in on the poker games and entered into their conversations. There were some intelligent guys among them but we didn't have much in common. I was no Puritan but their preoccupation with sex, booze, bodily functions and the female anatomy bored me stiff and I soon gave up this attempt at sociability.

The situation was relieved somewhat when Joe gave me access to his library which consisted of stacks of mystery, detective and Western stories.

Then there were the Sundays—the longest days in my experience. I would have enjoyed walking in the woods but that was out because of the deep snow. Hunting was out as I could find no pleasure in shooting animals. Which left fishing.

The camp was located on the edge of a sizable lake and most of the men enjoyed fishing through the ice. I tried it, of course.

The procedure was to erect a tent on the ice and place a kerosene stove in it to generate warmth. Then we'd saw great holes in the three-foot-thick ice. Baited hooks would be dropped into the holes, the lines attached to flag signals. And sitting in the comparative warmth of the tent, we'd suck on jugs of rotgut whiskey and wait for bites.

When a flag went up we'd rush out and haul up the catch, usually a three-to-four-foot-long pike or muskellunge. Bringing them up was about as exciting as hauling in a log. They put up no struggle at all and froze solid almost instantly after reaching the air. Baked with plenty of onions and potatoes, though, they were excellent eating.

Eventually I came to spend most Sundays in the office, shooting the breeze with Joe Bigelow and watching him drink himself into a stupor. I drank right along with him but for some inexplicable reason, unless it was that I had a hollow leg, the booze didn't seem to have much effect upon me.

The winter wore on with nothing particularly eventful happening until one icy morning when we rolled out to find the mess hall dark, the stove cold and the cook missing. He was a fat and surly German named Ferguson who was about fifty years old and a boozefighter.

We tracked him into the woods and found him frozen

stiff about a mile from camp. The poor, lonely old guy had drunk himself blind and sometime during the night had wandered into the woods to die.

The body was wrapped in a tarpaulin and stashed high in a tree. There it would remain until spring when it would be hauled out to civilization and the death reported to the authorities.

I was paid off in early May. Joe Bigelow drove me to the railhead. He told me that it would please him very much if I decided to go back to school. "A college education gives a man a big edge," he said, "but in case, just in case you should make the wrong decision, I want you to remember that you can always count on a job with me. You can find me through the Lumbermen's Association."

Joe Bigelow was one of the few people I have ever really liked and as the train pulled out I stood on the rear platform waving until I could no longer see him. And, like a small boy waving "Goodbye" to his Daddy, perhaps for the last time, I had to swallow a great big lump in my throat.

I arrived in Boston, happy, healthy and rich. I had close to three hundred iron men in my pocket. I lingered in the big city just long enough to buy presents for all of the family, then made tracks for home.

Feeling like a conquering hero home from the wars, I made a big entrance but was sadly disappointed by my reception.

Only my parents seemed to show any interest in my adventures. It seemed that my brothers and sisters were living lives of their own. My three brothers now considered themselves men of affairs; my oldest sister Ruth's full attention was devoted to a parlor-sitting suitor whom she subsequently married. My kid sisters had become beautiful young sirens. Esther, now sixteen, and Dorothy, fourteen, were much too involved with a swarm of admirers to be anything but bored by my tales of adventure in what they termed a dirty old lumber camp.

At that time I was well aware that I had reached a plateau of sorts. To progress, it was all important that I chart a course for my future. If engineering was to be my choice of profession, it was high time for me to resume my schooling. Thanks to my grandfather, finances were no problem. I planned to engage a tutor and prepare for matriculation at M.I.T.

For Johnnie O'Brien it was also a year of decision. His mother had died in the interim, and now, deprived of her restraining influence, Johnnie was like a ship without a rudder. Of one thing he was certain. He had no intention of going back to school and was appalled by my plan to spend at least four years at MIT.

He drew a dismal picture of my probable future. "What will you have to look forward to? You'll fall for some biscuit and before you know what's happening to you, she'll have her hooks into you and you'll be married. Then the kids will start coming and you'll be stuck for the rest of your life. You'll conform to all the stupid conventions, keep out of trouble and become a solid citizen. And if you're lucky enough to live that long, at the age of sixty you'll be a dull, dried up, frustrated old duffer, whining because life has passed you by. If that's what you want, go to it. But so far as I'm concerned, it's strictly for the Wonks."—"Wonk" being a word coined by Johnnie to designate what today is called a "square."

I must confess that the conventional pattern of life was as repugnant to me as it was to him. Consequently, I had little to offer in rebuttal except to stress the handicap of being adrift in the world without a trade or profession.

"So I'm a born drifter," he admitted, cheerfully. "Drifter, bum, call it what you like. I intend to get some pleasure out of life. And the first thing I'm going to do is to get away from this God-damned town. It was lousy to my mother and I hate it."

"Where will you go?"

"First, New York City. After that, I don't know. Everywhere . . ."

A few nights following this particular conversation, Johnnie and I were aboard a Fall River Line boat, bound for New York.

It had been a strictly inadvertent move on my part. I had gone to see Johnnie off and at the last minute decided to go along. I had no intention of accompanying him on an extended bumming tour of the world and planned, after a few days of sight-seeing in the big town, to return home and further my own plans.

The Fall River Line operated small coastal steamers between Fall River, Massachusetts, a town near Boston, and New York City. An overnight trip, the accommodations were inexpensive and correspondingly inelegant, but to us, embarking on our first ocean voyage—there were times when land was not in sight—the trip smacked of adventure and romance.

We spent most of the night on the boat deck, watching the moonlight on the water and speculating on the high old time we would have in the big town. Neither of us slept.

My first impression of New York was not very propitious. The morning broke warm and humid and as the ship veered in towards New York Harbor the air suddenly became permeated with a nauseating stench. Thinking we must be passing the putrifying carcass of a whale, we looked in every direction but saw nothing but water.

I asked a passing deck hand what was causing the stink. He sniffed, tentatively, then growled "What stink? You got complaints, tell 'em to the captain."

He continued on his way, leaving Johnnie and me gaping at each other. Then, concluding that the poor guy had lost the use of his smeller, we sought out another sailor.

"What's that awful stink," I asked.

"Stink?" He looked surprised. "I don't smell nothing." Then, suddenly comprehending, he continued, "Unless you mean New York."

"For Christ's sake," said Johnnie. "You mean that's New York we smell?"

The sailor grinned. "Don't let it throw you, kid. Coming in from the open sea, big cities always smell like that. Especially when there's an off-shore breeze, like this morning."

Suddenly New York had lost its glamour. But as the ship steamed up the harbor, the sights and sounds of the shipping, the bridges, and above all the magnificent Manhattan sky line excited me to the extent that I didn't notice the smell.

We found a room in a shabby old brownstone, somewhere in the west forties, where my first act was to write a note to my parents, explaining my absence and forewarning them that I might just do a little gallivanting and see something of the country before going back to school.

Then we set out to see the sights—and, what sights!

The throngs of hurrying people, the skyscrapers, the traffic, the thousands of pretty, smartly dressed girls, the variegated neighborhoods, the vista and the noise added up to make Boston look like a village. Each day as we discovered new and colorful districts to explore, my first unfortunate impression faded and I had to concede that New York was one hell of an exciting place.

Came the inevitable day when I had to face the fact that I was no longer wealthy. The two hundred dollars I had arrived in New York with was all but gone. We quit living it up and started job hunting. I went to work for a brewery as a striker, or helper, on a truck, hauling kegged beer from the brewery for delivery to saloons. the horses were a magnificent team of matched grey Percherons and I was highly elated when after a couple of days the driver, a two hundred and ten pound moron named Muller, allowed me to drive them. The work was hard and the kegs of beer were heavy but I liked the job. It paid forty dollars a week—not bad pay for that era.

Arriving home from work one evening, I found Johnnie very excited about a job he had landed.

He had been furnished with a salesman's kit, consisting of an impressive brochure—photographs of a beautiful lake and surroundings, drawings of a magnificent proposed club house, blue prints of a one-hundred-and-sixty-acre subdivision, indicating impressive lots, paved streets, lighting, sewers, and other features.

The brochure disclosed that this Garden of Eden was located in New Jersey, a beautiful mountain wonderland overlooking the Delaware river. The surrounding forests abounded in game and the crystal waters of a private lake teemed with fish.

The Dreamwold Hunting and Fishing Club, Inc., was

offering for a limited time only, membership in this exclusive club for one thousand dollars. The membership included clear title to a choice of the available building lots—first come, first served.

The salesmen were to be furnished leads obtained from return coupon advertisements in magazines and newspapers.

They were to be paid salaries of twenty-five dollars per week against commissions of thirty percent.

Johnnie was to work out of the main office in Newark and had been allotted the exclusive territory of East Orange.

I was nearly as excited about the setup as Johnnie. It sounded like a bonanza and in comparison made my poor forty-a-week sound like nothing.

Then Johnnie, delighted by my reaction, told me that he had already set up an interview for me with Mr. Herkimer, field sales manager of the organization.

In retrospect, I see Mr. Daniel Herkimer as a flashily dressed, shifty eyed, glib-talking con man but at that time he impressed me as a well-dressed, affable and businesslike gentleman. After asking a few questions about my background, he handed me a typewritten sales pitch, a sales kit, an envelope full of leads, and allotted me the city of Elizabeth, New Jersey, as my territory.

Johnnie and I left the office together and after congratulating each other on our good luck, set out to make our fortunes; he to his territory in East Orange and I to Elizabeth-town.

Two weeks passed. Neither of us had closed a deal. Mr. Herkimer's affability had lessened and it was clear that if we didn't deliver soon, we'd both get bounced.

As all of the other salesmen were earning good money,

two of them averaging well over two thousand dollars a month, I knew the fault must be our own. Cornering one of the top salesmen, I asked him to listen to my spiel and tell me what was wrong with my approach.

He was very accommodating and after listening to my sales talk told me there was nothing wrong with it. "Don't forget," he said, "you're working virgin territory and it's bound to be rough going until after you sign up a few prospects. People like to know who their fellow club-members and neighbors are going to be."

Those few words furnished the key. One of my first leads had been a prominent Elizabeth surgeon who had been sufficiently interested to have me revisit him. I re-called that he had asked about the present membership and that his interest had faded when I replied that the project was just getting under way.

Taking the sub-division blue print from my kit, I asked the sales manager to check off the lots that had been sold and to write in the names of the buyers. There were more than fifty names but not one from Elizabeth. Nor were there any from East Orange.

Again I called upon the surgeon. Showing him the blue print, I pointed out the names of prominent citizens of Newark, Irvington, Montclair, Bloomfield and other towns. I emphasized the fact that Elizabeth was not rep-resented and explained that because it was still virgin territory, I was prepared to make him a proposition. I offered him a club membership and his choice of any available lot in return for the names of four friends who might be interested in joining the club.

He went for the deal and while I was filling in the necessary forms for his signature, he made several phone calls which resulted in two sales on that very day.

That evening I found Johnnie singing the blues but he segued into *Glory Hallelujah* without missing a beat when I showed him the three signed contracts and the checks for two thousand dollars. When I told him the full story of my day, he wouldn't have it that I was anything less than a bloody genius. He decided to emulate me.

There was one fly in the ointment. It was quite possible that when I reported in to the sales manager, I'd be fired on the spot.

On the following morning Johnnie waited in the outer office while I had my session with Herkimer. If I came out in one piece, he would then ask his approval to follow my procedure.

Herkimer sat silently and stared at me while I explained in detail what I had done to sign up the doctor. I had seen more warmth in the eyes of a dead cod fish.

And when I handed him the doctor's contract, he didn't even look at it, but asked, very quietly, "Just what do you expect me to do about this?"

"I hoped you would O.K. it, sir," I said.

"I see," and he really looked very angry. "And what in hell do you think we're running here—a charitable institution?"

"Please hear me out, sir," I said. "If it had been a conventional deal, my commission would have amounted to three hundred dollars which leaves seven hundred I owe the company. Right?"

"Right. And I suppose you expect to pay us out of future commissions."

"Yes, sir. And here's the first six hundred."

With that, I handed him the other two contracts and the two one-thousand dollar checks.

His eyes bugged and for a long moment he examined

the papers. Then, murmuring "Well, I'll be God-
damned," he got up and, still holding the papers, went
quickly into the vice president's office.

Five minutes later he reappeared, smiling, and called
me in to meet the vice president, Mr. Blackmer, a roly-
poly, benevolent looking man.

Mr. Blackmer informed me that although my procedure had been highly irregular, it revealed a rare initia-
tive which should be rewarded. Therefore he had decided
that the company would cancel out the hundred dollars
still owing. Pulling an enormous roll of bills from his
pocket, he handed me two fifty-dollar bills as an extra
bonus for my good thinking.

For the next couple of months Johnnie and I lived like
pigs in clover. Johnnie had gotten the green light to copy
my procedure and the two of us were doing all right. Not
a week passed without each of us ringing up at least one
sale. One week I scored a record three. We were a pretty
cocky pair of kids, firmly convinced that we were on our
way to riches.

But it was not to be.

One morning, as we approached the office, we saw a
couple of police cars parked before the building. There
were a few bystanders, among whom were two of our
fellow salesmen. They broke the sad tidings that the
Bunco Squad was raiding the offices of the Dreamwold
Hunting and Fishing Club, Inc. Mr. Herkimer had already been nabbed and the cops were waiting for Mr.
Blackmer to show.

They couldn't tell us what the charges were and Johnnie and I decided not to wait around to find out. We got
away from there fast.

The whole set-up had been a swindle and it had been

one of my customers, a certified public accountant, who had spilled the beans. He, feeling the urge to inspect the development, had motored to the alleged site only to discover that although there was plenty of beautiful scenery in the area, no one had heard of the Dreamwold Hunting and Fishing Club, Inc. Not only were no land deeds registered to the company, no such corporation was listed at the State capital.

It occurred to neither of us that we might be adjudged accessories to the crime. Nor that the money in our pockets—twelve hundred in Johnnie's and over two thousand in mine—rightfully belonged to the swindled victims. Our only regret was that the bubble had burst.

Carefree and by our standards filthy rich, we again prowled the streets of New York. Because of its central location we had checked into a little hotel on West Forty-Fifth Street where, for thirty-seven-and-a-half dollars per week we shared a two-room suite, complete with kitchenette and bath.

It didn't take us long to learn that the joint was jumping with chorus girls, a discovery which, to our unsophisticated eyes, transformed the shabby little flea-bag into a glamorous *palais de joie*.

Nor did the voracious young houris delay in their discovery that sizable rolls were burning holes in our pockets.

The inevitable result was that after living it up for a few weeks our pokes were sadly depleted. It was clearly indicated that the time had come for us to stop making like a couple of butter-and-egg men and find jobs.

Work was scarce but after a few days of weary hunting I was taken on as a barker and guide for Chinatown bus tours. I wangled an interview appointment for Johnnie.

But the easy money he had made in New Jersey had spoiled him and he scorned the job. He had come to the conclusion that the business world was a pretty soft nut to crack. There was plenty of easy dough lying around just waiting for smart operators like us to pick it up. And while what I did was my own business, he had no intention of wasting his time as a five-dollar-a-day spieler on a Chinatown bus.

Our long friendship was too firm to shatter on such an issue but we did quarrel violently and for the next few weeks saw little of each other. My working hours had something to do with it. From twelve o'clock noon to twelve midnight each day, Sundays included, I guided gullible tourists through opium dens, houses of prostitution and gambling hells—all phony and set up by the company to make the "wonks" believe they were being conducted through sinister and dangerous dens of iniquity.

These synthetic examples of human depravity were staged for the most part in dank and dismal cellars, dimly lighted and with sinister looking Chinese hired by the company slinking about in the shadowy halls.

During the last part of each tour, I steered the suckers into certain Chinese curio and art shops. These were stocked with authentic, made-in-Brooklyn, Oriental merchandise, and operated by scrupulously dishonest Chinese merchants who paid me five percent of all monies spent by my victims.

As these commissions boosted my take to well over a hundred dollars a week, the financial aspect of the job was gratifying. Not so the work itself. The palpable fakery, naïveté of the customers, the dishonesty of the merchants and everything about the operation made me feel like a con man. And, worse still, a bored-to-exhaustion con man.

About one o'clock each morning, I would arrive back at the hotel disinterested in anything but falling into bed. Johnnie was usually conspicuous by his absence, or, if he was there, had already hit the hay.

Then came a morning when I arrived to find him waiting for me. Thrusting a gallon can and tin sprayer into my hands, he dramatically informed me that the can held liquid gold and that we were about to become millionaires.

The label on the can was self explanatory. Against a bright yellow background, huge red letters spelled out the attractive title, "KILLEM."

The fine print claimed that the preparation, sprayed around sinks, bathtubs, bedsteads and bars, was guaranteed to drive all lurking insects into the open and destroy them. It was further warranted not to stain fabrics and to be non-poisonous to humans.

Having spent an entire day on the lower East Side, accompanying a KILLEM salesman into saloons, cheap cafés, rooming houses and hotels, Johnnie was prepared to vouch for the fact that not only did the stuff do everything claimed for it, it also sold like magic.

He had watched the salesman write orders for forty gallons of KILLEM, plus twelve sprayers. As the price was two dollars a gallon and seventy-five cents per sprayer, the man's fifty percent commission added up to forty dollars and fifty cents—all for one day's work.

And as Johnnie had been offered Albany, New York, as his exclusive selling territory, his enthusiasm was understandable.

My reaction was one of skepticism. There were many

similar preparations and the market was highly competitive. And after our experience with the Dreamwold Hunting and Fishing Club, Inc., I was inclined to cast a suspicious eye upon any outfit offering lucrative selling deals to green kids like us.

Even so, I wasn't quite as doubtful as I pretended, the truth being that I was still burning because of his attitude toward my job. I was determined to cut him down to size.

So I talked tough. I panned the project, belittled the product, and accused him of exaggerating the sales figures.

Johnnie's Irish temper flared.

"You stupid bastard," he roared. "You are shooting your mouth off about something you don't know anything about. This is a great proposition. Look, I'll show you how this stuff works. This is a fairly clean joint we're living in. Right?"

I agreed.

"Okay. Watch."

Rushing into the tiny kitchen, he sprayed the stuff into the crevices around the sink and baseboards.

Roaches—a battalion of them, staggered into view, turned up their toes and expired.

"You see what I mean?" he crowed. "You didn't even realize the place is crummy. You have to admit the stuff is effective. Right?"

"Okay. It's effective. So what?"

"So I'll show you how easy it is to sell. I'm going to call Madame Puccini up here and show her those dead bugs."

"What do you expect her to do, pin a medal on you?"

"She'll order a batch of the stuff, that's what."

He went back into the living room and, as I listened to him on the phone, it occurred to me that it would be most interesting to study the reaction if when Johnnie entered the kitchen with Madame Puccini the *corpus delicti* had disappeared.

I quickly gathered the defunct roaches and placed them in my pocket.

The evidence thus disposed of, I sauntered into the living room where, to keep Johnnie's attention occupied until the arrival of Madame, I embroiled him in a specious argument concerning business ethics, taking the righteous position that in the present instance his technique smacked of blackmail and was therefore immoral and undeserving of success. I further badgered him into a hundred dollar bet that the Madame wouldn't go for his pitch.

Madame Puccini was, of course, the proprietress of the hotel. Petite, sweet-faced and sad-eyed, she looked exactly like someone whose name should have been Angela.

It was.

And she lived up to the title. Widowed and childless, her life was dedicated to the wellbeing of her boys and girls, mostly vaudeville performers and chorines, many of whom were chronically on the cuff.

Eviction for non-payment was unheard of. She even underwrote their credit with the Italian restauranteur who leased the hotel basement and, in addition, saw to it that they didn't want for cigarettes.

So impressed was I by the kindness of this lady that long after I made the big time and until after her death, I continued to make her hotel my New York headquarters.

This then was the gentle creature who, after Johnnie's brusque summons, hurried into our apartment concerned only by her desire to be of service.

Although I was rooting against Johnnie, I had to admire his sales technique, evidently plagiarized from the KILLEM salesman. After apologizing profusely for bothering her at such an hour, he assured her that the importance of the revelation he was about to make justified the imposition.

Her curiosity thus piqued, he spouted some fast double talk which had to do with hygiene, public welfare and the board of health.

As she listened, Madame's serenity gave way to mounting anxiety until finally she was pleading for him to tell her what was wrong.

Only then did he hit her with the awful truth.

"Madame Puccini," he declaimed, "your hotel is crawling with vermin."

Madame's reaction to this earth-shaking revelation was totally unexpected. Momentarily startled, she stared at him incredulously. Then, after a great sigh of relief, she laughed.

Disloyal pal that I was, so did I.

Johnnie was not amused. "I'm glad you think it's funny," he said. "Or perhaps you don't understand what I'm telling you?"

"Oh, but I do," she said lightly. "You have seen a bug or two. In old buildings such as this there are always bugs. But do not be alarmed. It is nothing."

"I am not alarmed, Madame. I'm just trying to do you a favor. And it's not a question of seeing a bug or two. The joint is crawling with them."

Grinning triumphantly at me, he yanked aside the curtain which served as a partition of living room and kitchenette.

"There you are, Madame! See for yourself."

I don't know which amused me more, Johnnie's bewildered double-take as he gazed at the bare floor, or Madame's change of face as she came to the conclusion she was being kidded. One thing was certain. She'd had it. Drawing herself up to the full extent of her five feet three inches, she said imperiously, "If this is your idea of a joke, young man, you've picked the wrong subject."

Johnnie was chastened. "Please, Madame Puccini. It's not a joke, believe me. They were right there on the floor. Dead cockroaches. Dozens of them." Then, referring to me, "Ask him. He'll tell you the same thing."

"Don't drag me into this," I said, quickly. "It's your party."

That tied it. Madame was on her way, pausing at the door just long enough to give us a twelve-noon deadline for our departure and suggesting that we might find the Astor or the Ritz more to our liking.

I immediately pressed Johnnie for payment of the hundred dollars I'd won so fairly. Then, leaving him to puzzle over what had happened, I went downstairs to try and square things with Madame Puccini.

It took all the charm I could turn on to break her down but after a full confession of my duplicity, supported by the sight of the roach remains, her sense of humor tipped the balance. She rescinded her order for us to get out and, for good measure, ordered twenty gallons of KILLEM.

This, incidentally, was the beginning of a friendship which lasted for many years.

I arrived back in the apartment to find Johnnie still

racking his brains to solve the mysterious disappearance of the dead bugs. Having had my fun proving whatever it was I had set out to prove, I told him the truth and waited for the laugh. But he was as sore as a boil. Even the news that I had squared things with Madame and sold her twenty gallons of KILLEM didn't reconcile him.

Characteristic of Johnnie was his penchant to make snap decisions. He made one now. He swung from the floor. When I came to, he was gone, bag and baggage.

After a couple of days it was apparent that he'd flown the coop for good. I felt bad about it. Particularly so as I had precipitated the blowup. I decided to try and find him.

I hadn't the slightest idea where to start. I knew he was close to being flat broke which meant that he had probably checked into some flop house. But as there were hundreds of such places in the city, it was like searching for a specific grain of sand in the Mojave desert. It wasn't until after I had spent hours phoning cheap hotels that I got the flash. The label on the KILLEM can bore the company's address. Certainly Johnnie in his enthusiasm for the project would have contacted the company again and someone there could direct me to him.

The company occupied one of a cluster of soot-blackened, one-story structures nestling in the shadows under the Manhattan end of the Brooklyn Bridge. The building fronted on a dark, cobbled alley and as I turned into it I came face to face with Johnnie. With him were two bowery bums, each laden with ten gallons of KILL-EM.

The bums grinned appreciatively as Johnnie and I greeted each other like the great pals we were.

"Hi," said Johnnie. "Fancy meeting you here. How'd you enjoy your sleep?"

"Great," I answered pleasantly. "And how's all your folks?"

The amenities over, I belted him. It was my Sunday punch and right on the button. Johnnie went down but not out and in a flash was up and at me. As we were well matched, it developed into quite a party, ending in a forced armistice. The cops arrived.

Johnnie and I were loaded into the Paddy Wagon and by the time we arrived at the precinct station the temporary truce had developed into an *entente cordiale*.

The desk sergeant happened to be a nice guy by the name of O'Hara and after listening to Johnnie explain that we were not really fighting but had simply been settling an argument over which of us could hit the hardest, he let us off with a warning.

Back at the alley we discovered that the bums had made off with the twenty gallons of KILLEM which, as Johnnie explained, had been destined for delivery to Madame Puccini.

Three days later the executive officers of the Bickford and O'Brien Exterminating Company (I insisted on top billing, having supplied the necessary capital), together with a thousand gallons of KILLEM and three hundred sprayers, were aboard a Hudson River boat en route for Albany.

The venture was successful from the start. Within two weeks we had wired a rush order to replenish our stock, and by the end of the first month had established a standing order for six hundred gallons a week.

And as the business continued to grow, Johnnie emerged as an astute business man. Thinking big, he was

well on the way to secure distribution rights to upper
New York State.

Certainly the prospects were bright for the firm of
Bickford and O'Brien, but try as I might—and I really
did try hard—I could not share Johnnie's enthusiasm. I
really detested the business. The prospect of spending the
better part of my life in the stinking atmosphere of cheap
hotels, rooming houses, restaurants, and saloons began
to weigh me down. I began to think of myself as a God-
damned bug exterminator. Johnnie was not sympathetic
and our friendship faltered.

The business was six months old when we closed the
distribution deal and it was at the same time that it
dawned upon me that peace of mind was more important
to me than making money.

Shortly thereafter and after a violent quarrel, I turned
over my interest in the business to Johnnie and with
some five thousand dollars in my kick headed West. I
never saw Johnnie again.

Hiking, riding freights, sometimes riding first class, I
went where I pleased and how I pleased, prancing the
boulevards and prowling the back alleys of Chicago, Detroit, Cleveland, St. Louis, Kansas City, New Orleans
and Denver.

I worked briefly at many jobs, hustling freight on the
docks, driving trucks, harvesting wheat, mining copper
and checking steers.

Sometimes I slept and ate in the best hotels. At other
times I slept in hobo jungles and ate Mulligan stew.
There were times when I was forced into combat with
characters who would slit anybody's throat for a dollar.
Had it been known that I was carrying a poke of over
five thousand bucks, I'd have been a dead pigeon

If I were to be asked today what I was seeking, I could only answer that I was indulging a yen for adventure. I was going places and seeing things. I was learning something of life and of people.

I asked nothing and expected nothing but the chance to make my own way in my own fashion. I was extremely lucky—I was a healthy, happy hundred-and-ninety pounds of self-reliant masculinity; I was living in the grand old days of the American Tradition, the great days of free enterprise and opportunity.

The dollars I carried in my pocket were mine. I had earned them and they were worth one hundred cents each. There had been no deductions from my earnings. I had not been forced to participate in pension, hospitalization and insurance plans. Nor had I been forced to join any unions.

I was not subject to confiscatory income taxes; nor was I taxed for everything I purchased, whether a loaf of bread or a Cadillac motor car.

Oh yes, I was lucky indeed. At that time my government was not posing in the Big Brother image and promising, in exchange for my vote, to coddle, wet nurse and care for me in my doddering old age. I was really and truly an American boy. Free. Proud. And Happy.

The youth of today should be so lucky.

The day came when I arrived in that wonderfully exciting city of San Francisco, California. It was in the late summer of Nineteen Eleven and the city was still in process of rebuilding after the great fire of Nineteen Six.

I didn't look for a job, it being my intention to see what there was to see, then, and this time for sure, head for home and school.

There was plenty to see. The place was seething with

activity. For days I tramped the streets, revelling in the cosmopolitan atmosphere.

At night I prowled the back alleys of Chinatown and the Barbary Coast like a stray pup. The strange smell of opium smoke plus the eerie effect of swirling fog never failed to give me an exultant sense of derring-do. The blaring of German bands, the chatter of pitch men enticing suckers into the joints along Pacific Street, the staggering drunks, the painted prostitutes and the motley throng of seamen from many nations thrilled me to the core. This, I thought, was one of the exotic, far places Grandfather Tom used to talk about. This was life in the raw.

I spent several days exploring this colorful sink of corruption and then, one night, came the happening that changed the course of my life . . . I went to a burlesque show.

It was above the average in quality, boasting a really funny comedian and a chorus of girls still below crowbait age. One of these girls was very pretty and it seemed to me that each time she came on stage she looked at me and smiled. I was sitting in the first row.

Nineteen, footloose-and-fancy-free, brimming with vim and vigor, I decided to investigate the situation.

After the final curtain I went to the alley leading to the stage door and waited. Or perhaps I should say that I sweated it out. For my youthful arrogance did not extend itself to women. I still looked up to them as superior beings, of much finer stuff than men and therefore worthy of greater respect and solicitude. Not that I was ignorant of the birds and the bees. In fact, young as I was, I had more than a nodding acquaintance with some of the raciest whores in America. And even they, in my book, rated a place on the pedestal.

And so, standing in that dark and filthy alley, waiting to accost a girl who didn't know me from a bull's foot, I suddenly got the feeling that I was being presumptuous and insulting, even while accepting the fact that some of these girls eked out their incomes by doubling in brass after the show.

The feeling grew as I looked about me at the leering faces of several characters, each of whom was waiting—as in truth I was—to knock himself off a floozy from the "Burly" show.

I had decided to chicken out and was turning to go when she appeared, accompanied by the soubrette of the show who was also a looker.

As they walked toward me along the alley, I determined not to let on by word nor gesture that I was lurking there to pick her up. But she saved the day. As they neared, she smiled and greeted me, "Hi, Red. I'm so glad to see you again."

I, of course, expressed my happiness at the opportunity of renewing our acquaintanceship, whereupon she introduced herself as Maizie and her best friend as Elsie. Niceties attended to, we proceeded to a restaurant where we were apparently to meet someone named Billy.

The restaurant was situated in an alley and from the outside looked like a dump. A few steps led down to a shabby door which opened into a huge basement room. It was one of those red-checkered-table-cloth, sawdust-on-the-floor places, dimly lit by candles stuck in bottles. The whole was dominated by a huge bar, extending the length of the room. Entertainment of a sort was provided by a

piano player who intermittently gave forth with a sentimental ballad. The place was crowded but a table had
been reserved for Billy's party and we were seated immediately.

Billy soon joined us and I recognized him immediately
as the comedian of the show. A runty little guy with a
Puckish face, it was soon evident that his reason for
being was to keep 'em laughing, on or off. Inveterate
ham though he was, his humor was contagious and I
found myself a sucker for his corny gags.

In addition to being the star of the show, he was its
entrepreneur, and Elsie, the featured soubrette, was his
lady love and constant companion.

It was because of Elsie that the incident occurred
which, I think, firmed Billy's regard for me. A burly
drunk at an adjoining table, a local yokel of the type that
considers theater women fair game, had sent a waiter to
our table with complimentary drinks for Maizie and
Elsie. The drinks were politely refused, whereby the
drunk, considering himself insulted, came to the table.
Addressing himself to Elsie, he became abusive, calling
her, among other things, a blond slut.

Billy came to his feet, swinging, but the guy back-
handed him, and Billy went down.

Mine was purely reflex action. I automatically swung
from the floor and belted that poor slob into forgetful-
ness. Once done, I thought nothing of it.

But to hear Billy carry on, I was nothing less than Sir
Lancelot, Frank Merriwell and Bob Fitzsimmons rolled
up in one package.

What had been casual camaraderie on his part
changed to sincere interest. He plied me with questions,
wanting to know all about my background, my present

activities and my plans for the future. I told all and by
the time the party was breaking up, he knew more about
me than my mother ever had.

Then he wowed me by suggesting that I join his company and become an actor.

I thought he was kidding and the idea struck me as
being ludicrously funny—Until I noticed the hurt expression and realized the wonderful little guy was trying to
help. He was actually offering me a job.

Trying to make amends, I thanked him for the offer
and explained that I was laughing at the mental image of
myself as an actor.

"I'm just not the type, Billy," I said.

"What's that mean? What in hell has type to do with
it?"

"Plenty. I'm just a big roughneck kid. I'm not artistic.
I don't know how to dress. I don't even speak good
English. Most of the actors I've seen were, well, different
—kind of precious. When I was in New York I got so I
could pick one out of a crowd. They all wear velour hats
and carry walking sticks. That's not for me, for Christ
sake."

"In other words, you think we're a bunch of fags."

"You're the one who said it."

Billy laughed long and loud.

Then he proceeded to straighten me out. He assured
me that the percentage of queers in show business was no
higher than in any other business, that for the most part
show people were normal, hard working members of a
noble and respected profession and that it was a highly
lucrative calling for those who made the grade.

"And speaking of type," he said. "If I had your build,
that attractively homely puss and that mop of red hair,

I'd put it together with my talent and retire in ten years with a million bucks. How about it, girls?"

Elsie agreed that I had a very striking appearance while Maizie, by this time a bit plastered, insisted I was so pretty that I gave her the hiccoughs.

"You see?" said Billy. "You'll knock the dames for a loop."

So persuasive was he that at ten o'clock on the following morning, I reported at the theater for rehearsal.

Billy introduced me to the assembled company, gave me some typed sheets and, after explaining which were my lines as opposed to the cues, started me in rehearsal. After a few moments, the proceedings were stopped while Billy explained the character. "You see," he said, "you're an outrageous fairy. We'll dress you in white flannels, red necktie, and a blond wig. You're always on the make for me, as the tramp. Like this."

He proceeded to simper and camp around the stage, drawing gales of laughter from the other actors. I laughed, too. I thought this was his way of getting back at me because of my crack about actors being fags, and went along with the gag.

But when it developed that he really expected me to play this character, my ears went flat and I balked.

"You're out of your mind," I said. "I'd be ridiculous trying to do that. They'd give me the hook, for Christ's sake."

"You're wrong, kid, they'll love it. A big rugged bloke like you, camping this part—you'll lay them in the aisles. Do me a favor and try it my way. What the hell, if it doesn't work out, you can quit and no hard feelings. How about it?"

I agreed to try. Soon I began to get belly laughs from the other actors and dropped my inhibitions.

I rehearsed all that week and on the following Monday night made my debut in Oakland, California. Much to my amazement, I got some tremendous laughs and on one occasion, after an exit, a round of applause.

Billy was tremendously pleased and after the show that night, we made a deal. The fairy bit was to be retained. In addition, he was to write some patter for my appearance with him in the olio. I would play straight for his comedy and sing one number. He would write a second skit for the second half of the show in which I would play a barefoot, country boy character, opposite the soubrette. My salary was set at twenty-five dollars a week.

On the following day I bought myself a dark green velour hat and a malacca cane.

I had become an actor.

Book
TWO

I HAVE NEVER known if I chose acting as a profession or if it picked me. In any case, after playing that first week in Oakland, I loved it. The show soon hit the road and four weeks later in Minneapolis my salary was raised to forty dollars a week.

I added spats to my wardrobe.

For the next twenty-five weeks we toured. Perhaps the most noteworthy happening insofar as I was concerned was the departure of Maizie. In Duluth she met a loaded mining man and eloped with him. I was happy for both of us. Maizie was a nice enough kid but she sure did crave respectability.

Billy's romantic status also changed, due to Elsie's catching him chiselling with one of the chorus girls. She swore she'd never speak to him again, and as far as I knew, she never did, except on stage during the show.

Billy and I, therefore, finding ourselves delightfully unencumbered, became excellent bottle pals and usually after the show could be found bellying up to some bar. There were a few incidents when some yokel would recognize me as the nance in the show and become offensive. Usually I would try to kid him into a friendly mood but if he became too obnoxious I would belt him out. These encounters delighted Billy who got a kick out of seeing me in a brawl. I hit a guy one night and failed to flatten him. Billy was much concerned about this. He thought I must be sick or something.

The weeks became a succession of stinking trains, grubby theatrical hotels and lousy restaurants. It added up to sheer hard work and if there was any semblance of glamour connected with it, I certainly did not detect it. Nevertheless the whole experience imbued me with a sense of secret, unexplainable excitement and as the season drew towards its close I knew I would miss it, my intention still being to go home and resume my studies.

The show closed in Brooklyn, N.Y. and during that last week Billy offered me a contract to rejoin the show the following season. The offer was of such a flattering nature—sixty dollars per week and second-feature billing—that although I refused it, its implications induced me to take a new, hard look at myself in regard to this strange setup called show business. Sixty dollars a week and feature billing was big stuff for a burlesque juvenile in those days. Perhaps, as Billy insisted, I had something to offer as an actor.

I knew of experienced construction engineers who earned no more than sixty dollars a week; only the eminently successful ones made big money, and they were relatively few. In comparison, here was I, a tyro in show business, being offered sixty a week. I had heard that there were successful actors in the dramatic theater who earned a thousand per week and more.

I decided to investigate further so I stopped over in New York for a few weeks, checked into Madame Puccini's Hotel and proceeded to haunt Broadway and various bars and restaurants where actors hung out. During my thirty-week experience I had learned enough theatrical jargon to pass as a professional; I was well enough heeled to quickly build a reputation as a check grabber with the result that I was soon surrounded by quite a retinue of hungry and thirsty pals from whom I learned the ropes. In a short time I knew the office locations of producers and agents, the mechanics of registering with the agents, the layoff periods of no casting and the periods of activity and when new shows were going into production. I went to all the shows currently playing on Broadway and after studying the techniques of the leading men and male stars, I came to the conclusion that I could make the grade, providing that I acquire the proper training and experience.

Alas for the engineering profession! I had arrived at the cross roads and I chose the theater. I would become a dramatic star on Broadway. Not that I had acquired an urge to express myself, nor did I feel any compulsion to deliver world-shattering messages to a breathless public. I was thinking in cold, hard terms of money. I knew that my decision would probably entail many years of hard work, frustration and poverty; but I also knew that in the end, if I made the grade, it would all add up to property, possessions and wealth. And in my book, these are not dirty words.

Within a few days after coming to my momentous decision I was home again. Admiral Dewey's reception on his return after the Battle of Manila Bay had nothing on my greeting by the Bickfords. All it lacked was ticker tape and a few Navy bands. My father and brothers cocked their eyebrows at the velour hat, the cane, my undeniably snappy suits and particularly at the spats. But they were genuinely glad to see me and dutifully joined my mother and my sisters to become a captive audience for my saga of adventure.

Their general reaction was one of relief that I had had my little fling and was now ready to settle down and prepare myself for the conventional existence of a respectable square.

Their presumption weighed me down with a sense of guilt to the extent that I hesitated to disclose my real

plans. But inevitably the subject came up and when my
father suggested that there was very little time left if I
was to enroll at M.I.T. for the fall semester, I braced
myself and told all, precipitating a minor explosion.

My brothers scoffed, demanding to know by what
right I assumed that I had talent for the theater. They
derided my experience, stating that burlesque was at best
a debased branch of the theater and that any bum could
get by in it. My father was vehement in his disapproval,
pointing out that actors were vagabonds and in some
states were subject to arrest, having no visible means of
support. My mother and sisters were my only supporters;
they were mildly pleased with the idea of having an actor
in the family.

At this time, there was in Boston a dramatic stock
company, the Castle Square Theater, which was owned
and operated by John Craig and his wife, Mary Young.
The pair headed the acting company as leading man and
woman and were tremendously popular. This company
had earned the reputation of being one of—if not *the*—
finest of hundreds of stock companies playing throughout
the country. "What a perfect setup for a beginner," I
thought, realizing that if I could work in any capacity
with a troupe of fine actors, rehearsing and performing a
different play each week, I must of necessity learn something. I knew the theater was closed for the summer but I
located Mr. Craig who was gracious enough to grant me
an interview.

He listened to my plea then informed me that his entire company had already been engaged for the new season. I thanked him and was about to leave when he
stopped me, saying that he liked my attitude in regard to
learning and that if I were willing to accept what
amounted to a token salary, fifteen dollars a week, he

would make a place for me as a second-assistant stage manager. My duties would consist of calling overture and the acts, holding the script at rehearsals, acting as supernumary whenever needed. Occasionally I would be given small parts to play. In the meanwhile I could watch and learn.

No trout ever struck a fly harder than I hit that offer. This was one time in my acting career when money was of no account. I had sense enough to realize that. I was about to acquire training and experience that money could not buy.

And so I became a member of one of the finest acting companies in America.

Almost immediately I knew I was home. I took to the atmosphere of that old playhouse like a duck to water and although as bottom banana I was relegated to duties that any errand boy could have performed, I was filled with the same haunting sense of new horizons that I had thrilled to in San Francisco's Barbary Coast and New Orleans' Bourbon Street.

Only this time I knew what I was looking for and where I was headed. My days of uncertainty and procrastination were over. I had matriculated, not at M.I.T. but at the Castle Square Theater. I would graduate, not as an engineer but as an actor and my target was Broadway.

Al Roberts, the stage manager and my immediate boss, was a stern task-master. He was one of those show people who had actually been "born in a trunk" and his respect for the traditions of the theater amounted almost to reverence. He maintained a discipline in the company that was military in its rigor and woe to the actor who stepped out of line. He was a great stage manager and as his assistant I learned much of the theater and its mores. This knowledge proved invaluable to me in subsequent

years. Al was also a fine actor and comedian and one of
the many from this troupe who became Broadway
names. John Craig, Mary Young, William Powell, Donald Meek, George Hassell, Florence Shirley, Theodore
Friebus, Walter Walker, Mabel Colcord and Alfred Lunt
were all John Craig Stock Company alumni. Two more
names that were to become famous on Broadway were
Chamberlain and Lyman Brown. They failed to make it
as actors but made it big in New York as Artists repre-
sentatives.

When the season closed in early May, I could con-
gratulate myself on having made an excellent investment.
My eight-month apprenticeship had been a rewarding
experience. I had been cast in nineteen plays, my roles
becoming increasingly important as the season progressed. The last five weeks were taken up with a cycle of
Shakespearean plays, in three of which I was cast—I
played Tibalt in *Romeo and Juliet,* Laertes in *Hamlet*
and Cessio in *Othello.* "Not too bad," I thought. "From
burlesque to Shakespeare in one easy season." I cite these
three plays because of gratifying mention I received in
the newspaper reviews, notably from the Transcript's
Parker, nationally recognized as a top flight critic. A
good notice from Parker was supposed to mean something.

So far, so good. I had learned much, had proven to
myself that I possessed a modicum of talent and had
acquired a measure of authority and assurance. I felt that
I was now equipped with the basic tools of my trade and
could hold my own as a journeyman actor. If I were to
become a master workman, I must learn to use my tools
to the greatest effect; I must acquire the finesse which
comes only with experience.

My first engagement after closing at the Castle Square

Theater was as leading man with a repertoire company which was organizing to tour Maine, New Brunswick and Nova Scotia. I had discovered it by answering an ad in "Billboard," the theatrical publication. There was an opening for a young, handsome and virile leading man. He must have an extensive, up-to-date wardrobe and must be able to play cornet, trombone or drums. Photographs were to be enclosed with applications and were to be mailed to an office in Augusta, Maine. The repertory was to consist of eight recent Broadway releases; salary was fifty dollars a week and the billing was first feature under the leading lady star. I reasoned that although the setup had all the earmarks of being strictly from hunger, it afforded the priceless opportunity of playing eight leading roles in up-to-date Broadway plays. In answering the ad, I stressed my recent engagement as "Juvenile Leading Man" with the Castle Square Theater Stock Company and enclosed copies of my good notices by Mr. Parker. I was honest about my lack of talent as a musician; in spite of the deficiency, I got the job.

I reported at Augusta in early August. We were to rehearse three weeks and open on Labor Day in Bangor, population of about 26,000 and the largest city on our itinerary. The entrepreneur was also the director and the Broadway plays turned out to be shockingly inept, things he had written himself and labelled as "Broadway Hits." The leading lady and star was a coy little ingénue of some fifty years who doubled as the producer's wife. The cast of players was incredible. They were beyond any doubt the shabbiest, hammiest troupe of hungry thespians I have ever seen, and I've seen some lulus. The scenery consisted of painted cloth which would be tacked on to walls or flats, if there were flats. Slip covers transformed kitchen chairs into elegant furniture.

After the first day of rehearsal, held in a hay barn on the edge of town, my reaction was one of stunned disbelief. My first thought was to escape. But perhaps because of my proneness for the unusual, I stayed with it and opened to capacity business at the Odd Fellows Hall in Bangor. To my amazement business was near capacity everywhere. For twenty years this troupe had been playing through the territory to nearly full houses at ten-, twenty- and thirty-cent prices. The uncritical, show-hungry natives turned out *en masse* to welcome the show folks as we heralded our entry into each new town by a parade down the main street. The leading lady and I, being the only members of the troupe who did not double in brass, rode side-by-side in a surrey with fringe on the top.

I barnstormed with this company for twelve weeks, playing mostly one-night stands which meant that much time was spent on trains—locals, always late, and usually made up of passenger coaches and freight cars. It was not unusual to ride in a car sandwiched between a carload of potatoes and a carload of hogs. The only heating was supplied by a wood-burning iron stove set up in one end of the coach. Many of the towns did not boast hotels, so bed and bait was only to be obtained at private homes. The beds were . . . beds, and the food was . . . wholesome. The people were . . . Down-Easters.

Despite the hardships entailed—the trashy plays with their pirated titles, the pathetic company of actors with the leading lady who was addicted to kippered herring and limburger cheese, which made the playing of love scenes a torment—I enjoyed this tour and when the end came, unexpectedly, in Truro, Nova Scotia, I was sincerely regretful.

The company was forced to close because my short, chubby, coy, fiftyish, blond-wigged leading lady discovered her husband in *flagrante delicto* with a hotel chambermaid. Later that night she attempted to castrate him with what was evidently a very dull knife.

I remember Truro fondly because of the magnificent sea food on the hotel menu. I recall having a couple dozen lobsters packed in sea-weed and ice and shipped to my folks in Boston.

My next engagement followed almost immediately. From Truro I had gone directly to New York and on my second day there accompanied a chance acquaintance to an agency where, it was rumored, a play was casting. The agency occupied a shabby little office in an incredibly scabrous old building. The single elevator was out of order so we walked up. When we reached the twelfth story we found the corridor swarming with actors. There were tall actors, short actors, elegantly dressed actors and down at heel actors, pushing and shoving to get into the tiny reception room and each one brimming with hope—hope that the others would drop dead.

Suddenly a woman entered from the inner office. This was the agent. She was short and stocky—the perfect type for Mrs. five by five—with a prognathous jaw and gimlet eyes. She walked swiftly through the reception hall to the corridor, speaking to the actors individually as she passed. She had two lines, "Nothing for you today" and "You wait." There were about ten who were told to wait. I was one of them. My disgruntled acquaintance was not.

I was the fourth to be interviewed. The producer was a darkly handsome man of about forty-five. He wore a

thin black mustache and as I entered the office he was
twirling the end of it. "What a hell of a villain this guy
would make," I thought. Before there was time for an
introduction he said, "He's the right height and coloring.
My wife is a tall girl. But he looks pretty young."
Addressing me directly, he asked, "How old are you?"
"Twenty four," I lied.

He asked the agent, "What's his name again?" Before
she could tell him that she had never before set eyes on
me, I answered for her, whereupon he graciously informed me that he had never heard of me. I could, of
course, have bounced this one right back at him. I had
never heard of him, either. But I waited for the inevitable
"What have you done?" and my reply was chronologi-
cally truthful. I told of the season in burlesque, the season at the Castle Square Theater and the twelve week
tour with the repertory company. The mention of the
John Craig Stock Company hooked him. Such is the
power of prestige; applause from the Bostonians was the
criterion. In answer to his further questions I reeled off a
long list of leading roles which I had not played.

His reaction told me I was his boy and suddenly I was
gratified to find myself on the receiving end of a hard
sell. He was offering an engagement as leading man for
his Repertory Company which was to begin rehearsals in
Chicago within two weeks. After five weeks of rehearsal
the tour would begin at Madison, Wisconsin. The repertoire would consist of ten plays, all standard melodramas
such as "Queen of The White Slaves," "Chinatown Charlie," "The James Boys in Missouri," "The Great Dia-
mond Robbery" and "Deadwood Dick's Last Shot."
These plays all provided great roles for the leading man
and the salary was seventy-five dollars per week. The
leading lady and I would co-star. He assured me that it

was a golden opportunity for an up-and-coming young leading man.

I voiced enthusiasm for the project, with one reservation—I considered the salary much too little and demanded a hundred. We compromised on eighty and I left that office feeling like fortune's darling.

A week later I reported for rehearsals which were conducted in a gloomy old theater on Chicago's South Side. Most of the company were already assembled on the stage when I arrived and were, instead of the ragtag and bobtail group I had expected to meet, an obviously professional cast of experienced actors, all of whom worked out of Chicago. The producer also functioned as director and considering the type of plays he was staging, his direction was expert. The stage manager was a very businesslike, bantam-rooster of a man who knew his stuff. By the end of the first day's rehearsal I knew that this engagement was to be grist for my mill.

After weeks of intensive rehearsing, the company opened as per schedule and for the next twenty weeks we toured and played to excellent business at a dollar top.

Proper projection of the melodramas in our repertoire demanded a bravura-type of acting. A prevalent gag among us was to the effect that 'The best actor is the guy who can yell the loudest'. It was no great surprise to be interrupted during a scene by raucous demands from the gallery to be 'louder and funnier.' Consequently, we really socked those plays over and the audiences loved them. It was not unusual for them to evidence their enthusiasm by cheering the hero and hissing the villain. Sometimes they would yell warnings to the hero during situations when the villain was about to launch a dastardly attack from the rear.

All pretty corny, to be sure, but it added up to tremendously valuable experience for me.

Perhaps the most rewarding element of this engagement was my association with David Weston, the character man who was to become my closest companion and, to an extent, my mentor. David was past his seventieth year and a confirmed drunkard. Although a small man and fragile, he was an actor of great power and I admired his work tremendously. Our association had begun, I think, because he discovered that I could always be depended upon to supply him with a drink. I had acquired a taste for a certain brand of bonded Kentucky Bourbon and used to buy it by the case. There were many occasions when we sat far into the night consuming my whiskey and shooting the breeze. I never tired of listening to his stories of the theater and its people. He had been acting for more than fifty years and had never, as he put it, gotten within shooting distance of Broadway. Nor had he ever acted with a first class production. "I always worked out of Chicago," he explained, "and nothing but Turkeys emanate from there."

He constantly criticized my performances and berated me for ranting, with the result that my work gained in strength and control. I became much more restrained and in some degree developed an individual style. One of the reasons I enjoyed this old man's company so much was because he fed my ego. He insisted that I had the makings of a great actor. "Already," he declared, "you're capable of making a fine living as an actor. But that's not good enough. You must think big, raise your sights. Don't be satisfied with a bare living. You have what it takes and if you handle yourself correctly, you can be a big man in the theater."

Two more years, he told me. Two full seasons of dramatic stock and I should be ready to take a crack at Broadway. But they must be engagements with first class companies, playing the latest New York releases. "And when the time comes for you to invade New York," he told me, "you must be choosy. Don't accept any part unless it is a good one. And you must stick to your guns no matter how broke you may be. If you need bread and butter money, get a job outside the theater. Swing a pick. Do anything, but never play a bad part in New York because 'parts make actors.' A carpenter can't do a good job unless he has proper material to work with. The same is true of an actor. The finest actor living could go unnoticed in an unimportant part. On the other hand, any mediocre actor may deliver an adequate performance of a fine part and be hailed by the unknowing as 'great.'

"And by the unknowing, I am referring not only to the public but to most of the people who are connected with the theater, whether they be creators, such as actors, producers, writers and directors, or whether they belong to the parasitical horde, such as columnists and critics, which battens on the theater from the outside. There are very few of them who have enough knowledge of the actor's art to enable them to differentiate between an actor and his role."

David likened the theater world to a jungle. "It's a highly competitive profession," he said. "You are only one of thousands who are pushing, biting and clawing their fellows in the frantic struggle to reach the same target. Many are called but few are chosen. You damn well see to it that you're one of the chosen."

I didn't take David's pontifications too seriously at that time. I listened because I liked him and enjoyed watching him wax dramatic as he kicked sacred cows in the teeth.

He had a veritable mane of white hair which topped an extremely sensitive face and to me he looked like nothing less than some old prophet who had stepped directly out of the Bible. Incidentally, David had made application for admittance to the Actor's Home, and his principal worry was whether or not he would be accepted. "I'd hate to become a statistic," he said. "Just another bum found dead in an alley."

In subsequent years I came to realize that David Weston had taught me the facts of theatrical life.

Excepting Dave Weston there was nothing particularly exciting or noteworthy to relate. The tour was typical. Two full-week stands, several three-day stands and many one-night stands constituted our bookings which meant, of course, that most of the time was spent in travelling on bad trains, sleeping in cheap hotels and eating lousy food in inexpensive restaurants. There was a brief romantic interlude with the attractive, dark-haired second woman which came to an end because of her possessiveness.

The season closed in Altoona, Pennsylvania, and after the closing performance the producer invited us all to a farewell supper party. Fourteen of us gathered in a private dining room to say our 'Goodbyes' and to wish each other good luck. It was here that I first recognized an emotionalism which I believe to be peculiar to theater folk. There is a definite sense of finality in the breaking up of a theatrical troupe. People who have lived in close association for months suddenly become aware that they are about to scatter in different directions and in all probability never work together again. Petty jealousies, misunderstandings—any and all ill feeling which may have existed during the tour dissolves into thin air and is replaced by a sense of poignant nostalgia.

And so it was this night. The party progressed in an atmosphere of good-fellowship and when it came time to break up I found myself choked with emotion. I liked this group of real pros and was truly grateful to them for the knowledge I had gained by working with them.

Afterwards, Dave Weston dropped into my room for a final nightcap. He was leaving in the morning, by bus, to join a show boat troupe which was about to open its season on the Ohio River. It was to be his fourth summer season with this show which, he said, paid next to nothing. All of the actors were paid the same stipend—twenty-five dollars a week and found. They slept and ate on the boat. The plays were terrible, the acting was worse, but the company was congenial and it was a nice way to spend the summer.

He expanded upon the beauty of the Ohio countryside and then he began to stretch the truth. He lied about the Ohio River fishing, about the friendliness of the natives who inhabited the river towns and about everything else pertaining to the Ohio River basin. It wasn't until he began to describe the wondrous attractions of the female members of the show boat company that I caught on that he was throwing me a hard sell to spend my vacation on the Ohio River. I intended to spend the summer in Boston with my family but decided to go along with Dave and vacation on the Ohio for a couple of weeks.

After a long and exhausting bus trip we arrived at our destination—a town which shall be nameless.

It had been raining and excepting the paved Main Street the area was a sea of mud. The nondescript buildings of the single business block were depressingly shabby and the modest homes, to be glimpsed on the side streets, were drab and uncared for. There were, however, magnificent old shade trees lining the streets and several attractive churches, seven of them, serving this town of less than five thousand inhabitants. Five of them were of wooden construction and painted white; one was built of field stone and the seventh was constructed of red brick.

The bus paused before the one crummy hotel just long enough for Dave and me to get off, suitcases in hand. Then, with a clash of gears and emitting a blast of evil-smelling smoke from its exhaust, it roared on its way, leaving me with the feeling of being stranded in Siberia.

I remember standing there for a moment looking about me before turning to Dave and saying, "You have to be kidding." Shaking his head sadly, he said, "It's better than panhandling in Chicago." After inviting me to dine with him on the boat, he picked up his suitcase and trudged down the street toward the river front. A great surge of affection and pity came over me as I watched that frail and gallant little man stop and rest a moment before switching the weight of his suitcase to his other hand. "Fifty years in show business," I thought, "and there he goes, carrying everything he owns in that lousy suitcase." I vowed that it would never happen to me.

After checking into the Commercial House (rates: one dollar and a half per day, with meals), I headed for the water front. My spirits lifted at first sight of the QUEEN. She had obviously seen better days but ancient and battered though she was, this old side-wheeler retained traces of former grandeur. She was painted a rich turkey red, with white trim, and sported dozens of brightly colored little pennants, the general effect of which was an air of carnival gayety in sharp contrast to the miasma of gloom which pervaded the town.

I stood for a moment admiring her, and I believe,

smiling for the first time since my arrival in the town. Then, as I started across the rickety old dock towards her, a man carrying a shotgun appeared from the wheel-house and hailed me. "That's far enough, young fella," he said. "What do you want?" Before I could answer, a group of people erupted from the main saloon, Dave Weston among them. After being identified and vouched for by Dave, I went aboard and met the company.

Captain Walter Hunnewell, owner and entrepreneur, explained my startling reception. Arthur Paige, the young leading man, had been involved in what he insisted was a harmless flirtation with the seventeen-year-old daughter of one of the leading citizens.

Upon discovering the incipient romance, the father had accused Paige of the attempted seduction of his underage child and had used his influence with the town board of selectmen to the end that the QUEEN was branded a public nuisance and a menace to the morals of the community. Thereupon the town Marshal had ordered Captain Hunnewell to cast off and get out of town.

The Captain defied the order, showing evidence that he had paid dock rental in advance and refused to move unless and until it was so ordered by a court of law.

The following night, Captain Hunnewell had waked to discover that the boat was drifting down the river. The mooring ropes had been cut and a spilled can of kerosene was found on the deck. Obviously there had been an interrupted attempt to burn the boat.

A simple solution to this affair would have been for the Captain to avoid further trouble by mooring the boat at some point farther along the river but he was not capable of that kind of submission. He was a courageous man and stubbornly determined to defend his rights.

"I've got two weeks to go before the expiration of my dock lease and, by God, no bunch of God-damned hypocritical rubes are going to drive me out," he said and promptly stoked up the boilers and put back to the town.

Then he broke out the boat's arsenal which consisted of a shot gun, a rifle and a thirty-eight caliber revolver. In addition to these weapons, he distributed pick handles to the nine men aboard. Pick handles, in case you don't know, are very handy weapons during a Donnybrook. Then he set watches around the clock and declared war.

I found this situation a most intriguing one and volunteered to join the defenders, whereupon the Captain invited me to be his guest and dispatched one of the deck hands to bring my things from the hotel.

The boat's crew consisted of two deck hands, two firemen and a Negro woman who was a very good cook.

Captain Hunnewell was a man about sixty years of ago. He was short, stocky, vigorous and out-spoken. Of his background, I know nothing; but here on this old packet he was king. He was sole owner and held a Master's Ticket which licensed him to operate the boat. He wrote, produced and directed the plays which were his versions of old chestnuts such as, "The Old Homestead," "Under Two Flags," "The Two Orphans," "Lights of London," and "Rip Van Winkle." The writing was inspiringly bad and his direction worse.

The acting company was composed of eight people. A young leading man of about my age who was husky, handsome, inexperienced and devoid of acting talent. The Captain had pegged him as a sex pot; the women of the river towns would adore him. A leading lady of about the same age, blonde, pretty, also a tyro, but possessed, I think, of a modicum of acting ability. A second man—

villain to you—about thirty-five, dark, handsome, conceited and an abominable actor. The second woman was his female counterpart. The character man was, of course, Dave Weston and the character woman, about sixty, was chatty, motherly and evidenced much acting experience—all bad. There were two general business people, male and female utility actors who played all types of fill-in roles. Extra players and supernumaries were recruited as needed from local talent in each town.

The first couple of days I had little to do but fish, swim, stand my watch with a shot gun and watch the company rehearse.

The actors, bad as they were, approached their work with great sincerity and as the rehearsals progressed they seemed to exude confidence and self-satisfaction. I remarked on this to Dave and got slapped down. "Of course they're self-satisfied," he said. "What's wrong with that? If they weren't, they couldn't do it at all. There's not one of them who has the slightest inkling of how bad he is. They think these plays are masterpieces and they look up to Hunnewell as the Master. They are no-talent people, playing to tasteless rustics. And the rustics will pay their money, and they'll think the shows are great, and we'll all eat this summer. Don't knock it."

In addition to their acting, the actors were required to help with the chores—dish washing, house cleaning and what have you—and even these mundane tasks were performed with gusto. Not once did I hear a complaint. They were the happiest group of poverty-stricken thespians I have ever come across. Except for the ever-present tenseness induced by the feud with the townspeople, one could have mistaken this bunch for a carefree group enjoying themselves at a house-boat party.

And the tensity was justified. The danger in the situation was very real. This boat was actually besieged and threatened by a gang of bucolic bigots with a high potential for viciousness. Groups of sullen-looking characters were constantly hanging around the dock, gawking at the boat. My assigned time for standing watch was from ten p.m. to midnight and it was a weird experience to stand there in the darkness, loaded shotgun in hand, watching and waiting for something to happen that would precipitate violence and bloodshed.

It was on the third night, during my watch, that Dave and the Captain suddenly appeared in the wheel house. "We've come up," said the Captain, "to have a little talk with you." I knew immediately that Dave had been sounding off about me and that I was about to be offered a job. "I understand you were leading man with the Castle Square Stock Company in Boston," he said.

Who was I to make a liar out of Dave? "I played there," I said, nonchalantly. Then, looking quizzically at Dave, "How in the world did you hear about that?"

"Oh, things get around. Anyway, I've got an idea. I want to make you a little proposition."

"I think I know what you're going to say, Captain. And I appreciate it. But there's no spot in your company for me. You know that. Besides, I'm pulling out in a few days. I'm going to visit my folks in Boston."

"So Dave tells me," he said. "But there's no harm in listening to what I have to say."

Then he handed me a script and proceeded to outline his idea. Monday night business was traditionally light. If I was in agreement, he would present me every Monday night as a special attraction, billing me as the noted star of the famous Castle Square Stock Company of Boston, Massachusetts. The play would be his own version of

"The Count of Monte Cristo," a great play and a wonderful role. For this one performance per week he would pay me thirty-five dollars with the stipulation that I was not to let the other players know my salary.

I protested that it wouldn't work. I asked how he could possibly expect people to come to see an actor they had never heard of. Dave put in his two cents worth by telling me to leave that end of it up to the Captain. "People are like sheep," he said. "They believe anything you tell them. They'll buy anything if you give them the right pitch."

I promised the Captain that I'd read the script that night. Which I did. It was pretty bad, but for some strange reason I decided to accept the deal and thereby became, I think, the original 'Guest Star.'

The following morning Captain Hunnewell announced the plan to the company. Expecting resentment, I was pleasantly surprised by their enthusiastic acceptance. These simple people actually believed I was a 'Star' and there was a subtle difference in their attitude toward me. I had suddenly become something slightly apart. I was a big frog in a little puddle, and I ate it up.

Already burdened with the task of getting up in five plays, the company was now faced with a sixth. With the opening engagement only a week and a half away, the activity of preparation was stepped up to a hectic degree. Rehearsal periods were longer and more intensive. Costumes and props were strewn everywhere and the atmosphere of urgency and excitement mounted as the days passed.

The town's hostility continued to cast its shadow but somehow the threat of attack only added zest to the situation. The assault never did materialize. The closest we came to a physical clash was the day it was found necessary to replenish certain food supplies. Captain Hunnewell selected me and one of the deck hands to go ashore with him to procure them. As there was a town ordinance forbidding the carrying of firearms, we armed ourselves with pick handles.

We evidently presented a formidable front because the few citizens we encountered on our way to the general store gave us a wide berth.

We were in the store but a couple of minutes when the town marshal showed up. We paid him no attention and he just stood around watching us with gimlet-eyed suspicion. When the Captain had made his purchases, we each picked up a heavy sack of groceries and left. Word had spread that we were there and about a dozen rough looking characters were waiting for us. It appeared that we were in for a shindig. For a second we stood on the store porch and stared, then I put down my sack and got the pick handle ready for action.

It was at this instant that the marshal came out. Indicating my weapon, he said, "What's that thing for?"

"To beat the brains out of any son-of-a-bitch that starts . . ."

I was interrupted by the Captain. "Shut up, Charlie," he said, pleasantly. "Why, that's a walking stick, Marshal. All actors carry them. Didn't you know that?" Then, to me, "Pick up your sack, Charlie. Lets get out of this stink."

The three of us started down the road towards the river. "Don't look back," the Captain said. And we didn't. They didn't follow nor did they yell after us. Nothing at all happened. But I think that if the marshal had not been on the job, this episode would have had a different ending.

When the time came for us to cast off from this hamlet

of lovely churches, not a single citizen was at the dock to wish us Godspeed. I dubbed the place the Holy City.

We opened the season on schedule and for sixteen weeks played to near-capacity business. The Castle Square Theater Stock Company label was surely box-office that summer because every Monday night was a solid sellout.

The boat tied up at more than seventy towns along the river and there being no occasion for rehearsing, there was much leisure time for fishing, swimming, basking in the sun and what have you. This unique engagement turned out to be one of the most enjoyable I have ever experienced and when in late September it ended, I found it difficult to say "Goodbye" to the company. Lousy actors they may have been but they were real people, and I was richer for knowing them.

And, of course, for knowing Dave Weston. I had grown very fond of that grand old trouper. I suggested that he come along with me and try his luck in New York. But he refused, saying that it would be tantamount to starting all over again. If he was known at all, it was in Chicago and it was too late to change. He saw me off on the bus and as it pulled out I had the sad feeling that I would never see him again.

New York in late September is a dreary place for the unemployed actor. Most of the early-season plays had been cast and were in rehearsal. Some of them had already opened. Others had opened and closed. Most of the road companies were on tour. Stock companies were cast and in operation.

Any illusions I may have had of being 'Fortune's Darling' were soon shattered. I was Mr. Nobody. After registering at all of the agencies, I accustomed myself to the routine of 'making the rounds'—tramping Broadway, checking in every day at the agencies and producer's offices. For the next five months I went round and round like a Six-day Bicycle Racer. I met nary a producer nor did I see one. The area beyond the receptionist's desk was out of bounds and the invariable greeting was "Nothing today." I was disappointed, confused and frustrated. I began to feel that I was engaged in a meaningless rat race, that I was wasting my time. It seemed apparent to me that the producers were completely indifferent to new talent. The unknown was virtually a vagrant, begging for a handout.

Naturally, I became acquainted with many of my fellow vagrants and was appalled to learn that most of them were experienced actors whose average income amounted to three to four thousand dollars per year. There were misfits among them, of course, and also many starry-eyed, stage-struck tyros.

I often thought of Dave Weston and remembered what he had said about competition. "It's a highly competitive profession. You're only one of thousands who are pushing, biting and clawing each other in their struggle to reach the same target." And as I looked about me at the horde of hopeless hopefuls, I wondered if this was what he meant by competition. I asked myself what could possibly be gained by pushing, biting and clawing at this bunch of hungry, shabby innocents. I reasoned that he must have been referring to the faceless men in the inner sanctums, the producers, and I thought, "Okay, Dave. I'd love to tangle with *them* but how in hell do I start? How am I to claw somebody if I can't get near the son-of-a-bitch?"

The fact that I was staying at Madame Puccini's hotel helped a lot. Pleased that I had become an actor, she evidenced an almost maternal interest in me and was never too busy to listen to my beefs. Like Dave Weston, she insisted that one day I would make it. "You mark my words," she said. "One of these days some big producer will notice you, give you your chance, and you'll be on your way."

And one cold, gray, rainy morning in February, I learned via the grapevine that a play was casting at the Al Woods office. I arrived there to find the place jammed with actors of every conceivable type. After an interminable wait, a man came from Mr. Woods' private office and designated the people that were to be interviewed. Much to my surprise, I was among them and when my turn came to be ushered into the great man's presence my hopes were high.

Mr. Woods' office turned out to be small, cluttered and altogether unimpressive. He, a big cigar in his mouth, was standing by a window gazing reflectively into Forty-Second Street. I stood for a moment, waiting, then he turned and said pleasantly, "Sit down, Sweetheart, and tell me about yourself." The 'Sweetheart' jolted me slightly but as I was subsequently to learn, the epithet was characteristic of Mr. Woods. He addressed everybody as 'Sweetheart.' I proceeded to tell all, becoming painfully aware as I talked that mine was a depressingly undistinguished history.

He listened attentively and when I had finished, thanked me graciously. Unfortunately, although I was a perfect type for the role, I wouldn't do because the part was a very important one and demanded an actor of stature. An actor, that is, who had done things on Broadway. A short speech but a meaty one. My hopes were dashed.

I used every argument I could think of to change his

mind. With perfect logic I argued that if I were right
physically and personality-wise for the role it would seem
to make good sense to try me out. "Let me rehearse one
day," I said. "Who knows? You might have a new star on
your hands."

He remained adamant, however, and dismissed me
with the encouraging statement that I was a good type
and that he would keep me in mind when something
suitable came along.

It was at this point that my frustration boiled up and
over. "What kind of a God-damned stupid business is
this?" I demanded to know. "You tell me I'm just right
for a part, then turn me down because I haven't played
on Broadway. How in hell can I play on Broadway if all
the producers have that attitude? How do I get in?" I
ended my tirade by telling him that ever since I had been
theater conscious I had read about the theater being sick.
Now I was beginning to realize why. It was because of
the stupid characters who were running it. "I've seen
every play now running on Broadway," I told him, "most
of them are lousy. That goes for the actors, too. You
need new talent, brother, and you need it badly."

I made my exit, leaving Mr. Woods staring after me in
open-mouthed amazement.

Never again did I make the rounds. The following day
I went down town and got a job hustling freight on the
docks. I subscribed to a telephone answering service and
registered the number at all the agencies so that in case
the unexpected happened and one of them were to call, I
would get the message.

My work on the docks was no hardship. Tough, hard
labor it was but it paid enough to meet my needs and,
importantly, it kept me occupied. I think that another six
months of that devastating treadmill, 'Making the

Rounds,' would have landed me in Bellevue's Psycho Ward.

Perhaps because of my wanderlust, I enjoyed the atmosphere. The maneuvering ships, the rough and ready stevedores, the aromas and stinks of the warehouses and ships' holds all held a peculiar fascination for me, and despite my urge to make good in the theater, I was relatively happy.

My procedure was simple. After finishing work, I would go up town to my hotel and check with the answering service. But there were never any calls from producers. No one seemed to be clamoring for my services as an actor. Then I would go out to dinner, usually at some inexpensive actors' hangout.

Occasionally I would hear of casting activity. The following day would find me at the specific producer's office where it was going on. On one of these occasions I did gain admittance to the producer's presence but his interest lapsed when he learned that I had no Broadway credits.

Months passed and although I was not discouraged, I began to question the wisdom of continuing along these lines. In mid-July, after a particularly hot and exhausting day on the docks, my answering service informed me that the Chamberlain Brown Theatrical Agency had called me three times during the afternoon. I was instructed to get in touch with them as soon as possible. I called immediately and was told to be in the Al Woods office at ten o'clock the next morning.

I was delighted and at the same time extremely curious and slightly apprehensive. I recalled my brashness during the previous interview with Mr. Woods and wondered if I was about to be handed my head.

Promptly at ten o'clock the following morning I presented myself sopping wet—it was raining—at the Woods office and was surprised to find the reception room empty of actors. The receptionist greeted me by name and with a friendly smile ushered me into the private office. Mr. Woods was graciousness personified and "Sweet-hearted" me to an embarrassing degree. He informed me that he had a great part for me in a play which was to start rehearsing early in August. It was a great role, only second to the star role which was to be played by a big star name. I expressed my satisfaction and delight. He asked me what I had in mind for salary and I said that salary was a secondary consideration to me, that if I liked the part I had no doubt but that we could get together. I would prefer, however, that he discuss salary with the Brown office.

He then handed me one of his big cigars and for the next hour we chatted. I found him to be altogether unassuming and extremely likable, an impression which endured until his death many years later.

As I was leaving he handed me a script and told me that I would be notified as to rehearsals. A trifle dazed but proud and happy, I strode through the rain to my hotel. I was really building a castle in Spain. Opportunity. Broadway. This had to be it. This was my big chance.

At home, the first thing I did was to call Chamberlain Brown and report the result of the interview. He was pleased and congratulatory and said he would close the deal immediately. He was going to try for three hundred a week salary but because I was an unknown he might have to settle for a hundred and fifty, or at the most, two hundred. In my enthusiasm I told him that I would leave it to his judgment. "Don't worry about salary," I said.

"Close the deal." Then, still in my sopping clothes, I sat down to read the play.

After reading the first act, I took time out to shower, put on dry clothes and bolster my rapidly fading euphoria with an enormous slug of bourbon.

Mid-way through the second act I was interrupted by a telephone call from the agent, Chamberlain Brown, who jubilantly informed me that he had closed the deal at two hundred a week. I was also to get third billing, under the title. He thought that was a pretty damned good break for a newcomer. I thought so too but Chamberlain, who was a sensitive soul, detected a lack of enthusiasm in my response and demanded to know what was the matter. I told him. "I've read the first act and if the rest of it improves a hundred percent, it'll still be the worst mess of tripe I've ever read."

Chamberlain's reaction was explosive. He told me in no uncertain terms that it was the height of presumption for me, a nobody, to set my judgment of a play above that of Mr. Woods and insisted that I come over to his office and discuss the matter. I agreed to be in his office within the hour.

Reinforcing my shattered morale with an added four fingers of bourbon, I resumed my reading. If the first act had been a misdemeanor, the second act was a felony. I shall have to leave the third act to imagination. I did not bother to read it, therefore I cannot describe it.

I sat in that depressing apartment and pondered the situation. I tried to visualize myself playing the assigned part and decided that although it was the best-written part in the play, it was not one in which I could do justice to myself or to the play. I thought of Dave Weston's advice, "When the time comes for you to invade New

York, you must be choosy as to roles. Don't accept any part unless it is a good one."

My Castle in Spain crumbled into a pile of rubble. I would not do this play.

I will not go into a blow-by-blow account of what transpired at the Brown office, but Chamberlain and his partner-brother, Lyman, really gave me a bad time. Utterly devoted to the theater and steeped in its traditions, they could not accept the reality of an unknown actor turning down an important role in a Broadway production. It was unheard of. I must be out of my mind. I was passing up an opportunity that may never come again. And so on, *ad nauseum*. They did not succeed in changing my mind, however, and the discussion ended with their assurance that they would never again negotiate an engagement for me.

The following day I returned the script to Mr. Woods and asked him to excuse me, explaining as best I could that I could not see myself in the role and consequently my performance would be lousy and therefore hurt the play. Mr. Woods heard me out, smiled graciously, and said, "Okay, Sweetheart, if that's the way you feel about it. Good luck."

I left with the suspicion that I hadn't fooled Mr. Woods one little bit, that he knew exactly why I was walking away from his play.

The experience had a devastating effect on my morale. The more I thought about it the closer I came to agreement with Chamberlain Brown. I was just an inexperienced nobody, with nothing in my record to justify the assumption that my judgment of a play was sounder than that of Al Woods, an experienced and successful producer. My own stupid arrogance had caused me to throw away a tremendous opportunity. I was so bedevilled by these thoughts that for weeks I shunned my usual haunts along Broadway, fearing that word might have gotten around and that I would be pointed out as the damned fool who had just thrown a career out the window. Luckily I had my work on the docks to occupy my muscles, if not my mind, and I threw myself into it.

Meanwhile I watched the theatrical columns for news of the Woods play. In due time an item appeared, announcing that the play was in rehearsal. A high-salaried name actor had been cast in my role. This news deepened my depression and I vowed to myself that if he and the play hit, I'd cut my throat in the lobby of the theater.

And on one hot night in mid-August the play opened. I did not witness the disaster, spending the evening and most of the night riding back and forth on the Staten Island Ferry boats in an effort to keep cool.

At about one a.m. I came uptown, bought the papers, went to my apartment and had a ball reading the reviews. The play was a dismal flop. The critics had roundly panned the play and everybody concerned, making free use of such adjectives as puerile, inane, boresome, impotent, dull and uninteresting. The fog of uncertainty and depression that had surrounded me lifted and I was jubilant.

It was not that I was being inordinately cruel or insensitive to the distress of the people concerned in the play's failure. I think every professional deplores any flop even though he may not be directly concerned. My elation was due to the restoration of faith in my own judgment; most important, it set a pattern of independence of thought and action which has characterized my entire career.

And there's the gist of it. If it were not for this independence, arrogance, or just plain doggedness—call it what you will—my story would hardly be worth the telling.

In an effort to stay afloat on a sea of mediocrity, a creative worker, be he striving for fame or for material gain, must achieve a modicum of glory before he can gather in the shekels. Either way, he must of necessity set a standard of excellence and do his best to maintain it. All success is qualified, particularly that of the actor who, by the nature of his work, must be dependent upon the material he is given to interpret, material which is created by another worker, the writer.

The writer, too, is human. In his struggle to control the necessities of life his work often falls far short.

Really fine plays are the exception rather than the rule; consequently the actor in his search for fine roles to play must compromise. Basic necessity dictates that he must. There have been times when I have deliberately lowered my standards and accepted bad roles in mediocre vehicles simply because the sheriff was pounding on the door. I may say, however, that on each occasion I was completely aware that I was working with junk.

One evening, several weeks after the Woods fiasco, in a crowded little off-Broadway restaurant, I was shown to a table at which two girls and a man were already seated. My presence was scarcely noticed as I sat and unashamedly listened to a lively discussion among them. I soon gathered that one of the girls was an actress and currently engaged in rehearsing a dramatic vaudeville sketch. The man was the author and was staging it in preparation for an imminent tryout date. The second girl was his wife.

The actress was insistently demanding the replacement of an actor on the premise that he was so bad in the part that he jeopardized any chance of the act being booked. The man was in partial agreement but was equally insistent that there was not enough time to rehearse another actor.

This was on a Friday evening and the act was to open on Monday Matinee at an Eastside vaudeville theater.

Sensing an opportunity, I butted into the conversation, telling them that I couldn't help overhearing and explaining that I was an actor, an unusually quick study and that I was looking for work. I asked if I was at all the type for the part in question.

From the manner in which they looked at each other, I knew immediately that I had struck pay dirt. The wife spoke first. "It's amazing," she said. "The minute he walked in I said to myself, 'I wonder if this boy is an actor?' What a perfect type he'd be to play 'Ronnie.' " The man then asked a few pertinent questions as to my experience and, after dinner, we went to his apartment where I went through the act with the girl. The act was one of those tried and true, man and wife comedy sketches—the hen-pecked husband who finally turns. Hokum but sure fire.

I got the job. After intensive rehearsing through Saturday and Sunday we opened the Monday Matinee at Loew's Delancey Street Theater. This was a grind house on New York's lower East Side and played five acts of vaudeville, a feature picture and a newsreel. Our booking was for Monday, Tuesday and Wednesday and we were to play three shows a day. It was before the inception of play-or-pay contracts and whether or not you played out your time depended on the whim of the house manager. If your act flopped or if he did not consider it worthy of his house he would come back stage after the first show and cancel your act.

We went on for our first performance at about one-thirty p.m. The house was nearly a quarter filled and the audience consisted mostly of bovine-appearing women, screaming babies and yelling kids. No one attempted to quiet the kids who, during the fourteen minutes we were on, seemed to be playing football in the aisles.

Excepting one brief moment of pathos, the act consisted of the broadest type of comedy and we succeeded in playing it from curtain to curtain without the satisfaction of hearing one laugh, not even a snicker. When the curtain fell, not one person applauded.

My partner and I agreed that we had just laid a colossal egg. I went to my dressing room and waited for the manager to deliver the *coup de grâce.* A half hour passed and he did not appear. No one appeared. I came to the conclusion that the management, knowing it was our first showing, had made allowances and was giving us a second chance.

The second, or supper show, was scheduled at about five thirty, which meant that we had about three hours and fifteen minutes to wait. Taking advantage of that time we went over the act point by point trying to determine just where and why we had flopped. Try as we would, we could not find an explanation.

Determined to do or die, we went on for the supper show only to find a mere handful of people in the house. We died this time in silence, due to the fact that the kids had ended their football game and had gone home.

After this second debacle there seemed to be no question but that the act was doomed. We accepted the situation as a *fait accompli* and decided to play out the date as best we could and then forget it.

I had hardly reached my dressing room when the writer-producer burst in on me. To my astonishment, he was beaming and I sat gaping at him as he enthusiastically congratulated me for putting the act over with a bang. "That bang you heard," I said disgustedly, "was us falling on our cans. We didn't get a laugh out there. Not one lousy laugh."

He then explained that the seeming lack of response from the audience was because most of them did not understand English. The mere fact that they sat quietly and listened indicated that they liked the act. The proof of the pudding was that the bookers had caught us at the matinee and had liked it. We were already penciled in for six weeks in Loew houses in metropolitan New York and we were assured of at least thirty weeks to follow.

And so I became a vaudevillian and for the next fifteen months toured the country, playing over the Loew and Western Vaudeville circuits. Small time though it was and hard, wearing work, calling for three and sometimes four and five shows a day, it was nevertheless invaluable experience and could not help but rub off raw edges and develop some sort of style and stage presence.

And as I look back, vaudeville was to me the real "Show Biz." Here, among the midgets, trained seal acts, wire walkers, Salome dancers, monologists, girl acts and acrobats was to be found a sincere spirit of good fellowship and warm-hearted generosity. Gauche perhaps, and often ludicrous in their 'always on' efforts to impress, they were none the less people who always had their hands out, not to take but to give, whether money or whatever else might be needed to help a fellow in distress.

I found fewer sons-of-bitches among them than in any

other theatrical group. I have fond memories of vaudeville and its people.

Financially, the picture was not so bright. The act's
salary was two hundred and seventy-five dollars per
week. Of this, fifty went to the writer-producer, thirteen
seventy-five to the agent, leaving two hundred dollars
and twenty-five cents out of which we had to pay transportation expenses. And as our bookings consisted
mostly of split weeks, that meant twice a week railroad
fares which approximated sixty dollars per week. Then
there was the tipping. The stage hands had a racket operating which made it imperative for an act to tip. Otherwise, dire things could happen. I tipped an average of
five dollars in each house, or ten dollars a week. Other
and sundry expense amounted to another ten dollars a
week all of which deductions left a net amount of a hundred and thirty-one dollars and twenty-five cents to be
divided between my partner and myself.

If sixty-five dollars and sixty cents per week seems to
be niggardly reward for such rigorous endeavor, please
bear in mind that this all happened in the good old days.
Out of that sixty-five sixty I managed to pay my way,
send a few needed dollars home and even save a bit. In
short, I had no complaints save the constant awareness
that I was making no progress towards my Broadway
target.

It was this awareness which weighed in the balance
when the time came to end the tour. We had been touring thirteen months and the second February found us
playing a house in Duluth. We were to jump from there
to Minneapolis but for some unexplained reason our
bookings were switched and we were instructed to proceed to Winnipeg, Manitoba. After that we were to play

four more weeks in Canada in such places as Regina, Moose Jaw, Saskatoon, Medicine Hat, Calgary, Edmonton and Vancouver. This circuit was known among actors as "The Death Trail," and after playing the first date I could readily understand why.

Duluth in February is not exactly a place where one need worry about heat prostration. We were there for four days during which time the temperatures ranged from five to twenty degrees below zero.

Winnipeg had been experiencing a cold spell but when we arrived the weather had moderated and the mercury stood at only six below. Having been brought up in Boston I didn't consider that particularly excessive but when I read a news item stating that it was currently 22 below in Saskatoon, a town on our itinerary, I bought myself heavy woolen shirts, trousers, socks, underwear, a fur cap with ear muffs and a parka. I showed up at the theater looking like an Eskimo and was roundly razzed. Before we left Winnipeg, however, everyone in the five acts on the bill had followed suit.

We were to play the "Death Trail" as a unit. The headliner was an Hawaiian Dancer and her chorus of six girls. Her name was Mary Flynn. She was from Brooklyn and billed herself as "Princess Mauna Loa." The Hula was considered quite naughty in those days and the Princess was well named. She was hot stuff. There was a bicycle act, two men and a girl; a trampoline act, two men; a monologist and my partner and myself.

Our first jump after Winnipeg was to Regina, Saskatchewan and the night we left was one to remember. It had been snowing hard all day and the troupe rode together to the railroad station in a big, horse-drawn, open pung. Fortified against the weather by our arctic clothing and a few belts of potent Hudson's Bay Company whiskey, most of us were in festive mood and sang all the way to the depot thereby gaining the dour disapproval of the Scotch driver who was openly contemptuous of us as a pretty disreputable lot.

We had been assigned to a tourist sleeper which was parked on a siding by the station. A battered old relic, it looked like something that belonged in the Smithsonian Institution. It was fitted with narrow, built-in bunks with mattresses, or pads, which seemed to be stuffed with steel shavings. The dim illumination was furnished by some sort of gas lamps and its toilet accommodation consisted of a tiny cubicle equipped with a water closet and wash bowl, for the convenience of all. Later, when the car was rolling I discovered it had at least four flat wheels.

On the credit side I must report that while it was at the siding it was comfortably warm, being hooked up to a steam pipe. And, there was a porter in attendance.

Most of the troupe, including myself, turned in while the rest of them organized a poker game. Some of the boys were feeling no pain and were pretty noisy but I promptly went to sleep and it wasn't until the cold got to me that I came to. I woke up shivering and rolled out to find most of the others awake and freezing. While I had been asleep a switch engine had moved the car from the siding and it was now three miles down the track waiting for the train that was to pick it up and which was two hours late.

Away from the steam pipe at the station, the car had no heating facilities and even though the porter had distributed every available blanket, it was impossible to keep warm. It had stopped snowing and the temperature had dropped sharply, just to what degree we did not know as there was no thermometer on the car.

Aside from our troupe there were six other passengers and although they were Canadians and used to the climate, they too were shivering and agrccd that the situation was drastic. A council of war was held and it was decided that I and one of the acrobats from the trampoline act would hike back to the station for help. We set out, stiff with cold and bundled up like a couple of Arctic explorers. It was not long before we were limbered up and warmed by the exercise. Stimulated by the drama in the situation, the ham in me took over and I began to enjoy myself.

The sky had cleared and the stars looked like enormous diamonds flashing against a background of black velvet. As far as the eye could see the ground seemed to be blanketed by trillions of tiny diamonds that squeaked at every footstep. The air was so sharp and cold that every breath seemed to burn my throat and lungs and when my acrobat friend and I arrived at the railroad station we resembled walruses because of the icicles hanging from the lower rims of our parkas.

At the station we got quick action. The only person there was a telegrapher who immediately grasped the situation and phoned a division superintendent, whereupon a yard locomotive appeared, took us aboard and soon we were back at the scene of the crime.

The locomotive pumped steam into the car's heating apparatus and before long everything was back to normal. The locomotive stayed with us until the train arrived; after which we were soon rolling on our way to Regina.

It was a badly demoralized troupe that arrived in Regina the next day. Too late to play the matinee performance and with half a dozen of them coughing and sneezing. My partner came up with a bad case of laryngi-

tis necessitating cancellation of our evening performances. By the next morning she was running a high
temperature and that afternoon was hospitalized with
pneumonia. She was dangerously ill for three days, then
rallied and was discharged from the hospital two weeks
later.

In the meantime, I had been giving much thought to
my career problem. If I wanted the dramatic stock company experience that Dave Weston had talked about, it
was high time I went about getting it. This forced interruption of the vaudeville tour served to focus my attention on the matter and I made my decision. I would send
in my notice and end the tour.

I told my partner of my intentions, explaining that I
would stay with the act until she had properly rehearsed
my replacement. To my surprise she told me that she was
delighted at my decision, that she had been thinking
along the same lines and had been worrying about breaking it to me.

So ended my first flyer in vaudeville.

My next stop was Chicago, where I stayed over for a
few days in the hope that I might see Dave Weston. Not
having his address I made inquiries at the theatrical
agencies and learned that he was on the road with a
repertoire company.

The same agency that gave me this information offered me a week's worth with a stock company in Indianapolis. It was an excellent part in a good play and as I
had heard that the Indianapolis company was top flight, I
accepted.

The engagement was uneventful except that because
of it an idea was born.

It was truly a fine company and was playing nothing but recent Broadway releases. The play I was in, for instance, had ended a successful Broadway run less than six months previously. The plays were staged by an excellent director and were beautifully mounted.

I was playing the heavy and my more important scenes, including a fight scene, were with the leading man. A good actor and true matinee idol type; the Indianapolis Femmes were Ga-Ga over him. And did he know it? His attitude toward the other actors was highly contemptuous. I loathed him on sight. The feeling was reciprocated. To me—the fill-in chap from Chicago—he offered nothing but supercilious tolerance.

I not only detested him, I was jealous of his position. I wanted to be the leading man in a first class company like this. Perhaps that is why, although not consciously aware that I was doing it, I was a bit too realistic when rehearsing the fight scene. He was petulant about it and complained to the director whereupon I put on my best lace-curtain expression and promised not to play so rough—even as I was toying with the idea of laying him out at the dress rehearsal so he would be unable to play the opening performance. In which case, I figured, they might let me take his place.

I discarded the idea, however, after coming to the conclusion that if the customers went for a pretty son-of-a-bitch like him, they certainly wouldn't buy my type.

The play opened on Monday night as scheduled and went over beautifully. I received flattering notices in the newspaper reviews but the real kudos were reserved for the leading man. It was while reading these reviews that I hatched the idea of foxing the New York agents.

I went to a newspaper office and from its files copied a

half dozen previous reviews, selecting ones which extolled the work of the leading man. I rewrote them, eliminating the name of the stock company and substituting my name for that of the leading man. Later, in Chicago, I had these copies printed on newsprint paper.

I reasoned that these phony reviews, together with the legitimate Boston Transcript reviews, would serve as sufficient ammunition to enable me to crash the barriers and gain a hearing as an established leading man. Up to this time the only agents I had come face to face with were the obscure lady who had gotten me the Chicago Repertory engagement and the Chamberlain Brown Office which had figured in the Al Woods incident. My strategy would be to concentrate on the others.

It did not occur to me that what I was planning was at all reprehensible. I was a member of a profession which was teeming with people whose every waking moment was engaged in pretense. On, or off, they were constantly pretending to be something other than what they were. Consequently, if the agents were gullible enough to be taken in by my simple ruse, all the more power to me.

Back in New York, I lost no time in going about my nefarious scheme. I placed copies of the reviews in an envelope, wrote the name Wales Winter on it and went to the Wales Winter Agency, which, together with the Packard Agency and the Chamberlain Brown Agency, handled the bulk of stock company casting.

Handing the envelope to the receptionist, I told her that Mr. Winter was expecting it. She disappeared with it into the inner office. I waited, supremely confident, inasmuch as I had everything to gain and nothing to lose, and cast indulgent glances at the lesser mortals who crowded the reception room.

The receptionist was gone for a considerable time but when she reappeared and beckoned me in, I knew immediately that the first phase of my scheme had worked. I had crashed the barrier.

Mr. Winter was holding my reviews in his hand and it was quite evident that he was impressed. His interest, happily, was mostly in the legitimate reviews from Boston and we talked at length about the Castle Square Company and its virtues.

He was puzzled that he had not heard of me before and questioned me further as to my experience. I told him the truth of my experience in burlesque, repertory and vaudeville, after which he turned again to the fake reviews and asked, "And this company. Where was it playing?"

"Minneapolis."

"When?"

"I just closed there a couple of weeks ago."

"Strange. I hadn't known there was a company playing there."

At this point I was considering the advisability of making for the nearest exit, knowing that if he persisted on this line, I was sunk. But fate intervened. I was saved by the bell. His telephone rang, and by the time he had finished his phone conversation and turned back to me, Minneapolis was forgotten.

He dismissed me, asking me to return at two o'clock that same afternoon. I did so and after being interviewed by a stock company manager from Harrisburg, Pennsylvania, was engaged to join his company as leading man at a salary of a hundred and fifty dollars a week.

The Harrisburg engagement was important for it established me as a leading man. I played there for twenty weeks; it led to another engagement and I was soon in demand.

A couple of seasons later I graduated to the actor-manager class by establishing a company of my own in a city located a few miles out of Boston. This was a hard working project for me inasmuch as I functioned as leading man, director and producer. I took great pains in putting my company together, striving to emulate the excellence that had been maintained by John Craig at the Castle Square Theater. I was lucky to obtain the services of Al Roberts as stage manager. His vast experience and showmanship were invaluable to me in selecting players and plays.

In some small requital for having launched me as a leading man I engaged all of my players through the Wales Winter Agency. The first request I made of him was to locate David Weston whom I wanted to engage as my character man. I welcomed the opportunity of affording this grand old actor the pleasure of playing good roles in fine plays with a first rate company.

I was too late. Dave had died during the previous winter. What he had feared most had happened. He had died in a skid row flop house in Chicago.

The character actor I engaged was Donald Meek, a splendid actor who was destined to become famous on Broadway and in Hollywood.

My entire company, with one exception, was composed of experienced and reliable journeymen actors and I was proud of them.

The exception was my leading lady. She was relatively inexperienced and as she proved later not exactly what one might call reliable. In my search for a leading woman I had discovered that the names on my preferred list were not available, nor was there one among the many I interviewed whom I chose to engage. Finally Mr. Winter suggested that I look at a girl who was currently playing a small part in a Broadway show. "She hasn't had much experience," he said, "but she's young, beautiful and, I think, has talent. She's very anxious to acquire stock experience."

I went to see the play and was impressed, particularly by her poise and her looks. The agent arranged an audition and after having her read a couple of key scenes from our opening play, I engaged her.

She made a terrific impact on the town, arriving there in a chauffeur-driven Rolls Royce limousine, wearing a thirty-thousand-dollar chinchilla coat and sitting between two Russian wolfhounds. She leased a very expensive house on the ocean front and staffed it with a butler, French maid, house maid, cook and chauffeur. This on a salary of a hundred and twenty-five dollars per week.

It was great copy for the newspapers and they made the most of it, which was not at all displeasing to me. We opened to capacity business and the company went over in a big way, especially myself and my spectacular leading lady.

It soon became apparent that I was in for a very successful season, for which I was thankful and proud. Not to the extent, however, that my parents were. They were now living in Everett, a Boston suburb. I arranged to have a box held in reserve for them at all times. They never missed a play, coming sometimes twice or three times a week. My father, particularly, was an ardent fan. He, who had been most vehement against my becoming an actor was now ridiculously proud of me. My house

manager disapprovingly reported that my father would
prowl the lobby between acts, listening for comments
about me. He would bristle on hearing something derog-
atory and blossom like a rose if he heard a complimentary remark. If he heard neither, he would make conversation and ask people's opinion of my performance. On
receiving a favorable answer he would immediately in-
troduce himself as my father.

Undignified it may have been but I liked it and
wouldn't have had him act any other way. The old boy's
approval meant a lot to me.

We had been in operation less than a month when
scandalous stories anent my leading lady began to circulate. It was whispered that there were orgiastic goings-on
in her house of nights. It became common gossip that
certain prominent male citizens were romantically involved with the lady. The scandal became so open that I,
worried about its possible effect on my business, quietly
investigated the situation and found that the lady was a
bit of a nymphomaniac, plus being a smart business
woman, and was cutting a wide swathe through the ranks
of high society playboys, married and single.

Her morals were no business of mine unless and until
her behavior began to have a harmful effect on the box-
office at which time I would take action of some sort.

Several weeks passed. I was visited by a committee
representing a political party. In hush-hush fashion they
told me that a prominent young politician, an honored
and respected citizen of a nearby community and whom
the party was grooming as a gubernatorial candidate,
had been bewitched by the wiles of my siren to the extent
that a major scandal was in the making. He was married
and the father of two children. His socially prominent

wife was on the verge of suing for divorce. This action must be prevented at all cost else his political career was down the drain. They had come to ask my help.

I did not need them to tell me the disaster-potential contained in a scandal of this proportion. I did not care a damn about the politican but I was very much concerned for my theater. The only way in which I could help would be in firing the girl. This of course was what they had come to request. I explained that such an action in itself offered no guaranteed solution. "What happens," I asked, "if I fire her and she elects to stay in town?"

"We'll frame her and throw her in the can."

I considered this unfair treatment and said so. I suggested that the easiest solution was to ship their boy out of town for a cooling-off period. The answer was that they had already suggested this plan but that he refused to go along with it.

I then pointed out to them that apart from the manifest injustice to the girl, I must consider the danger to my business if I fired her. She was very popular in the town. A great number of my customers would resent losing her, might turn thumbs down on any new actress I brought in to replace her. And then I would be up the well-known creek.

"No, gentlemen," I said. "I have a fine paying little business going for me here and I don't intend to sacrifice it simply because your boy can't control his hot pants."

"You'll be through anyway, just as soon as the story breaks."

"I'll take my chances on that," I said.

The interview ended on that note.

The same day I called the lady in question (or the questionable lady) on the carpet and briefed her as to my

knowledge of her activities. I explained that I was interested in her personal life only when it endangered the
welfare of my theater. I told her of the visit by the political committee and stressed the point that the affair with
the politician could well result in closing up. I
pleaded, I cajoled, and finally threatened her with the
ultimatum that either she agree to end the affair immediately or she would have to go.

I have been told off many times, and by experts, but
never before have I been dirtied by a flood of Billingsgate
such as spewed from the mouth of that beautiful nymph.
A sense of decency prevents my writing a word-by-word
report of the tirade. Even as a kid I was never one to
scrawl dirty words on fences.

Divested of the lurid passages, her answer consisted of
a flat refusal to cooperate and a contemptuous dismissal
of my threat to fire her. Her exit speech was, "You won't
fire me. I'm all that's keeping this crummy, two-bit company alive, and you know it."

That evening I received a phone call from one of the
committee men. He said, bluntly, that he had been au-
thorized to make me a proposition. They were offering
me ten thousand dollars to cover any losses I might suffer
by firing the girl.

Inasmuch as I had already decided to get rid of her, I
was not faced with too difficult a decision. I agreed that
ten thousand dollars cash in hand by Saturday morning
would ensure her discharge.

These events took place on a Thursday. On Friday
morning the cash was delivered to me and on Saturday
night after the performance, I paid the lady two-weeks
salary in lieu of notice and advised her to get out of
town.

Her reply is unprintable.

At two a.m. on Sunday morning, the politicos, in connivance with the police, staged a phony raid on her house and she was faced with the alternative of leaving town, immediately and permanently, or being booked on the charge of conducting a disorderly house.

She wisely decided that a retreat was in order and, accompanied by her borzois, French maid and chauffeur, mounted her Rolls Royce and rolled out of my life. She was escorted to the county line by the police.

The lady had overestimated her drawing power. I issued brief statements to the press, explaining her sudden departure as due to family illness. The audiences took kindly to her replacement and we played on with no noticeable drop in attendance until the Lenten season.

I knew business would decline during Lent but was not prepared for a toboggan slide into a sea of red ink. A quick switch in policy helped in some degree. I cancelled late Broadway releases and booked old favorites, such as "Quo Vadis" and "The Sign of The Cross." I even put on a play which I had written, a terrible piece of tripe. I advertised it as a new play and offered a prize of five hundred dollars for the best title. The winning title was "Brown's Cows" which may give you an idea of its subject matter. It was, I confess, about Brown's cows. They got through the fence, you see, into Jackson's corn field and precipitated a feud. Brown had a daughter and Jackson had a son. I leave the rest to your imagination. I must report though, that "Brown's Cows" was the only play which showed a profit during the slump.

I considered the advisability of closing and decided to hold on until after Easter. Then, if business did not pick up, I would hang up the notice.

I did, however, close down during Holy Week, a traditionally bad time for theater attendance, and took advantage of the respite by organizing a fishing trip.

There were five of us: Karl Steiger, realtor; Joe Rankin, hardware merchant; Tom Kelly, hotel man; Donald Meek, and myself. We planned to leave early on the morning of Palm Sunday. Destination—a small island, situated three miles offshore. It was an acre-and-a-half of craggy rock, the highest point of which thrust up a mere forty feet out of the Atlantic Ocean. It boasted but one habitation, a dilapidated one room shack, built of driftwood and tarpaper. The only fresh water available was supplied by a cistern.

Although the official weather forecast had warned of a heavy storm approaching from the northeast, Palm Sunday morning dawned bright and clear and it appeared that we were to be blessed with lovely spring weather. Our holiday-bound group, two of whom, Kelly and Steiger, were feeling no pain, gathered at the shore in festive mood.

After loading into a rented dory five days provisions, including a case of bourbon and twelve cases of beer, fishing and sleeping gear, we shoved off; Donald Meek and Rankin at the oars.

I know of no safer or more seaworthy small boat than a fishing dory. Any Gloucester fisherman will attest that properly handled it will ride out the heaviest seas. It was instantly apparent, however, that our oarsmen didn't know the score and we were quickly turned broadside to the breakers. The situation was not helped any by the antics of our two drunks who were attempting to outdo each other in gymnastic stunts along the gunwales.

A dory is not easy to capsize but something had to be

done quickly if we were to avoid disaster. The surf was heavy and two of the men could not swim.

I grabbed the oars from one of the rowers and although I was no expert oarsman, instinct came to the rescue and I managed to get the boat headed into the seas.

When we had gotten beyond the surf and were progressing steadily over the long swells, Donald Meek suddenly shipped his oars and with an anguished groan collapsed across the gunwale and gave his all.

As if on cue, our two drunken shipmates turned green and followed suit.

Seasickness is a devastating malady and as those who have experienced it must agree, it is not a laughing matter. Perhaps because of a perverse sense of humor, I thought the situation very funny indeed and laughed heartily, much to the indignation of Rankin, whose face even as he was upbraiding me for my callousness was assuming the same ghastly pallor as the others.

I became hilarious.

Unfortunately as he suddenly let go, he was pointed in my direction and I received the full benefit of the upheaval.

I was no longer amused. To the contrary, I was instantly faced with the awful realization that my own stomach was doing flip-flops.

I did my best to fight it off. Closing my eyes to the sight of those four miserable wretches, I rowed like a madman. I sang at the top of my voice. I belted myself with bourbon.

All to no avail. The sight, the sound, the smell and the old rocking boat got me. I lined up at the rail with the others.

It was a greatly subdued group that finally put in at a

tiny beach on the leeward side of the island. We really didn't care if we lived or died. To add to our woes there had been a sharp change in the weather. The sun had disappeared behind a bank of black clouds and an icy wind was blowing in from the northeast.

Remembering the storm warnings broadcast by the weather bureau I knew we might be in for a rugged time and spelled it out to the others, suggesting that we turn back and try to beat the storm to the mainland. I was shouted down. I truly believe that they would have faced sure death rather than step back into that boat and to be frank about it, I put up a very feeble argument.

We proceeded to unload and secure the boat, then started the arduous task of packing the heavy stores up and over the slippery rocks to the shack. Because of our weakened condition, this necessitated several trips and by the time we had finished the temperature had dropped sharply, the wind was blowing very hard and it had begun to snow. Having been brought up in New England weather I could read the signs and realized that a real, block-buster of a nor'easter was in the making.

The shack was tiny, measuring about ten by twelve feet. It had a dirt floor and many chinks in the walls and roof. The furnishings consisted of two narrow built-in bunks, a kitchen table, two nail-kegs in lieu of chairs and an old kitchen range.

If the storm continued to develop we might be forced to hole up in this frail sanctuary, maybe for days. And if we were not to suffer from the cold, or freeze, we must gather a huge supply of drift-wood and chop it to fit the range. There was also the question of fresh water supply. Water must be carried in buckets from the cistern to a huge water barrel which stood just outside the door.

Kelly and Steiger had pre-empted the bunks. Rankin was seated on the floor beside them and all three were intent upon killing a bottle of bourbon. I pointed out the necessity for preparing against the storm and proposed that we all turn to and get the work done.

To my surprise and consternation my suggestion was greeted with Bronx cheers. They were on a holiday and had no intention of concerning themselves with such mundane tasks as hauling water and drift-wood.

It was at this point that I took over. I proclaimed my assumption of power together with a Philippic which would have made my grandfather justly proud. Such was the power of my egotism and self-assurance that they obeyed like little lambs when I finally snatched the booze away from them and ordered them out of the shack with instructions to bring in enough drift-wood to maintain a fire throughout the night.

Donald Meek promptly dubbed me "Wolf Larson," an epithet which persisted until the end of the ill-fated holiday and which probably was apt enough.

By nightfall an impressive supply of drift-wood had been gathered, the water barrel was full, everybody had worked off the effects of *mal de mer* and I had prepared a meal which consisted of thick porterhouse steaks, fried potatoes, canned peaches and coffee. We ate heartily and after cleaning up were ready to sit out the night.

And what a night! Eerie is the word to describe it. The storm developed into a raging blizzard. The wind, having reached gale velocity, threatened at times to pick up the shack and deposit it and us into the sea. It howled about the shack with the frenzied shrieks of a million Comanches and in combination with the thunderous crash of monstrous waves against the island cliffs created an ear-splitting cacophony of sound which made sleep virtually impossible.

Conversation was limited to monosyllabic shouts as, fully dressed and draped in blankets, we sat on the floor playing poker by the flickering light of a kerosene lantern. Despite a fire hot enough to keep the stove lids glowing red, the icy chill pervading the shack would have given a brass monkey cause to worry about his future. To further combat the chill we were drinking hot Kentucky bourbon, spiked with Jamaica ginger. And if ever you find yourself marooned on a tiny rock in the open sea during a rip-snorting blizzard, shivering with cold and fear, I recommend that you try this potent concoction. It will warm your blood and add at least three feet to your height.

By midnight we were all hilariously smashed. All fear gone, we were having the time of our lives and defying the storm gods to do their worst.

Someone up there must have heard us because suddenly we were startled out of our defiant confidence by the demoniacal shrieking as spikes tore loose from tortured wood and the entire roof disappeared into the night. The shack was instantly filled with swirling snow as the wind swooped and eddied about us.

After a moment of stunned surprise, Rankin panicked. Leaping to his feet he rushed to the door. As he lifted the latch the force of the wind slammed the door back against him and knocked him unconscious to the floor. It took the combined efforts of three of us to force the door shut.

The stove pipe had carried away, consequently the back draft created by the wind showered us with sparks, making it necessary to douse the fire thus leaving us completely exposed to the freezing cold except for the shaky walls of the shack which served to break the force of the wind and which undoubtedly enabled us to survive the night.

Our panicky friend's encounter with the door had left him with a broken nose which we treated by plying him with whiskey until he passed out.

As our immediate problem was that of survival, we stretched out and, huddling together like sheep, pooled the bedding which consisted of five blankets, and one cheap cotton comforter. The comforter was the property of Donald Meek who had brought it to insure protection against the cold for his bald head. He was allowed to keep it and so he promptly swathed himself in it, looking like an Eskimo squaw.

The blankets afforded shelter only in the crudest sense against the raging, ice-laden wind which penetrated them as though they were made of tissue paper. It was not until the blankets had been covered with a thick layer of snow, sealing in such heat as was generated by our shivering bodies, that our teeth stopped chattering and allowed us to relax in comparative warmth.

The hours until daylight seemed interminable. The howling of the wind, the constant thunder of mountainous waves crashing against the rocks, the iron-hard floor and the all-pervasive cold made it a truly torturous experience and when, at long last, it was daylight I, although blessed with rugged health and normally imbued with a wonderful feeling of vigor and well-being, found myself stiff with cold, bruised and sore from tossing and turning on the hard floor, exhausted from lack of sleep, and with the disposition of a wounded bob-cat.

There had been no abatement in the fury of the storm;

the wind was still raging fiercely, the temperature was subzero and snow was swirling into the shack so thickly that peering through it was like trying to see through a turkish towel. It was a foot deep on the floor and on our blankets. As self-appointed cook it was up to me to dish up some eats. So forcing myself to crawl out into the freezing temperature of the shack, I waded through the snow and uncovered the stove from a drift which reached nearly to the top of the wall.

Ordinarily building a fire is a simple chore and should require no special skill, nor should it pose any problem to tax the thinking apparatus of any but the veriest moron. But the conditions surrounding the building of this particular fire were somewhat unique. The only paper available consisted of the damp wrappings and bags containing our food supply. I gathered it together and laid it in the grate. Then, after splitting chunks of damp driftwood for kindling, I laid the fire and attempted to light it.

The wind had other ideas. Swooping down in all its frenzied fury it blew out the matches as I lit them. In my frustrated efforts to guard the feeble flames, I assumed postures that would have been the envy of a contortionist. Finally after consuming dozens of matches, the paper ignited and I was elated. Only for a few seconds. The paper merrily burned itself out, leaving the kindling pure and untouched.

My shoes were now filled with snow; my feet were wet and freezing; my teeth were chattering and my hands were numb. I had about decided to get back under cover when I remembered that our supplies contained a carton of toilet paper. I relaid the fire, using a roll of the paper as a base.

It worked. The paper ignited with a swoosh.

But the wind had become my mortal enemy. Shrieking in derision, it whisked the flimsy paper from beneath the wood, filling the air with sparks and flaming bits.

This time, however, I had made some progress. The wood was steaming.

I again relaid the fire, this time using three rolls of the paper. Then, my dormant intelligence roused enough to direct me to douse the kindling with kerosene from the lantern.

Success. The resulting eruption would have gladdened the heart of the maddest pyromaniac. Smoke and flames shot ten feet into the air, and even though I lost my eyebrows and most of my hair, I considered it a beautiful spectacle.

The wind, refusing to admit defeat, did its damndest to blow the entire fire into space, casting millions of sparks against the shaky walls and threatening to send the whole shebang up in smoke. But with breakfast in the making I couldn't have cared less.

There is something about the aroma of sizzling bacon and coffee as it comes to the boil which, when savored on a frosty morning in the open, is warranted to stir the senses of the soundest sleeper. And as the air became permeated by these heavenly perfumes, I expected the guys to rise up and with shining eyes and cries of gratitude rush forth to partake of the Lucullan feast I was preparing.

As nothing stirred under the snow-covered blankets, I sounded the tocsin by beating on a dish pan. Even then the response was less than enthusiastic.

All that appeared was something resembling a small mummy. As it crawled painfully from under the covers I identified it by the comforter in which its head and shoulders were swathed.

A great part of Donald Meek's success as a comedian was due to his appearance and his voice—short, bullet-headed, gimlet-eyed and with a mouth like a bear trap. His voice was high-pitched, querulous, and when he was excited, as penetrating as the screech of street-car wheels rounding a sharp curve.

He had taken off his boots and as his stocking feet met the deep snow, he began to hop from foot to foot, his piping voice railing at the cold and pleading for someone to hand him his God-damned boots.

Had every move been planned as a comedy routine he couldn't have been funnier.

Then, hampered by the comforter, he threw it aside and what had been merely funny became excruciating. The colors of the cheap print had run, transferring its rainbow-hued pattern to his bald head and face.

I yelled with laughter while Donald glowered at me in uncomprehending resentment. Unshaven, dirty, hung-over and shaking with cold, he was in no mood for levity and loosed a torrent of invective.

Fearing that he was about to blow a gasket, I explained the cause of my hilarity, at the same time shoving a mug of hot coffee into his fist. The coffee did the trick. He calmed down to his normal state of irascibility.

I turned to rouse the others and found three casualties.

Of the three, Rankin was in best shape. His nose was grotesquely swollen and both eyes had blackened but he was ambulatory and was easily coaxed to get up and eat.

But Kelly and Steiger were *hors de combat*. The long hours of exposure had been too much for them. Feverish, with sick eyes, runny noses and sore throats, they rejected all efforts to tempt them with hot coffee and shiveringly begged to be let alone.

I did just that. After covering them up again I saw to my own breakfast. It did not occur to me that these men might be seriously ill. In my youthful arrogance I considered them a couple of guys who couldn't take it. They had caught cold. So what? They'd get over it.

It was Donald Meek who startled us into the realization that allowing them to lie there in their soggy clothes and blankets was an invitation to pneumonia or worse.

Donald it was, also, who insisted that the sick men be kept warm and dry, probably saving their lives thereby.

As the storm raged about us we stoked up the fire and despite their pathetic protests stripped the men and placed their clothes in the oven to dry.

Then we dosed them with copious drafts of hot Jamaica ginger and bourbon, which portion Meek was now referring to as "Wolf Larson's Tiger Piss."

By mid-morning it had become painfully aware that our plight was critical. The condition of Kelly and Steiger had worsened. Both of them were running high fevers and in spite of the fact that we had succeeded in drying their clothes and blankets, they were racked by spasms of shivering. As our fuel supply neared exhaustion the problem of keeping them even relatively warm became more difficult by the minute.

Meek and Rankin volunteered to brave the wind in an attempt to gather drift-wood but I refused to allow it. The fury of the blizzard could easily have blown them into the sea.

As I laid the last sticks on the fire, I found myself eyeing the leeward wall of the shack. There were enough boards to keep the fire burning for hours. As it stood, the roofless shack was pitifully inadequate as a shelter and the loss of the back wall couldn't make it any more so.

It was clear that Kelly and Steiger would check out unless we could keep them warm.

I posed the question to Meek and Rankin and within minutes we had started the job of demolition. It turned out to be a major project. We had but the one axe and our numbed hands to work with and as each board came loose the wind did its damndest to wrench it from our hands. By the time the wall was down and the boards hacked into stove lengths we were near exhaustion and our hands were bristling with splinters.

We were delighted with the results, however. We now had fuel enough to last through the coming night; the remaining walls were standing firm and actually afforded better protection than ever. The wind continued to blow with hurricane force but it no longer eddied about us. Instead, it swept down over the seaward wall and continued on out through the open end of the shack carrying its freight of snow along with it. Also, we were now able to clear the knee-deep snow from the floor.

As this second murderous night closed in, the savage white maelstrom raging beyond the open end of the shack was weirdly beautiful and with its accompaniment of shrieking gale and booming seas suggested a perfect background for some fantastic science-fiction drama.

But to us, the flesh and blood cast of characters who completed the bizarre ensemble, the drama was all too real. Against tremendous odds, we were engaged in an all-out slugging match with nature; the lives of our helpless companions hanging in the balance.

In addition to my concern for the sick men, I was weighted down by a sense of responsibility for this tragic situation. I had organized the outing. It was at my invitation that they were here. I had arbitrarily assumed leadership of the group, a position which obligated me to find a way out of this desperate situation.

The frustration of it, the inability to do anything for these stricken men left me with a feeling of utter inadequacy. I felt like a babe in the woods.

Illogical reasoning perhaps, but quite understandable to me. Less comprehensible was my emotional attitude towards Kelly and Steiger.

In their anguish, they seemed to be putting forth an aura of infantile pettiness, recrimination and fear that repelled me. While I was keenly aware of the misery they were suffering, there were times while administering to their needs that my concern for them was tempered by disgust and, I think, by contempt.

In brief, I had formed an active dislike for them.

There was no question of friendship involved. Up to this time our relations had been merely those of acquaintances. Beyond the dictates of common decency, their fate meant nothing to me. I was disturbed that I could not force my mind to stop struggling with devastating thoughts of guilt and sorrow, that I could not accept the dictates of fate and let it go at that.

But the ball didn't bounce that way and when I had finally settled down under the covers, I pictured their gaunt faces and the unmistakable stamp of mortal illness and I wept a little. And I was thankful for the all-concealing darkness. It would have been most embarrassing had Meek and Rankin seen Wolf Larson sobbing his heart out.

I was becoming inured to the frightful racket raised by the blizzard or, as was more likely, perhaps exhaustion was taking its toll. I fell asleep almost immediately and

remained out of this world until some four hours later
when an excited Donald Meek jolted me back to awareness. He was clawing at my shoulder and yelling that
Steiger was dying.

I have heard it said that a doctor trains himself to
regard a seriously ill patient not as a person but as a case.
Thus, if a case goes sour and the patient dies, the doctor
is not racked by emotional strain.

I choose to believe that the doctor really trains himself
to hide his emotions.

Steiger showed every evidence of being in the process
of dying. He was unconscious. His eyes were rolled back
in his head. His skin was a ghastly blue and as he fought
convulsively for breath his mouth was wide open and
rimmed with mucus.

My reaction was a combination of nearly all the
emotions.

I could see that his throat was choked by a mass of
greenish-white mucus which seemed to rise in gurgling
bubbles as he frantically gasped for air. The same agonizing feeling of inadequacy overwhelmed me as I crouched
helpless in my ignorance of what to do and watched him
approach complete cyanosis.

Meek contributed to my frustration by repeated pleas
for me to "Do something. For Christ's sake, do something."

Then, after what seemed an interminable length of
time, I instinctively thrust my fingers into Steiger's throat
in an attempt to grasp the slimy stuff. I could as easily
have picked up a handful of quicksilver.

I tried again with the same dismal result, except that
this time his teeth closed on my fingers. I still bear a scar
as a memento of the occasion.

Meanwhile, his time was running out. I made a third

desperate attempt. Wrapping my hand in my handkerchief, I thrust deeply into his throat, crooked my fingers
and gently but firmly pulled. I brought forth a huge gob
of ropy phlegm that could have choked a horse.

Steiger shuddered, coughed convulsively and began to
breathe, sucking air into his lungs in great gulps.

I rushed to the open end of the shack and threw up.

We watched over Steiger until the blue receded from
his skin and he was breathing easier. As we could do no
more for him and because we were rapidly being transformed into human icicles, we retreated beneath the
covers.

The rest of the night was uneventful. I slept fitfully
until after daylight when I was startled by the squawk of
a sea gull. I opened my eyes to see him staring at me
from atop the seaward wall. For a moment my numbed
brain only registered wonder that the bird could perch
here so effortlessly in defiance of the wind.

Then he squawked again and the realization came that
my ears were no longer being deafened. Only then did I
grasp the fact that there was no wind. And it had stopped
snowing.

The hurricane was over.

I yelled like a madman, scaring hell out of Meek and
Rankin, who came up standing, demanding to know
what was happening.

For a quick couple of minutes we were a joyful trio
but a check on Kelly and Steiger soon chilled our enthusiasm. They lay comatose and barely alive, the snow-
covered blankets covering them in a shocking suggestion
of winding sheets.

We all knew that the one slim chance for these men to
live was to get them to a hospital, and fast.

We were also aware of the awesome turbulence that

was the ocean; a vast expanse of mountainous waves on which a small boat had little chance to survive.

There was no discussion and no hesitation. We'd have to try.

Meek went ahead to ready the boat. Rankin and I followed, carrying the unconscious Steiger. As we came out of the shack door Meek had started the descent over the rocks to the beach.

A second later we heard him shout, then he reappeared, running fast and yelling. We figured he'd been goosed by an electric eel.

Our boat had been carried away by the storm.

Someone once said or wrote something to the effect that God protects fools and babies. To some extent I must agree with the good wisecracker whoever he was. God does sometimes, and perhaps too often, take care of fools. He does sometimes, and not often enough, protect babies. I do believe that God intervened to save our lives.

Only a fool would have entertained the thought of rowing a dory across that three miles of watery chaos. Had the boat not been lost and if we had embarked, I am positive that we five orphans of the storm would have been scratched within minutes after the launching.

But at that time I could only view the loss of the boat as complete disaster. There were perhaps two dozen people who knew of our outing and I could think of no reason why any of them should be particularly concerned for our safety. We were grown men, plentifully provisioned and in possession of a staunch boat. The natural deduction would be that we would sit out the storm in comparative comfort and come home at our leisure. They could not know, of course, that we were marooned and that two members of our party were dying of illness and exposure. Rescue in time to save the lives of Kelly and Steiger seemed very remote.

We couldn't have been more isolated had we been on a meteor fragment in outer space. Less than three miles away were warm beds, doctors and nurses but until the giant seas subsided the three miles might as well have been three million.

After circuiting the island twice in a futile search for the dory, we resigned ourselves to the frustrating realization that we could do nothing more than wait, and hope.

As the morning wore on the temperature dropped to a degree that would have overpowered the cold resisting capacity of a Polar bear and by ten o'clock our fuel supply was again running low. As the wind had swept the island clean of everything that wasn't nailed down, including drift-wood, the shack again became the source of life-sustaining warmth.

We demolished both side walls, reducing our erstwhile shelter to something resembling a false front on a poverty-row movie set. It took the rest of the day to accomplish this task, during which time we were constantly harassed by sea gulls. The birds had come out in force and instead of going about their own business, whatever that might have been, they circled above us, squawking back and forth to each other like a squadron of Navy pilots, meanwhile using us as targets for bombing practice.

In spite of their uncanny accuracy, we were undeterred by this impolite heckling and carried on with our work, our heads unbloodied but bowed.

Actually they served to lift our morale to the degree that every hit scored by a bird called forth a ribald remark by one or the other of us, depending upon which one of us was the recipient of the package.

By late afternoon the seas had subsided to an encouraging degree. We kept an eager eye to the shore hoping every moment to see a rescue boat heading our way. But the sea remained empty and our hopes faded with the daylight. Even the gulls disappeared and as the icy darkness enveloped us our brief elation of the afternoon turned to utter dejection. Near exhaustion, chilled to the bone, our muscles lame, our hands swollen and bloody from splinter wounds, we hovered over the fire and through black-rimmed eyes expressed the unspoken thoughts that haunted us. Not an unnecessary word was said as we set about the meager preparations for the night.

Because of the intense cold we decided to keep the fire burning, making it necessary to split the night into watches. I elected to take the first four-hour shift, and after caring for the sick men, Meek and Rankin turned in.

During that melancholy vigil I reached the lowest point of my dejection. The cold was almost unbearable and even though the stove glowed ruby red, to keep from freezing I stood close to it, revolving slowly like a chicken roasting on a spit, my mind churning with thoughts of death.

I actually searched my mind for appropriate phrases of sympathy to use when delivering the corpses to Mrs. Kelly and Mrs. Steiger.

"The darkest hour comes just before the dawn." Corny? So what. It's been proven out time and time again that the old corn-merchants had something. Certainly I was in my darkest hour when I saw the light. At least, I thought I saw it. Far off toward the shore it seemed to hover over the sea for a brief moment. Then it was gone.

Not sure that it hadn't been a figment of wishful thinking, I put a damper on my hopes, held my breath and crossed my fingers. Then, like a little kid, I stared into the darkness and tried to conjure up a boat.

And who is there to say I didn't do just that?

Suddenly the light twinkled again. Just as suddenly it again disappeared. But I knew now that there was a boat out there.

I roused Meek and Rankin. We quickly carried a heap of our precious boards to the highest point of the island and built a fire.

Within minutes we heard a gun shot and knew that our signal had been seen and acknowledged. Our guess was that it was a Coast Guard boat.

Our guess was a miss. Two hours later we were aboard a lobster boat and chugging full speed ahead (eight knots an hour) toward safety.

Our rescuer was Luigi Ferrago, the little old fisherman who had rented me the dory and shack. He had worried all through the storm, not about our safety but about his property. As soon after the storm as it was safe to navigate he had put out in his lobster boat to investigate.

He was infuriated by the loss of his dory and when he saw what had happened to his shack he was apoplectic with rage. I was forced then and there to make a deal, promising to pay through the nose, before he would allow us to put Kelly and Steiger aboard.

That little old man was, however, among the least of our worries.

Kelly and Steiger were rushed to a hospital and were

deemed critically ill, Kelly with pneumonia and Steiger with pneumonia plus diphtheria.

Rankin was treated in emergency for his broken nose and allowed to go home.

Meek and I were besieged by reporters. The storm, one of the worst in New England history, had been front-page news for three days. It had created havoc up and down the coast, demolishing boats, sea walls and water front buildings.

We had hit the headlines the night of our rescue, word having gotten out that day that we were on the island. The press made a big story of it on the presumption that we were long gone.

Kelly and Steiger both recovered. Steiger's vocal cords had been injured, however, and from then on he went through life, whispering. He blamed me for the damage and threatened suit but finally accepted the advice of his lawyer and dropped it.

Rankin came out of it with a slightly crooked nose.

It was several weeks before the dye faded from Meek's head and face. Outside of that he suffered no ill effects.

Donald and I never trouped together after that season but the expedition to the island cemented a lasting friendship. He has long since gone from my horizon but I shall always remember him fondly as a fine actor and as the biggest little man I ever knew.

Incidentally, the resulting publicity boosted my theater business tremendously and we played to near capacity for the rest of the season.

The next few years provided but slim pickings for me. There were some routine stock engagements and one short season on the road with a second-rate company.

My dream of taking Broadway by storm began to fade.

Then one afternoon, in New York, I learned that the Shubert office was having trouble casting a leading role in a new Lionel Barrymore play.

I went to the Shubert office where much to my surprise I was ushered post-haste into the casting director's office. After a short interview the casting director accompanied me into the presence of Lee Shubert, a gray, little man. Shubert didn't even acknowledge the introduction but after sizing me up like a prize bull nodded his assent.

We returned to the casting director's office where he instructed me to report at once to a Mr. X, at the Broadhurst Theater. Mr. X being the director who was staging the play and whose name I have forgotten.

I have also forgotten the title of the play. It was a period piece and one of the worst plays I had ever read. The role offered me, however, was a flashy one and of equal importance as the Barrymore role. Not the great star-making part of my dreams but one in which I could score even if the play was a disaster.

The play had already been in rehearsal for a week and a half, leaving only ten days before it was to open cold on Broadway.

During the last run-through before dinner on the afternoon of my fourth day of rehearsing, Jack Barrymore sat out front and watched the rehearsal.

At the finish, Lionel went out and sat with Jack. After a few minutes the cast was dismissed for an hour-and-a-half dinner break. The stage manager notified me that the call did not concern me and that he would call me at my hotel.

I attached no particular significance to this exclusion,

figuring that they were going to work on scenes that I was not in. When the evening passed, however, and I received no call I began to wonder and about midnight, I went to bed with the premonition that something was cooking, something that was not going to be my dish.

My phone rang at eight-thirty in the morning. It was the stage manager calling to tell me to report to the Shubert office at ten o'clock. Whatever was cooking began to smell pretty bad.

At the Shubert office I found Mr. X waiting for me. As soon as I looked at him I knew I was about to get the gate.

Mr. X was personally officiating as executioner because he wished to soften the blow. He wished to tell me exactly why I was getting the axe and to express his indignation that it was happening.

He told me that Jack Barrymore, after watching the rehearsal had said to Lionel, "Get rid of that red-headed son-of-a-bitch or he'll steal the show right out from under you." That's all it took. I was out.

Mr. X had unsuccessfully protested the discharge and, nice guy that he was, became concerned that it might have a harmful effect upon my morale. Therefore he had decided that I should know the truth.

After thanking him for his kindness, I went my way, my pores oozing hatred. I did not realize then that this sort of unfair treatment was common practice among the great-hearted theater folk.

Ten days later I was revenged. The play opened. I could not have hoped for a more dismal flop. The critics tore it to shreds. The stars fared little better. Barrymore was roundly panned and the actor who had replaced me, an established Broadway leading man, was drawn and quartered. I must confess that my joy was unconfined.

The following season I accepted an engagement to replace George Abbott in "Zander the Great," starring Alice Brady.

I emphasize this engagement specifically because not only was it my most important job to date, it was also instrumental in landing my first great role on Broadway.

I joined the show in Detroit where I was to rehearse during its week's engagement there. We were to open the following week in Chicago where we were scheduled for a summer run.

Shortly after my arrival in Detroit I was contacted by the director who had been sent from New York to rehearse me and at the same time tighten up the show for its Chicago opening. He instructed me to catch the show that evening and to pay close attention to George Abbott's performance. George had registered strongly during the Broadway run and the idea was that I imitate him as closely as possible.

Again the Bickford individuality asserted itself, with disastrous results. I told the director that I preferred not to see the show for the very specific reason that I did not intend to be influenced by Mr. Abbott's performance. I wished to invest the role with my own personality and technique.

I precipitated a tempest in a tea pot. The director, a rather pompous little man, was enraged to the point of stuttering verbosity.

He was articulate enough, however, to deliver his message which, boiled down to its acrid pith, informed me in no uncertain terms that I was a presumptuous nobody and that he, as director, would tell me exactly what was expected of me and teach me exactly how I was to do it.

I told him not to get his bowels in an uproar.

"It is very clear to me," I said, "that this engagement does not call for an actor. It cries to Heaven for an automaton. Consequently, the answer is quite simple. Just count me out, little man, and wire New York to send you a robot."

Later that evening the company manager called and requested my presence at a conference to be held in Miss Brady's hotel suite after the performance.

At the conference, the manager and the director teamed up in a concerted, and in my opinion, stupid attempt to bully me into conformity, only to be frustrated by my unequivocal answer, "Get yourselves another boy."

The abortive discussion was brought to an end by Miss Brady who suggested that everything be held in abeyance; that the morning rehearsal be held as planned, at which time they would see what Mr. Bickford had to offer and judge accordingly.

Her suggestion was followed. They liked what they saw and I opened the following week at the Powers Theater in Chicago. The play was adjudged a hit. And so was I. My personal notices were flattering beyond any expectation and I was particularly gratified by a rave review from Ashton Stevens, one of the top critics of the day.

The play had a twelve week run in Chicago. It was in the heyday of Al Capone's reign. Violence was rampant and nocturnal Chicago afforded unlimited short cuts to trouble. The leading man of our company was a handsome, two-fisted guy named Victor Sutherland, a fine actor and my alter ego. Kindred spirits and good pals, we prowled the wide open town and brought many gray hairs to the head of our company manager.

That we did not become involved in any really serious trouble was due not to our circumspection but, as we subsequently learned, to the doubtful distinction of being under the protection of Al Capone. He had seen our show and was so impressed by Vic Sutherland and me that when we began to show up at the night spots, primed for a fight or a frolic, he passed the word that we were right guys and good friends of his.

For instance, about two o'clock one morning we were in a big rathskeller-type combination café and gambling joint. We had been shooting craps and, strangely enough, winning. However, because we were to play a matinee the next day, we knocked it off early.

On the way out we stopped at the bar for a last drink. There we were accosted by two hard-eyed but handsome girls, both of them slightly crocked and one of them amorously inclined. The object of her affections was Vic who responded to her advances by drawing her to him and kissing her.

At this moment three big tough-looking characters walked into the scene. One of them ordered the girls back to his table and called Vic an unprintable name. Vic slugged him and the brawl was on.

We were doing all right against the three but when two more bruisers joined them, the tide turned and we began to take a real clobbering.

Suddenly two more men materialized. One of them barked the terse order, "Lay off," and the fight was over. The lot of them melted out of the place, including the dames.

One night after that incident we visited a fabulous establishment in Cicero, a Chicago suburb, reputed to be the site of Capone's headquarters. This elegant palace of joy dispensed dope, liquor, female companionship and almost every form of gambling.

We started to buck the roulette and had been playing only a few minutes when a major-domo called us aside and said, "The boss says for you to lay off the gambling, fellas. This is strictly for the chumps. You can't win."

I said, "Thanks for the tip but who is the boss?"

"Al, of course."

"Al?"

"Don't be a wise guy. Al Capone. Who else?"

"Oh. Well, thanks again."

"Think nothing of it. Enjoy yourselves, fellas. See you around."

There were many such incidents which indicated that we were under the aegis of the Big Boy.

Years later while visiting Alcatraz, voluntarily that is, I met Capone for the first time. He recognized me immediately and while chatting about the good old days in Chi, it became evident that he regarded me as an old buddy.

After its successful run in Chicago, "Zander the Great" went on tour and finished out the season to excellent business.

The following season found me again trouping with Alice Brady, this time in vaudeville. The vehicle was an adaptation of her old Broadway play, "Drifting," and I was delighted to secure the engagement, feeling that it was a step up the ladder. For the first time I was playing leading man opposite a major star. And with feature billing.

The act was booked for twenty-four weeks, opening at the Orpheum in San Francisco. The date there is memorable because of the nostalgic kick I got from visiting my old haunts, particularly the old burlesque theater in Oakland where I had made my theatrical debut.

The next date was at the Orpheum in Los Angeles. The movie people rolled out the red carpet for Alice Brady and there were parties scheduled for every night of the week. I was invited to some of them and so got my first close look at Hollywood and its personalities.

For the most part I liked what I saw. I was as impressed as any glamour-struck kid to meet such charmers as Gloria Swanson, Vilma Banky, Clara Bow, Estelle Taylor, Laura La Plante, Blanch Sweet and Beverly Bayne.

I got a kick out of meeting such personalities as Rod La Roque, Tom Mix, Harry Cary, Milton Sills, John Gilbert, Francis X. Bushman, Lew Cody and Lon Chaney.

At that time it was the practice among legitimate theater people to disparage the work of screen stars. I had heard many of them pontificate on the subject of acting, drawing odious comparisons between stage and screen techniques and heaping scorn upon the heads of screen stars, dismissing them as mere dispensers of sex and personality.

I never could accept this, there being in my opinion too few people in or out of the profession who really knew enough about acting to justify their oracular criticisms.

I admired the work of screen stars. As I watched them on the screen, I thought of them not as actors but as fabulous creatures surrounded by an aura of glamour which lifted them to the stature of demi-gods. I considered them as God's gift to the millions of ordinary people seeking escape from the emptiness of humdrum lives.

Meeting them in intimate contact I fully expected them to shrink to the petty frustration-ridden stature of most of the sad-sacks I had met in the theater.

I was pleasantly disappointed. Some of them did shrink to an extent but most of them exuded such an air of well-being, of health, gaiety and prosperity that I began to wonder if I shouldn't shift my sights from Broadway to Hollywood.

The week sped by all too swiftly and when the time came to leave I was greatly disappointed that no producer had shown the acumen to offer me a fat film contract.

During several weeks of the tour, Jim Corbett, the ex-heavyweight champion of the world, played on the bill with us. We became good companions in spite of the fact that he, a fanatic on the subject of keeping fit and a teetotaler disapproved of my way of life.

He worked out every morning and whenever feasible boxed at least three rounds. His problem was that there was seldom anybody around who would box with him, so he was delighted when I volunteered to act as his sparring partner.

I thoroughly enjoyed these workouts. I weighed about a hundred and eighty-five pounds. I was fast, a fairly good boxer and was not afraid of taking a punch. Jim considered me nothing less than manna from Heaven.

There were times when the bouts got pretty rugged. I, exhilarated to be boxing on even terms with one of the greatest champions in ring history and a little unmindful of the fact that he had forgotten more about the game than I could ever learn, would try to sneak over a haymaker.

Jim was as gentle as any nice old lady I ever knew—

except when he was boxing. Then his reflexes were so conditioned that his reaction to a stinging blow was almost automatic. And he was a great counter puncher.

Consequently stinging him was comparable to touching off an explosion. I would find myself flat on the deck or halfway through the wall of the building. Twice, he knocked me cold.

It was Alice Brady who called a halt to this pastime. She objected to having her leading man show up for a performance nursing a black eye, a split lip or a swollen nose. When I appeared for a matinee with two black eyes, she blew her top. She really told me off, accusing me of jeopardizing the act, and threatened to have me replaced if it happened again.

When you hold the aces, you usually win the game. Alice held the aces.

I had boxed with Jim Corbett for the last time.

Shortly after this episode, Jim's bookings took him out of my orbit. I have fond memories of him.

Career-wise, a vaudeville tour, even over the bigtime, was relatively unimportant to a supporting actor. I considered this engagement, however, as extremely important to me. Our closing date was at the Palace Theater in New York and as featured leading man playing opposite an important star I could expect to command some attention, favorable or otherwise.

The Palace symbolized the best in vaudeville. It was the ultimate goal, the Mecca of every vaudevillian. To play the Palace meant recognition. It meant performing before what was perhaps the most critical audience in the country.

The importance of our date there was emphasized when, the week before our scheduled appearance, the

Brady management sent us an important stage director to tighten up our performances.

An appearance at the Palace could very well turn out to be a springboard to fame. Not that I expected to be so favored, not this time. The role was not that good. But many important people of the theater regularly viewed the Palace bills and it was within the realm of possibility that some Broadway producer might catch the act and discover me as the ideal type to play a magnificent starring role in an important play.

And although it was to be the final week of the tour, I looked forward to it with all the anticipation that precedes a Broadway first night.

It was an exciting week. Every time I passed the front of the theater I got a charge out of seeing my name featured, and second only to that of the top-liner, Alice Brady. I was also proud to be assigned the number two star dressing room, on the door of which was a star and my name.

The act went over with a bang, every performance evoking many curtain calls. Many theatrical celebrities came back stage to pay their respects to Miss Brady, and I was most gratified when a few of them expressed the desire to meet me.

But my pipe dream of being discovered did not materialize. To the contrary, the following season turned out to be one of my worst. My career settled into the doldrums and for many weeks I waited for calls that never came.

Then I was inspired by an idea for a dramatic sketch, calling for a cast of two. I wrote it, put it together and secured six-weeks booking in cities where I had formerly played dramatic stock. Those six weeks constituted my employment for the entire season.

Among the few possessions I had acquired was a small piece of land in Massachusetts. It was located but a few miles from Boston and fronted on the Charles River. A truly beautiful and secluded spot and an admirable retreat. The closest telephone was eight miles down river.

Sometimes when the going got rough I would head for this spot like a homing pigeon. Such a time was the spring of nineteen twenty-five. Because of the long intervals between jobs my bank balance was sadly depleted and there was no engagement in sight.

Not that I was discouraged. Far from it. My optimism about ultimate success was enviable. I had no doubt that my chance would ultimately come, and after fourteen years apprenticeship I was supremely confident in my ability to take it from there.

But my target was not yet in sight and my impatience might well have turned to indignation and self-pity if I had chosen to sit it out in my squalid little New York apartment. Nobody loves an indignant man.

Thence my retreat to my Massachusetts Eden. I arrived there in late March and for the next four-and-a-half months mothballed my ambition while I revelled in the sheer joy of living. I never tired of swimming in the cool fresh water of the Charles, of the fishing, canoeing, and the long hikes through the piny woods. As the weeks sped by I built up a priceless store of radiant health and vitality.

In June my brother Jack spent a couple of weeks with me and during his stay told me of a big construction job his firm was starting in Brooklyn, N.Y. Through Jack I arranged for a job there as a materials inspector, my work to start on September fifteenth.

I had intended to leave for Brooklyn on September twelfth but in the middle of August I received a wire from Chamberlain Brown, the agent who had vowed never to negotiate for me again. The wire instructed me to come to New York immediately to start rehearsals in an important Broadway production.

Needless to say I was surprised and delighted, but not being one to buy a pig in a poke, I launched my trusty canoe, paddled eight miles down the river to the village and called Brown on the phone.

The play was "Outside Looking In," adapted by Maxwell Anderson from Jim Tully's book, BEGGARS OF LIFE. It was being produced by Kenneth McGowen, Robert Edmond Jones and Eugene O'Neill and was to be directed by Augustus Duncan. They were interested in my playing the leading role.

This was exciting news. A dignified management, an author who, with Laurence Stallings, had recently chalked up a tremendous hit in "What Price Glory?" and a starring role. What more could an ambitious nobody ask?

I was about to say that I would catch the first train for New York when Brown spilled the beans. He said that time was of the essence, that I must be in New York early the following morning as he had arranged for me to read at ten o'clock.

The word "read" did the trick. I immediately ordered him to cancel the appointment, as I refused to audition for any part.

I have never been able to interpret the quirk in my character that compels me to place obstacles in my own path. I have been described as stubborn, obstinate, dogged, determined, intractable and pertinacious. Any or all of these adjectives might be applicable. I must admit, in all honesty, that I have a wide streak of something or other. I choose to call it "integrity."

I could be wrong, of course. It is possible that my mother, while carrying me, had her path crossed by a black Missouri mule. In which case the proper word is stubborn—or it could be that I'm just plain old hard to handle.

I recall one erudite gentleman of my acquaintance once suggesting that a suitable epitaph for me would be: "Get yourselves another boy."

Chamberlain Brown chose to call it, "God-damned stupid foolishness." He informed me that the role in question was a tremendous one that could result in a triumphant *tour de force* for me. The play was already in rehearsal and they had tried out and rejected every actor in New York who could possibly fit the part. I had been suggested by the author, Maxwell Anderson. Anderson had seen me in "Zander the Great" while it was playing in Chicago. Brown insisted that the audition was a mere formality and that the part was in the bag for me.

In spite of this pitch, which from an agent of Brown's standing should have clinched the argument, I insisted that he send me a script. If I approved it, I would be happy to consider a deal.

Brown again stressed the time element, maintaining that delay would blow the deal.

I remained adamant.

The following day a script of "Outside Looking In" was delivered to me via U.S. Mail, special delivery.

The play, called by its author a comedy, was in my opinion a hard-hitting, razor-edged social satire, constructed loosely of episodes and conversation and held together by one vibrant character. My reaction to the play was negative.

The leading character, Oklahoma Red, was a horse of another color. Well-written, many-faceted, vital and picturesque, it was a truly magnificent role and I recognized it as the great star-making vehicle I had dreamed of for fourteen years. It presented the first real challenge to my ability as an actor and I was fully prepared to meet it head on. I knew that the impact would be terrific.

As quickly as I could make it I got to the telephone, called Chamberlain Brown and instructed him to make the deal and on any terms.

The following morning I was in New York and at ten o'clock started rehearsing at the Greenwich Village Theater. There were eighteen characters in the cast; seventeen men and one girl, the latter played by Blythe Daly. Playing opposite the girl was a little red-headed guy named James Cagney. It was his first role in a dramatic play.

During the first rehearsal it became apparent that the director and I were poles apart in our ideas of interpreting my role. This led to an extensive discussion during which it was tactfully hinted that my sins had found me out. Word had been passed to this worthy gentleman that I was an extremely arrogant and opinionated young man.

Thus forewarned he was prepared to exert his prerogative as director, and in scholarly but no less inflexible fashion reminded me that the play was to open cold in less than two weeks time and that therefore there was no time for experimentation. He stressed the fact that staging the play was his responsibility and asked that I grant him my complete cooperation.

He was so amiable in his attitude that I felt like a small boy who had just been told that father knows best.

But behind the velvet-glove approach I sensed an unqualified ultimatum which precluded further argument. I was to play the part his way, or else. And I wanted desperately to play this rare part.

And yet I knew that the great opportunity it offered could only be realized if my performance equaled its potential. Failing this, the character could emerge as a ludicrous caricature.

The director was a man of experience. I respected his knowledge and intelligence. I had to consider the possibility or probability that his approach to the character was correct. If so, I would go along with him all the way.

That night I carefully analyzed the character, compared the two interpretations and came up with the decision that mine was the correct one. The director's approach was purely intellectual and tended to reduce the character to a pale carbon of the real thing, a paper man which could not possibly spark an audience to enthusiasm.

I was convinced that the character would be believeable only if invested with utter realism and projected with tremendous vitality and brute force.

Having come to this conclusion I found myself perched precariously on the horns of a dilemma. I must accept direction or be replaced.

Again I recalled the words of my old mentor, Dave Weston, "You are only one of thousands who are pushing, biting and clawing their fellows in a frantic struggle to hit the same target." I decided that now, with the target in sight, I must ruthlessly disregard the niceties of theatrical tradition and go for broke.

As the rehearsals continued, no one—director, management, nor member of the cast—was aware of any difference of opinion between the director and myself.

Although inwardly seething, I followed his direction to the letter, posing no arguments and objecting to nothing. I became wax in the director's hands and he, well pleased, worked very hard indeed to mold a piece of pliant material into his conception of Oklahoma Red.

Meanwhile with the guile of a serpent, I laid my plans. After every rehearsal I went to my hotel and by myself rehearsed the part as I intended to play it. No actor could have worked more diligently than I to prepare for an opening performance. In addition to my own part I learned every word and bit of action in the entire play, planning to dominate during every second of the time I was onstage. I experimented with makeup until I hit on exactly the effect I wanted to achieve. I had special body and shoulder pads made and installed inch-and-a-quarter lifts in my shoes to achieve the effect of immensity. I ransacked the Seventh Avenue second-hand clothing stores until I found the exact suit to fit the character. I was fanatically meticulous in my attention to every detail and when the date of the opening arrived was as finely tuned as any thoroughbred, ready and poised to make his "Run for the roses."

The fateful date was September sixth, nineteen twenty-five. I arrived early at the Greenwich Village Theater and smuggled my special costume and accessories into my dressing room. Three quarters of an hour before curtain time I made the rounds, expressing my good wishes to the cast, then retired to my room and locked the door. The room was a tiny cubby hole and was situated in a right-hand corner of the stage, which was in turn so shallow that once a set was up, the dressing room was inaccessible without crossing through the set.

Opening the door to no one, I arrayed myself for my

imminent onslaught against the bastions of the New York Theater.

My excitement was intense. *This was it*. The stakes were all or nothing. If I were right, it meant fame and fortune. And if wrong, it was going to take one hell of a long time to live down my unorthodox behavior.

The half-hour was called. I began to have misgivings. I wondered if I were really as good an actor as I thought, or just an egomaniac who was about to stick his head in a noose.

Then came the fifteen-minute call. Now made up and dressed, I tensed up and was nervous to the point of nausea.

As curtain time approached, my pulse began to gallop. I was bathed in perspiration. My lips were parched and I had a frog in my throat.

Worst of all, I began to fear that I could not remember my lines. I got out the script and frantically studied scenes that I knew by heart. Convinced that my performance was going to be a failure, I became jittery.

Then came that breathless moment as the curtain went up. I stepped out of my dressing room and waited in the wings. My entrance cue would come in about five minutes. And as I waited, my jitters disappeared and I became as nerveless as an oyster.

The set represented a hobo jungle at night. A group of tramps were discovered as they waited for a freight train to come through. I was to appear from the darkness under a railroad trestle.

My cue came and as I made my entrance I was as cold and deadly purposeful as an animal engaged in stalking its prey. Nervousness had been replaced by supreme confidence and I was indeed the master of my fate.

A first night audience, when sensing a smash hit begins to generate a contagious excitement that becomes electrifying in its intensity. I had been on the stage but a few minutes when, my sensory apparatus being keenly alert, I began to feel the vibrations emanating from the audience and by the end of the first act I knew that this was my night.

When the second act ended, the excitement was electric. And the end of the play brought forth a standing ovation, with the attendant "Bravos," calls for the author, and—for "Bickford."

After an opening, theater people, anxious to read the reviews, usually wait up until the morning papers hit the street. En masse, in groups, or singly, they go to favorite haunts and make merry or mourn, whichever may be indicated.

On this occasion, I, though highly elated, spurned all invitations to make wassail, went directly to my hotel and to bed.

Not that I was disinterested in the reviews. To the contrary. Audience reaction to my performance meant little unless it was gold-starred and documented by the critics. It was my modest hope, and expectation, that critical acclaim would serve as the catapult which would hurl me over the ramparts and into the center of the golden circle.

The performance had left me physically and emotionally spent and realizing that my notices would be no better nor any worse if I read them at ten o'clock in the morning, I left a wake-up call and went promptly to sleep.

The next voice I heard was that of the switch-board operator. Her voice fairly dripped honey as she heralded the joyous tidings that it was ten o'clock and that I was the toast of the town.

Then came effusive congratulations from the bell-boy who brought me the newspapers together with a sheaf of messages and telegrams, most of the wires being from tradespeople including one from a famous Broadway mortuary which read, "Congratulations and best wishes for future success. At your service."

The reviews? I can best describe the critics' reaction to me by modestly offering a few excerpts:

"The real achievement is the finding of a tall, ruddy actor named Charles A. Bickford to play the ruthless Oklahoma Red. He was treasure trove. . . The hat of your correspondent . . . goes up in the air (where it belongs) for the welcome newcomer."

— Alexander Woollcott

"The performance of Charles A. Bickford is worth braving the trip to the village in the inclement weather."

— Walter Winchell

"Most of the vitality of 'Outside Looking In' comes from the acting of Charles A. Bickford as Oklahoma Red. He is swaggering and burly, glib of tongue, mocking and reckless all at once. What had seemed too gentlemanly for a hobo play before he appeared on the stage began to show color when he walked on, and through the remaining acts he is the center of activity."

— *New York Times*

"Charles A. Bickford's acting as the brilliant and disheveled Oklahoma Red is a wonderwork of fluent comedy, and is as satisfactory an impersonation as you will find in years of playgoing."

— Percy Hammond

"If you are interested in mean, noble, cruel and witty vagabonds, there is a chance . . . to see one of them in 'Outside Looking In.' Mr. Charles A. Bickford, as Oklahoma Red, impersonates a frontier Villon, and he does it so well that you can renew your waning faith in the art of histrionics. He and Mr. James Cagney as his adversary, Little Red, do the most honest acting now to be seen in New York. I believe that Mr. Barrymore's effective performance of Hamlet would be a mere feat of elocution if compared to the characterizations of either Mr. Bickford or Mr. Cagney, both of whom are unknown."

— Burns Mantle

"Mr. Charles A. Bickford illustrates brilliantly the profits of the training in stock and vaudeville that the other players need. Oklahoma Red, a sort of playboy of a cynical, wild hobo world, a knock-'em-out philosophic child of the road, written very well indeed by the author, loses nothing at Mr. Bickford's hands. He is a fine actor with a good sense of timing and a self-assurance that contributes greatly to his present role. He takes his points unfailingly well and keeps himself well in scale with every scene."

— Stark Young

"One of the eighteen characters in the play stands out vividly enough to go down in theatrical history. This is the part of Oklahoma Red, the big bullying bad man of the hobo world, portrayed by Charles A. Bickford. If any stage character ever did justice to the art of profanation, Oklahoma Red, as played by Charles A. Bickford. is that character. He swears, not like the ordinary man does, but whole heartedly, with a rich and robust feeling for color, emphasis and sting. Two thirds of his vocabulary consists of words never used in respectable conversation, but they roll off Bickford's tongue as trippingly and with as much ease and grace as the

coloratura warblings of an innocent debutante. Not that
the glib utterance of strong talk is Mr. Bickford's only
attribute. He has a physique, a slouch and a cluster of
red hair that go a long way towards making him properly impressive in his role. Bickford and his Oklahoma
Red are to 'Outside Looking In' what Louis Wolheim
and his Captain Flagg are to 'What Price Glory.'

"Alongside this imposing character portrayal by Bickford almost every other member of the cast is reduced
to minor importance."

— Don Carle Gilette

"Wherever Mr. McGowen found two redheads like
Charles Bickford and James Cagney, who were evidently
born to play Oklahoma Red and Little Red, he was
guided by the hand of the casting God. Mr. Bickford's
characterization is the first important one of the year
and is likely to remain at the top for some time."

—Robert Benchley

As anyone with perception can see, the critics unani-
mously agreed that I was a wow.

A search of the world would not have disclosed a happier actor than I was that morning. Not only had I hit the
target—I had shattered the bulls-eye.

At long last I was in the winner's circle.

And so, because of "Outside Looking In," I found
myself on the inside looking out, an extremely novel and
thoroughly enjoyable vantage point.

I got a real boot out of being lionized. I enjoyed the
sycophantic flattery that was part-and-parcel of sudden
celebrity, at the same time being aware that the trucklers
now patting me on the back would as soon kick my
brains out if I fell from grace.

I loved having taxi drivers and head waiters address

me by name. I enjoyed being besieged by autograph hounds. I got a real kick from seeing my caricature on the wall of Sardi's restaurant. Above all, I was thrilled by the sudden recognition of producers who began to submit plays for future consideration. There was no question in my mind that I had it made . . .

It was only after "Outside Looking In" had finished its run that I realized, to my distress, that maintaining my newly-won niche in the theater was not going to be all beer and skittles.

There was no play among the many submitted to me that I could appear in without minimizing the effect of that first terrific impact. In each script either the role was good and the play bad, or vice versa.

The immediate benefits of my triumph could only be measured by prestige, and unfortunately fame alone makes for very tough eating. I was faced with the problem of earning a living while waiting for a satisfactory vehicle.

As the weeks passed, my obligations mounted. My bank roll slimmed and I decided it was high time to get myself a bread and butter job. Fortunately my exposure to the aesthetics had not rendered me a victim of preciosity, and being quite able-bodied I could still earn enough to buy the groceries, whether by carrying a hod or by driving a truck.

I secured a job as a laborer with a contracting company which had started excavation work for a big building project on Broadway, in the heart of the Rialto.

For some inexplicable reason, New York City pedestrians seem irresistibly attracted by the spectacle of thirty or more laborers shoveling muck at the bottom of an open pit. At any hour of our working day there would be a group of rubbernecks gazing at us from the sidewalk, forty feet above.

The crew was a heterogeneous group of thirty strong-backed Italians, Irishmen and Bohunks—rough, illiterate and in the main good-natured.

It was back-breaking work, presided over by a slave-driving foreman but occasionally diversion was afforded whenever a goodlooking woman happened to be standing in the first rank of sidewalk watchers. Looking up from our angle left little to the imagination.

The men were constantly on the watch for such an exhibition and the first man to spot one would give the signal by a sibilant "pst," followed by the utterance of one unprintable word. In low tones the word would be passed on until every man in the pit knew that the show was on.

One afternoon, after I had been on the job about a week, work was nearly brought to a standstill as the men, exchanging ribald and obscene banter, gawked unashamedly at a beautiful girl on the sidewalk above. She, aware of and pleased by the attention she was attracting, stood there for several minutes, chatting serenely with her escort.

Her serenity might have been shattered had she realized that the men were not at all interested in her beautiful profile. They were fascinated by the obvious fact that, while dressing that day, she had forgotten to don her pants.

My interest in the subject, although not entirely negligible, was overshadowed by my recognition of her escort, who was none other than Chamberlain Brown, the agent. He had spotted me, as was evident by the way he kept staring at me, but I knew from the puzzled look on his face that he was not quite sure. At first I pretended not to notice him but finally grinned up at him and waved.

His reaction was surprising. Instead of returning my friendly gesture, he stared at me with a look of absolute unbelief then, taking the girl's arm, he hurried away. I shrugged his action off on the presumption that he had not recognized me after all.

I was wrong. On reaching my hotel after work, I found a message from Chamberlain requesting that I contact him at the earliest possible moment. I went to his office, which incidentally was just across the street from my hotel, and found him and his brother Lyman waiting for me.

Chamberlain had recognized me all right. And he was outraged. With Lyman joining in the attack, he arraigned me with all the ferocity of an enraged butterfly. I was amazed to learn that by my undignified actions I was belittling myself and making mock of my fellow artists, the theater, my precious art and all the ships at sea.

He was shocked to the depths of his artistic being that I, who had just made theatrical history and who was being sought by every producer on Broadway, would cheapen myself by what he termed an undignified and stupid publicity stunt.

Astonished by his extreme indignation, I innocently explained that it was no publicity stunt, that it was simply the case of an out-of-work actor attempting to make an honest living.

This revelation horrified the brothers. I had just confessed to the greatest of all sins—poverty.

Chamberlain became lyrical as he reminded me that I was now one of the exalted beings that dwell in that wonderful never-never land of make-believe, where there is no such word as adversity. He spelled out the enormity of my offense. In earning my bread by the sweat of my brow, I had stepped beyond the pale. I had become common game and had placed myself at the mercy of every predatory producer in New York. He hoped to Heaven that his were the only professional eyes to have witnessed my earthy activities and insisted that I renounce all such ill-advised actions as of then and forevermore.

He offered to advance monies to the extent of two hundred dollars per week if I would sign a personal management contract, the terms of which would guarantee me ten weeks employment per year at a minimum salary of a thousand dollars per week.

I would have accepted the contract but for a stipulation that I must accept such employment as and when he secured it for me.

I was touched by the evident interest in my professional welfare and capitulated to the extent of a promise to cease and desist from shoveling muck under the eyes and noses of the producers. I gave my solemn word that henceforth my pick-and-shovel production would be strictly off-Broadway.

The great follow-up role I had been hoping for never did materialize. I appeared in five plays during the next three years, and each engagement represented a compromise on my part. I thought it unwise to allow too great an interval between appearances and each of the plays was offered at an expedient time. In my opinion, no one of them was a fine play but each provided a role showy enough to ensure critical acclaim.

I managed to sustain my prestige as an actor but was worse off financially than I had been as a stock leading man. There were times when if it had not been for my avocation as a manual laborer, I would have been in real distress.

During the years of my climb to recognition, two great mediums had caused radical changes in the character of mass entertainment. By the middle 1920's, show business, from the Atlantic to the Pacific, had become almost completely dominated by motion pictures and radio.

Because of the ruinous competition from these giants, good dramatic stock companies were as extinct as the dodo. Except for rare instances, touring companies no longer paid off, and vaudeville was on the way out.

The only real theater left was concentrated in New York and it was sick. It was a rough period indeed for actors who loved the theater.

Inexplicably, I, whose motivation for becoming an actor was a hundred percent commercial, chose to place myself in that category. As I look back at those three frustrating years I can only wonder at my stupidity. Unless one is extraordinarily sagacious, or very, very lucky, attempting to make money as a stage actor is equivalent to betting on a three-legged horse.

The first evidence of my mental derangement came when immediately following the run of "Outside Looking In," I was offered a co-starring role in the motion picture "Beau Geste." It was to be shot as a big-budget, silent picture with an all-star cast and to be directed by Herbert Brenon, a top-flight director. The salary offered was five thousand dollars per week with a guarantee of ten weeks.

In any man's language, fifty thousand dollars for ten weeks work is real folding money. To me at that time it was a fortune, the pot of gold at the end of the rainbow. It was my *raison d'être* as an actor.

And did I grab it? Not this mule. I remained steadfast in my evident determination to starve in a garret. I turned it down for the declared reason that I had just won a niche for myself on Broadway and did not care to jeopardize my position by acting in the movies.

La-di-da-da-da. Just how dim-witted can a guy be?

Nothing worthy of particular mention happened to me during 1926 and 1927. There were a couple of plays, "Glory Hallelujah," a flop; and "Chicago," a hit.

Then, early in 1928, things began to happen. There had been a revolution in Hollywood. Excitement over talking pictures had seethed up and boiled over. The picture industry was in a turmoil. Most of the silent picture stars were on their way out and the studios were grabbing for stage personalities.

I was offered long term contracts by every studio in Hollywood. I played it true to form—stupidly. Even though some of the offers were unbelievably generous, I turned a deaf ear to all of them. I had to think of my career in the theater, you know.

I will say in my own behalf that there were mitigating circumstances. Maxwell Anderson and Harold Hickerson were writing a play based upon the highly controversial Sacco and Vanzetti case. The Sacco role was being tailored to my measurements and according to Anderson the play would deal boldly, fervently and savagely with the terrible and sad case. The play was to be produced in the Fall.

So, while I was turning a deaf ear to fabulous picture offers, this provocative prospect of a hit play was in the offing.

The play, "Gods of the Lightning," opened at the

Little Theater on the night of October 24, 1928, and was the second most memorable and exciting opening night in my experience; to me, nothing could equal the excitement of the "Outside Looking In" opening.

The following quote is representative of the play's reception by the critics and fairly descriptive of what happened that night in the theater:

> "It's an overwritten, overwrought and tremendously effective play which Maxwell Anderson and Harold Hickerson have fashioned from the life, death and resurrection of Sacco and Vanzetti. They've fashioned it in the only way it could be fashioned, with a heart full of bitterness and a thoroughly one-sided point of view. You may not admire 'Gods of the Lightning.' But, as it's to be seen in the Little Theater, you can't ignore it.
>
> "From curtain to curtain it is special pleading. From curtain to curtain we worshippers of, as the phrase goes, law and order, are permitted no word of protest. From curtain to curtain Sacco and Vanzetti are martyrs in a great crusade—holy men who live, suffer and burn for a holy cause, latter-day saviours who'd drive the money changers from the temple which is the world, twin messiahs who actually believe in the brotherhood of man.
>
> "The story of 'Gods of the Lightning' is the story of Sacco and Vanzetti. As the moving finger writes, as it progresses relentlessly from the Lyceum Restaurant to the office of the District Attorney, from the office of the District Attorney to the courtroom of the Supreme Court, from the courtroom of the Supreme Court to the electric chair, you follow it with fascinated eyes. You hadn't realized that Sacco and Vanzetti were merely human beings—foolish, stubborn, mistaken human beings, even as you and I.
>
> "Don't imagine that Sacco and Vanzetti are Sacco and Vanzetti in the Anderson—Hickerson play. In the Lyceum Restaurant you meet them as Capraro and Macready. In the courtroom of the Supreme Court it's

Capraro and Macready who are found guilty of a murder they have not committed. It is as Capraro and Macready that they die. Not once are Sacco and Vanzetti mentioned on the Little Theater stage. Mr. Anderson and Mr. Hickerson are clever propagandists.

"But, where a croupy and uncomfortable audience is concerned, Sacco and Vanzetti are on every tongue. In the lobby, between the acts, it's Sacco and Vanzetti this, Sacco and Vanzetti that, Sacco and Vanzetti the other thing. 'Sacco and Vanzetti are dead,' says one. 'Why not let well enough alone?' says another. 'Let the dead bury its dead.' 'Sacco and Vanzetti are not dead,' says a third. 'Sacco and Vanzetti have just begun to live.'

"The acting is little short of perfection. As Macready, Charles Bickford is the strong, bold, outspoken, acrid anarchist. In the courtroom scene, he rises to heights. You believe in his Macready without believing in his point of view. We are wise, we tell ourselves, to get the Macreadys out of our way. But, as we hang them and burn them, we respect them. If they really are mistaken they're mistaken magnificently.

"As Capraro, Horace Braham is the weak, timid, sentimental anarchist. You believe in him, even as you believe in Macready. As Rosalie, the girl to whom Macready is engaged, Sylvia Sidney comes into her own.

"Last night, as I left the Little Theater, a well-dressed, well-fed, hundred percent anti-anarchistic audience was cheering Mr. Bickford, Mr. Braham, Miss Sidney and the tremendously effective play which has been fashioned from the life, death and resurrection of Sacco and Vanzetti."

This reviewer neglected to mention that following the second-act curtain some fifty or more indignant customers had hissed, booed and stomped their way out of the theater.

"Gods of the Lightning" could have been called, in all

justice, a one-sided, blistering piece of propaganda, directed against the judge, jury and prosecutor in the case. Nevertheless it was terrific theater, an exciting melodrama that moved audiences to stand and cheer for minutes after every performance.

It should have been a smash hit. It wasn't.

This play marked a turning point in my career, for it caused me to reappraise my attitude toward the theater with the result that my sense of loyalty, or whatever it was that had chained me to Broadway, dropped away . . .

BOOK THREE

SHORTLY AFTER "Gods of the Lightning" folded on Broadway, I was approached by an agent regarding a starring role in a forthcoming Cecil B. De Mille picture. It was to be De Mille's first talking picture and would be made in conjunction with Metro-Goldwyn-Mayer at the MGM studio in California.

I was most receptive until it developed that it was to be my first picture under a long-term contract. Not being interested in a term contract, I answered that I would be happy to read the script. If I liked it, I would be interested in discussing a single-picture deal.

This was out of the question as the story was still in work; therefore the deal must be made on faith.

Being a man of little faith in these matters, I sadly but unequivocally turned the deal down.

The following morning I received a call from an MGM executive. He asked if I would lunch with him and discuss the De Mille matter. I acceded.

I found him to be most affable, quite polished and very, very sharp. Coming quickly to the point he laid his cards on the table, telling me that De Mille had seen my work on Broadway and was very desirous of signing me for the part of Hagon Derk in his first talking picture. He frankly admitted that De Mille had tested every suitable actor in Hollywood and had rejected all of them.

Sketched for me was a glowing picture of MGM's importance in the motion picture industry, the prestige of Cecil De Mille as a director-producer; and great stress was made of the tremendous opportunity for me to make my motion picture debut under such a distinguished aegis.

It was explained that the reason for contacting me

directly was because of the time element. De Mille was holding up work on the script until a star was set to play the protagonist. If it turned out to be me then the role would be developed with me in mind.

The man from MGM was aware of my reluctance to commit myself to a long-term contract and made it very clear that the studio would not sign me for such an important engagement without a firm option for further and exclusive services.

I assured him that I was flexible on that point provided that an equitable and mutually agreeable contract could be worked out. However, I would sign no contract before appraising the material I would be expected to play.

I was asked if I had any objection to listening to Mr. De Mille outline the story over long distance. I had no objection and within a few minutes Mr. De Mille was on the phone from California.

He too was most amiable and after effusive compliments on my work in "Outside Looking In" and "Gods of the Lightning," spent the next forty minutes telling me the story of "Dynamite."

I thought the story was contrived and corny but the role offered me had hit-potential and in consideration for De Mille's undoubted flair for producing successful theater for the masses I assured him that I would play the role, providing of course that I could work out a deal with the studio.

So far, so good. Everyone concerned was happy. All that remained was to work out the deal.

Time was of the essence. In New York I discussed the contract and in an amazingly short time had reached agreement as to compensation and most other points.

It was not until I proposed a clause which guaranteed

me the right to approve my roles and stories that the hitherto benign climate changed abruptly. I was assured, with considerable acerbity, that MGM as a matter of policy had never granted such right to an actor and probably never would.

It was the harshness in the delivery of this dictum that triggered my equally acerbic response to the effect that under no circumstances would I enter into the contract unless such a clause was part of it.

The issue became the crux of the deal and we argued at length.

MGM's attitude aroused all of the stubbornness that has been characteristic of my entire career—a trait which has been an important factor both in my retardation and in my survival.

They knew nothing of the mental processes, attitudes or actions that motivate the obstinacy of a Missouri Mule, otherwise they would not have revealed their awareness of my impecunious position, nor have called me a God-damned fool for turning my back on a fortune.

It appeared that we had arrived at an impasse.

Time was important and we wrangled for six more weeks before a compromise agreement was reached.

MGM yielded to the extent of a verbal promise that if the picture hit, and if I hit personally, they would grant me reasonable approval of my roles and stories. They flatly refused to incorporate the clause into the contract on the grounds that to do so would establish an undesirable precedent.

The real compromise was mine in accepting this promise in good faith. I did it because I knew that the story, hokum though it might be, would be blessed by the Midas touch of De Mille. And, never handicapped by self doubt,

I also knew that I could smash my way through to a personal hit. In which case I had no doubt that the studio would hold to its promise since it would be to our mutual advantage.

And so it came to pass that in the week before Christmas of 1928, I became a prime piece of MGM property. Everybody was happy—including myself.

During the three thousand mile trip to the West coast, my sense of importance was titillated by the lush accommodations furnished me. First, a drawing room on the crack Twentieth Century Limited to Chicago, followed by a suite at a swanky hotel in that city, where I rested comfortably between trains, and finally, a drawing room on Santa Fé's de luxe train to Los Angeles.

It was the first time I had travelled in such extravagant fashion. I revelled in the luxury and it was a fat cat indeed that on the day before Christmas, 1928, descended, purring, at Pasadena, California.

Even the bored MGM publicity man who, with rare condescension, posed me on the Pullman steps for the conventional "Star arrives in Hollywood" shots, did not succeed in diminishing my sense of well-being.

At the Roosevelt Hotel in Hollywood I changed into light sports clothes, the temperature being a salubrious seventy-eight degrees, and left the hotel to take a look around. I found Hollywood about as interesting and exciting as any small town in the country. The much publicized Boulevard, for instance, had all the distinctive qualities of Main Street, USA.

Returning to the hotel in mid afternoon, I was pleased to see my mug plastered on the front pages of the evening papers. It surprised me that there were no messages. Not one person had called to say "Hello," "Merry Christmas" or "Go to hell." While I could think of no one in the vicinity whom I could truthfully call "friend," I did have many acquaintances and was slightly perplexed that the announcement of my fat contract had not enhanced my popularity to the extent of at least one voice calling to say, "Welcome to Hollywood."

It was while pondering this weighty circumstance that my phone rang. The call was from Cecil De Mille and his first words were, "Hello Charles Bickford. Welcome to Hollywood."

Those few kind words made all the difference. My self-esteem was restored and I again had the world by the tail. After an exchange of amenities, he invited me to an open house Christmas party which was in progress at his office on the MGM lot. I accepted, of course, and he said that a studio car would pick me up within a half hour.

Each year, on the day before Christmas, open house prevails at most of the studios. Feuds are laid aside and daggers are sheathed at twelve o'clock, noon, when people go the rounds, from office to office, exchanging gifts, compliments of the season, and toasting everybody from the watchman at the gate, to the president of the company.

Inevitably, as the afternoon progresses, the casualty list rises. Thus, when at four-thirty that afternoon I was driven onto the MGM lot, I got the impression of arriving late at a Hibernian come-all-ye.

The party at the De Mille bungalow was merry, but decorous. Of the twenty or more celebrants present, I spotted but one drunk. The others, sun-tanned and dressed in sports clothes, were standing around in groups as they vivaciously discussed the important question of the day, namely, Who is doing it to whom?"

The buzz of conversation stopped abruptly as I en-

tered the spacious conference room and stood, the cyno-
sure of all eyes, waiting for someone to say, "Hallelujah—it's the great man himself."

Nothing of the sort happened, however, and after what
seemed an interminable time, I, feeling somewhat as a
prize bull must feel while on exhibition at a county fair,
put on what I hoped was an ingratiating smile and said,
wittily, "Don't shoot, anybody, I haven't got a gun."

This clever stratagem proved effective, serving both to
break the ice and to establish me as a friendly and very
funny fellow. I hadn't figured to be that comical but must
have been because everybody laughed hilariously.

Then a sturdily built, sun-bronzed man came toward
me with his hand extended in greeting and although I
had never met De Mille, nor seen a picture of him, I
knew that this must be he. The pongee sports shirt, well-
tailored riding breeches, leather puttees and Napoleonic
stride seemed to proclaim the fact that here was the director to end all directors. "My God," I thought. "It's an
American Benito Mussolini."

Restraining a compulsion to give him the fascist salute, I grasped his hand. The man had a grip like a bear
trap. I thought nothing of it, having shaken hands with
powerful men before.

Although he was smiling, I detected the glint of antagonism in his eyes. It was difficult for me to believe that a
man of his position would resort to such an infantile
method of intimidation but as the pressure continued I
realized that he was serving notice to me that he was king
of the mountain.

I rose to the challenge and matching him smile for
smile, I bore down. Unfortunately for De Mille, my own
meat hook was an instrument of considerable power and

my own smile broadened as the challenging glint in his eyes changed to one of respectful dread.

The watchers seemed to sense that something dramatic was happening and for a long moment there was absolute silence in the big room as De Mille and I, both approaching middle age and two prime examples of rugged individualism, waged our juvenile battle for psychological advantage.

He quickly recognized that his force was not as irresistible as he had supposed and slackening his grip, pressed the charm button, becoming forthwith as gracious a host as could be desired.

After extending me a warm welcome, he introduced me to the gathering, which was composed of writers, directors, technicians and a few actors, among whom were Joel McCrea, then a tyro, Carol Lombard also a beginner, and Lon Chaney.

The latent antagonism between De Mille and me was particularly interesting to me because of the mutual respect and admiration we held for each other's talents.

I considered his work extraordinary. It could be argued that most of his pictures were without reality, logic or artistic expression. They were, nevertheless, put together with consummate craftsmanship. And considering the possibility that they were consciously made to appeal to the great mass of infantile intelligence, they were, in my opinion, indubitable masterpieces.

I hold no brief for conscious artistry, in the theater or on the screen. I believe in sound stories, clearly and logically written and honestly projected as well-constructed plays, or screen plays. I object to so-called aesthetic approval, or criticism of any artist's work.

In my estimation De Mille was in a class by himself.

As there was only one P.T. Barnum, so there was only one C.B. De Mille. Beyond any argument, he was a great showman. And I believe it was his opinion that I was a great actor.

But in spite of our mutual admiration, our togetherness in the desire to make "Dynamite" a huge success, we could not prevent a challenging defensiveness toward each other.

Having recognized each other, so to speak, and after a sociable drink and a few minutes of small talk, I said my goodbyes and left.

As I stepped into the limousine that was to carry me back to my hotel I found that something had been added. It was about twenty years old, blonde, very pretty, startingly female, and very, very drunk. In fact, she was the one drunk I had noticed at De Mille's party. She was dressed in black silk, Mandarin-style pyjamas, with a chinchilla coat slung carelessly across her shoulders. Her fingers and wrists were weighted with about seventy-five thousand dollars worth of ice and she was sucking on a quart bottle of champagne.

This angel-faced creature, unrestrained by inhibitions and possessed of a gutter vocabulary that would be taboo in any well-regulated whorehouse, nearly floored me with her opening gambit. In one sentence she addressed me as a red-headed son-of-a-bitch, invited me to park my ass and informed me that she was riding into town with me because she was too God-damn drunk to drive her own fucking car.

The drive to my hotel took about thirty minutes, during which time she chattered continuously, castigating her boy friend, a prominent MGM producer, and describing in revolting detail the poor sucker's frenetic attempts to satisfy her insatiable sexual desires.

She said that I was the answer to a maiden's prayer; a great big, beautiful hunk of stud and she had made up her mind to knock me off before the studio man-eaters got to me.

Fascinated and repelled by the unceasing stream of filth spewing from her pretty lips, I listened in silence until the car was well into Hollywood, when I asked where she desired to be dropped.

The inquiry elicited a torrent of abuse, this time directed at me. Among other things she called me a dumb bastard not to have realized by this time that she was not about to be dropped anywhere. Where I was going—that's where she was going.

I wanted no part of this, and as the car turned onto Hollywood Boulevard and rapidly neared the hotel I made plans for a fast getaway.

The car stopped opposite the hotel entrance. The doorman opened the door and I was off and running. But she was fast too and before I was halfway across the sidewalk we were running neck and neck. I skidded to a stop. The driver had turned on his ignition. I yelled for him to hold it, then turned on the girl and ordered her to get back in the car. She refused, telling me in her unique fashion where I could go and what I could do when I got there.

Passersby were beginning to linger and gawk. I lost my temper, grabbed her by the shoulders and started to push her toward the car. She turned suddenly and landed on my nose with a left hook that would have done credit to Jack Dempsey. My nose spouted blood. The gawking natives laughed. Resisting the impulse to belt her, I told her what I thought of her, making it very clear that if she were the last female on earth I wouldn't touch her with a ten-foot pole.

I then started for the door. She followed. Through the door, along the corridor, and into the lobby, she followed.

And as she came after me, she screeched. At the top of her lungs she screeched, telling the world that I was a God-damned fake. I wasn't a he-man at all. I was nothing but a God-damned pansy, a faggot.

There were about a dozen people in the lobby, guests, bell boys and clerks. Like figures in a *tableau vivant* they stared in amazement as I, seething with anger and more embarrassed than I had ever been in my life, stalked to the desk, my screeching nemesis close on my heels repeating over and over again that I was a God-damn faggot.

Turning from the desk, key in hand, I came face to face with a big man whom I recognized as Noah Beery. With lifted eyebrows he leered at me, saying, "Well, for Christ's sake. A fag, huh?"

Exhibiting what was for me remarkable self-restraint, I did not punch him in the nose. I just stood there, speechless. Then I began to feel sick at my stomach. I ran for the elevator and as I stepped into it I heard him say, "And that's the kind of character they are bringing out here to take over our jobs."

Several slugs of bourbon later, I had recovered my sense of humor and concluded that if the happenings of this, my first day in Hollywood, were any criterion, my picture career was to be anything but dull. I had really started with a bang, having in all probability alienated De Mille, one of the most powerful men in the industry, and for good measure having had it broadcast to this gossip-loving town that I was a queer. Nice going, Charlie.

Later I found out that the fabulous slut was not an actress. She was the expensive plaything of an important producer who, ironically enough, was one of the few who could have been honestly classified as a member of the intelligentsia; a man of culture and well versed in the realms of literature and the theater. I've often wondered what they could have talked about between times.

On the day following a drearily nostalgic Christmas, De Mille called again. Via the studio publicity department he had learned that January first was my birthday. In his most courtly manner he assured me that he would consider it a privilege and a pleasure if I would celebrate by being his guest of honor at a New Year's party to take place at his mountain ranch, Paradise.

I appreciated the gesture and accepted, with thanks. He instructed me that a car would pick me up at my hotel at three p.m. on the afternoon before New Year's Eve. Dress was to be informal but I was to bring dress trousers and shoes. He stressed the point that dinner jacket and black tie would not be necessary.

He asked if there were any specific wines or liquors I was partial to and topped the quiz by asking my preference in women.

Slightly startled but none-the-less intrigued, I answered facetiously, "Why, Mr. De Mille, your hospitality overwhelms me."

"Oh, come now, Mr. Bickford," and though his tone was jocular I sensed a challenge. "Don't tell me I've overestimated you."

My mind flashed to the screaming virago who had denounced me as a fairy. "It's gotten back to him," I thought, "and the bastard is testing me out."

I rose to the bait. "It's not that, Mr. De Mille. It's just that you're the last man in the world I would have expected to concern himself about my sex preferences, and it throws me."

He chuckled, appreciatively. "Don't get *me* wrong, Charles. I strive to please. I want you to have a good time. Which is it to be—blonde, brunette or redhead?"

"Make it one of each," I said, modestly. "All I ask is that they be dainty, feminine, shapely, beautiful, intelligent and passionate."

I scored a belly laugh. "That's a large order in more ways than one. I know of only one such pearl of great price and unfortunately she's already wearing a brand."

"Heaven forbid that I should step on anyone's toes," I laughed. "But it might simplify matters if you just tag the three with my initials—C.B. That should prevent any clash of interests. Or should it?"

The conversation ended on a note of amiable hostility. My suspicion that the New Year's party had been a long-planned affair did not lessen my appreciation of De Mille's gracious gesture in terming it my birthday party. But I wondered what it was in this man that made my back itch.

Was it because my impression of him was that of a ruddy stallion, pawing the earth and proclaiming himself monarch of all he surveyed? It was possible of course that I projected much the same image to his eyes, in which case each of us, by manifesting an aggressive superiority, posed a challenge to the other. In any case, my instinct warned me that De Mille and I were destined to clash.

I looked forward to the party with great eagerness, and for two reasons. The first was the hope that our close contact over the weekend at the ranch might lead to better understanding of each other and consequent co-operation and accord during the making of the picture.

The second was because of my very human curiosity concerning the nature of the party. De Mille was reputed to be something of a sybarite. His reputation, our bald dialogue concerning feminine companionship, the secluded ranch in the mountains—all these factors added up to the possibility that the party might turn out to be one of the legendary orgies. Could it be that I had been nominated for membership in the fabulous fraternity of Hollywood voluptuaries?

Certainly it was an exciting prospect for a guy with a strong streak of Yankee Puritanism.

The day of departure arrived and I was ready and waiting when my phone rang at exactly three p.m. The awe-stricken voice of the operator informed me that Mr. Cecil De Mille's car was waiting.

Cecil B. De Mille was also waiting. And seated beside him in the glittering black town car were three gorgeous girls—one blonde, one brunette and one redhead! All three were dainty, feminine, shapely and beautiful. I could only presume they were passionate and hope they were of reasonable intelligence.

Each of them wore a small blue ribbon on which was emblazoned in gold the letters: C.B.

With a flourish De Mille performed the introductions, referring to me as that distinguished, dynamic, he-man star of the Broadway stage. And with a gleeful twinkle in his eye, he sat back and watched for my reaction.

The three lovelies, obviously his answer to my request for one of each, vied for my attention.

I, thoroughly appreciative of the humor contained in

this delicious bit of Oriental hospitality, decided to top
the gag. I responded to the adulation with Olympian reserve, giving it the cultured Bostonian bit and adding a
dash of lavender for good measure.

I went over big with the girls who pegged me as a real
classy gent. Particularly effective was my pontification
upon the theater and literature.

I remember dissecting the latest best-selling novel,
which I hadn't read but of which I could speak with
supreme authority, having read the *New York Times*
review.

For an hour and a half I displayed my erudition and
took delight in watching De Mille's anticipatory twinkle
fade to puzzled disappointment and finally to a fixed
feral glare. By the time the car turned from the highway
onto the winding mountain road leading to Paradise, De
Mille, whom I suspected read neither books nor reviews,
had come to the disgusted conclusion that I was Queen
of the May.

As it was no part of my plan to drive the man into a
decline, I decided the time had come to let him off the
hook. Reverting to my natural manner, I said abruptly,
"Mr. De Mille, I've got to hand it to you. You sure know
how to judge a man. Your taste is impeccable."

Caught slightly off balance by my sudden reversal of
form, he started to smile but quickly restrained it. He
snarled at me.

"What are you talking about now?"

"Women," I said with a grin. "But there's only one
thing that bothers me. I'm wondering what you have to
offer for the second night."

That wonderful clown, Red Skelton, couldn't have
gotten a bigger reaction. Seldom have I seen a man laugh
so heartily. It started with a snort. Then he chuckled.

The chuckle developed into a guffaw. He huffed and he puffed; he coughed and wheezed until I feared he was about to have an attack of asthma. Finally he managed to speak. "Bickford, you're a miserable snake in the grass. What a bastardly thing to do to me."

I think that if we had really been kindred spirits, this moment would have given birth to a life-long friendship. His relief at finding me normal opened him up like a flower and for the rest of the trip he treated me like a long lost son. He subsequently told me that up to the time I tipped the gag, he had been planning ways and means to cancel my contract.

De Mille was justly proud of Paradise Ranch. Nestling in a secluded mountain valley and but a few miles out of Los Angeles, it afforded everything it takes to make a perfect hideaway. I fell in love with it even before I saw it. As the car turned into De Mille's private road, we were suddenly engulfed in a subtle perfume, emanating from acres of lime, lemon and orange trees. This fragrance, blended with the sharp mountain air, made the simple function of breathing a sheer delight.

The road ended at the center of this enchanted forest, disclosing an attractive sprawling ranch house, a pool, handball and tennis courts.

Radiating from the major house were several shady lanes, or lovers walks, each leading to a picturesque little guest bungalow.

De Mille led us into a spacious living room, the salient features of which I remember as great comfortable-appearing divans and arm chairs upholstered in red leather, an enormous fireplace, and—most impressive in those prohibition days—a practical bar which boasted a breath-taking stock of pre-war liquors.

Exclusive of the staff of white-clad, Filipino house

boys, there were some sixteen people present. I recognized a former Broadway matinee idol, a notorious swordsman who was equally famous for his portrayal of romantic roles and his facility at evading irate husbands. Also two screen *femmes fatale;* two hopeful juveniles, one quite manly; and several screen starlets, one of whom was destined to become a top-ranking star.

Here, certainly, was high potential for orgiastic activity but after casing the joint carefully I reluctantly came to the conclusion that in decorum these people were indistinguishable from convivial groups I had dallied with at the Westchester Country Club. All were personable, gay, and believe it or not, engaged in animated conversations about many things, from cabbages to presidents.

I did not rule out the possibility of high jinks to come, however, particularly when, after the introductions, De Mille led me into the library where with great enthusiasm, he showed me his collection of erotica. I presumed it to be priceless and recognized that most of the volumes were beautifully bound and illuminated. Because of my streak of inherent Yankee Puritanism, I suppose, erotica was to me synonymous with pornography and I was square enough to be embarrassed by it. I'm sure he was disappointed at my reaction.

I managed to display a modicum of phony interest by expressing admiration for a privately printed three-volume edition of shockingly illustrated works of Francois Rabelais. De Mille, in what I was to learn was a typical gesture, insisted that I accept it with his compliments. I still have the set. It rests on my library table and occasionally shocks the hell out of visiting New England Blue Noses.

After rejoining the group it soon became evident that De Mille, true to his word, had designated me as the lion of the occasion. It was indeed my party and as it progressed I enjoyed myself hugely.

When at seven o'clock we were shown to our respective quarters to dress for dinner, I was in a mellow mood. My room was in De Mille's personal bungalow which consisted of a huge playroom and four spacious bedrooms; one for his personal use, the others for special guests.

I found my things unpacked and a Filipino house boy in attendance. Laid out on the bed were my dress trousers and a red silk Russian blouse. I looked at the thing in amazement and asked the house boy, "How come?"

He explained that it was Mr. De Mille's custom to have the male guests wear red blouses at dinner. "Very pretty," he volunteered.

"I should imagine so," I said. "What an eccentric idea. And what does Mr. De Mille wear?"

"Russian blouse," he answered. "Only always white, yellow or black."

It occured to me that here was a perfect opportunity to pull another gag on the master. I instructed the Filipino to go to Mr. De Mille's room and tell him that I could not wear the blouse. "If he wants to know why," I said, "Tell him it's too small."

He reappeared shortly, accompanied by my concerned host. He explained that the blouses were tailored in three sizes—small, medium and large. The one in question was indubitably large. However, he politely accepted my statement and was about to send the house boy for another blouse when I interrupted.

"Don't bother sending for a red one. It would still be too small. The only Russian blouse that will fit me tonight must be white, yellow or black."

For an instant temper flashed in his eyes. But remembering he was the gracious host and I the guest of honor, he favored me with a quarter smile and said seriously, "Please don't think I'm arbitrary about this, Charlie, but it's traditional here at Paradise for my male guests to wear the red blouses at dinner. Put it on. You'll find it very comfortable and you'll look stunning in it."

I continued in serious vein. "I'm sorry, C.B. I certainly have no wish to appear ungracious but that shade of red clashes terribly with my hair. Besides, as guest of honor, I think I should be allowed to co-star at the dinner table. Or, you go ahead and star solo in white, and I'll settle for the feature spot in black."

The gag fizzled. He didn't dig my humor at all. But after a moment of serious consideration he decided my idea had merit. "Nice showmanship" he called it and sent for a black blouse.

It was not only becoming but comfortable; much more so than the conventional dress shirt and dinner jacket. The master went up a notch in my estimation. There appeared to be method in what I had deemed mere eccentricity.

Together we walked back to the main house, or perhaps I should say we marched. He always seemed to be leading a parade. During that short walk, in semi-darkness and with no one watching, I got the impression he was attempting to keep one pace ahead of me.

As we entered the house, or rather as we squeezed through the door side by side, the assembled guests broke into a round of applause. Evidently they had the impression we'd been racing and were ending up in a photo finish.

Dinner was served promptly. Several tables had been pushed together, forming a half circle before the great fireplace in which a log fire was now blazing. The flickering firelight, augmented by the mellow glow from dozens of candles, provided the only illumination resulting in a subtle change in the atmosphere of the great room.

There was an aura of mystery, romance, and for good measure, barbarism. The girls' eyes seemed unnaturally bright and the men had taken on the aspect of satyrs—an exotic effect produced in part by the red blouses.

Or, more probably, I was beginning to feel my liquor. Anyhow, I listened for the clash of cymbals and watched for the grand entrance of dancing girls and camels.

The dinner was a lively affair, with much gossipy conversation and good-natured banter. De Mille, a superb host and skillful raconteur, saw to it that the ball was kept in the air; there were no dull moments.

In line with the general atmosphere, I had expected the menu to consist of a profusion of rare and exotic dishes. I couldn't have been more wrong. The *pièce de résistance* was corned beef and cabbage.

After dinner two teams were organized to play charades. I was chosen to captain one team. De Mille headed the other. The orgy image was receding into the dim distance. My aunt Sarah used to throw wilder parties than this one, I thought.

Yet, champagne flowed like water and as the witching hour approached some of the boys and girls developed a hot and bothered gleam in their eyes.

"Of course," I reasoned. "It's New Year's eve. Something other than corks will start to pop at midnight."

And so they did. But only in terms of noise and enthusiasm. There was an abundance of noise makers, tin horns and whistles and at twelve o'clock everybody cut loose. The din was terrific.

When everyone was breathless from trying to scream "Happy New Year" louder than the other guy, the toasts began. De Mille toasted me. I toasted De Mille. We toasted the New Year, the motion picture industry, "Dynamite," President Hoover and the United States of America, winding up with a maudlin rendition of *Auld Lang Syne*.

Perhaps because by this time my vision was slightly out of focus, De Mille appeared to resemble old Bacchus himself as, surrounded by his votaries, he passed out long slim candles to the Bacchae.

He explained that they were called Brides Candles and according to old Spanish custom were to be used to foster the romantic spirit among the señoritas and caballeros. If a girl were in the mood for dalliance, she had but to light her candle and place it outside her door. The caballeros would take it from there.

Having expounded this quaintly naughty bit of folk-lore, he announced that he was about to retire to his quarters, making it clear, however, that the party was by no means over and that he would take it very unkindly if we allowed his absence to spoil the fun.

The revel continued but the spark was gone. With the great man no longer present, the necessity for impressing him was no longer existent. Within a few minutes several of the guests drifted.

Someone turned on the radio and tuned in Ben Bernie's band, broadcasting from Catalina Island. And so we danced, flirted, smooched and went through all the motions of having a gay old time. We resembled the New Year's parties in New York night clubs, where sad-eyed people appear determined to have a good time if it kills them.

After about a half hour of this, the major-domo ap-

proached me and whispered that Mr. De Mille was expecting me at his bungalow. I welcomed the summons.
My thinking was that De Mille wished to discuss "Dynamite" over a sociable night-cap. In my half-stewed
condition I saw nothing incongruous in holding a story
conference at one o'clock of a bibulous New Year's
morning.

But this man of constant surprises had again thrown
me a curve.

I walked into his bungalow to discover that I had been
called, not to a story conference but to a party. Or perhaps I should say to *the* party, for it was plain to be seen
that this was the center ring; the star performers were
assembled and the main show was on.

The big play-room was in semi-darkness except for a
pool of light in the center, cast from the ceiling by an
artfully concealed spot-light. A girl, beautiful, blonde
and petite, was dancing. She was nude but for a diaphan-
ous veil which she cleverly manipulated as she writhed,
python-like, to the beat of Ravel's *Bolero*.

Three men: De Mille, the Broadway leading man, and
one of the juvenile actors—the manly one—watched
avidly as they sprawled on the carpet just outside the
circle of light.

Three girls, the cream of the crop, catered to the gastronomical desires of the men from a table laden with a
Lucullan display of food and drink.

The performer was blessed with an exquisite body; she
was a bumper and grinder *par excellence*. She finished to
enthusiastic applause from all of us, but De Mille's fervor
caused me to wonder if somewhere on her anatomy she
wore a brand. In an effort to find out, I tried, unsuccessfully, to persuade her to encore without the veil.

With great sincerity she explained her refusal on the

premise that the veil made all the difference between artistic interpretation and indecent exposure.

She was indeed a dedicated little artist . . .

After the dance we played games. First, a marble rolling contest for prizes. Quite innocuous, but lucrative. I won an expensive Leica camera and a matched set of hammered silver flasks.

Then we engaged in a sort of strip-tease dice game. Very naughty but lots of fun, evidenced by howls of laughter from the men and squeals of outraged modesty from the girls as, piece by piece, the losers were forced to discard bits of clothing.

Luck was with me, or against me depending upon the point of view, and the game ended with me fully clothed surrounded by semi-nude nymphs and satyrs. It developed into quite a shindig and there were some cute capers cut.

Incidentally, the dancer was innocent of brands.

My first major purchase in Hollywood was an automobile and although my taste ran to the latest model Dusenburg, which, in view of my prospects I could then have afforded, I decided to buy a used car just in case I should wake up some morning to find I had been living in a world of fantasy.

So, sharpening my Yankee wits, I hied myself to automobile row in Los Angeles. There I was surprised to learn that my horse-trading instinct would not be needed. I had not realized that America's most honest citizens had migrated to Los Angeles to become used-car dealers.

Among others, I met Honest Mike, Honest John, Honest Louie, Honest Charlie and Honest Joe and was deeply touched by their avowed eagerness to do me good. I was, in fact, so affected by their efforts to please that I did no business with any of them, having come to the conclusion that it would be manifestly unfair for a man of my sophistication to take advantage of their innocence.

Instead I chose a dealer who made no claims to honesty and who frankly advertised to the world that he was insane. Mad Man Munch he called himself and explained to me that he was so titled because of his policy in selling cars for half their real value, thereby atoning in part for the wrongs done the public by unscrupulous dealers.

Here, I decided, was a *bona fide* philanthropist worthy of any man's patronage. So after test-driving a snappy looking Cadillac roadster and finding it in excellent condition, I started negotiations.

The asking price was thirty-two hundred dollars. But because of my sympathetic personality Munch was willing to make me a gift of it for the niggardly price of twenty-four hundred.

I countered with an offer of fifteen hundred and thereby precipitated a crisis. The Mad Man was extremely disappointed and highly offended. He wept. He tore his hair. He gnashed his teeth and beat his breast as he berated me for attempting to ruin him.

Finally as he paused for lack of breath, I applauded and praised him for the hammiest imitation I had ever seen of David Warfield in "The Auctioneer."

This appeased him, for although he had never heard of David Warfield, he recognized the note of sincere approval in my voice and from then on we settled down to normal throat-cutting haggling which resulted in a deal. I paid him seventeen hundred and drove the car away.

Subsequent expert appraisal set the value of the car at fourteen hundred . . .

In terms of enjoyment, however, I had made an excel-

lent buy. Driving the open road was one of my greatest
pleasures. That was, of course, before the dreadful mi-
gration to California had made the highways a nightmare
of death and destruction. In the weeks that followed I
raw-hided that roadster over the highways and byways of
the Golden State, experiencing keen delight in its scenic
wonders. In the process I became a dedicated camper-
outer.

My camping outfit consisted of a tarpaulin, blankets,
cooking utensils, aluminum dishes, a zinc-lined basket
which was partitioned to hold ice and provisions, a couple of canteens, fishing gear and a thirty-eight caliber
Police special.

This simple but efficient equipment was kept in the car
and was therefore available at such times, and there were
many, when away from the beaten path, I would happen
on lonely and lovely spots and decide to linger a while.

It was also convenient equipment to have at hand in
case of inadvertent delays because of such things as
washed-out roads and bridges, or as on one occasion, by
becoming stuck in deep sand. This happening is noteworthy because it occurred on a trip during which I
made my first intimate contact with the desert and
straightway fell in love with it.

After my memorable New Year's party, weeks passed
with no word from the studio, nor from De Mille. My
theatrical background having accustomed me to a certain
degree of collaboration with writers, directors and producers, I had begun to champ at the bit. It annoyed me
that I had read no part of the "Dynamite" script, that I
had not been invited to sit in on story conferences and
that none of the MGM executives had taken the trouble
to meet me.

In view of the fact that each week saw a fat check deposited to my account, I don't know why I should have cared a tinker's damn about these real, or fancied slights but the fact remained that I was building up a head of steam.

It could be that I had fallen victim to that horrible disease, forever rampant in the acting profession, self-importance.

Whatever the cause, the effect upon me was anything but good. I took to sulking in my hotel suite, sucking on a bottle and waiting for the phone to ring. As each day passed, my restlessness increased until one morning when I awoke, rationalized the situation, and saw myself as a prisoner of my own unreasonable impatience. I decided to escape.

No sooner said than done. I rolled out my trusty Cadillac, patted her on the carburetor, pointed her nose in a vaguely northeasterly direction and rambled.

Mid-morning found me driving through the incredible vastness of the Mohave Desert. I became fascinated by its almost lunar emptiness. On and on it rolled with occasional small mesas, clumps of mesquite and sage affording the only relief from the expanse of sand—sand without end, dust-colored, golden yellow, chocolate brown and black; the colors merging into a purple haze in the far distance.

Mysterious, sinister, beautiful and incredibly hot. The sun, shining down from a cloudless sky, threatened to burn me to a crisp until, in self-defense, I was forced to put up the top of my chariot. The car metal was blistering hot to the touch. I'm sure I could have fried an egg on any rock in the vicinity.

In the afterglow of a spectacularly colorful sunset I

rolled into a town called Baker. The heat had subsided
with the sun and a gentle breeze had sprung up. The
evening promised to be so fine that I elected to stock up
with provisions, then go on from there and camp out
under the stars.

Leaving the car to be serviced, I found a market and
filled my refrigerated basket with ice, bacon, eggs, cream,
butter and a couple of porterhouse steaks. I also bought
bread, crackers, coffee, milk, fruit, and a five-gallon bottle of spring water.

Thus fortified against hunger and thirst I pressed on in
the fading twilight. A few miles out of Baker I came
upon a bullet-riddled road sign which designated a side
road as the shortest route to Death Valley.

The little I knew about Death Valley consisted of
some rather grim statistics. I knew that it was a deep and
arid basin, about a hundred and forty miles long and
four miles wide, lying between two mountain ranges, the
Panamints on the west and the Armagosa on the east. It
boasted the lowest point in the Western Hemisphere, two
hundred and eighty feet below sea level, and had at one
time recorded a temperature of a hundred and thirty-four
degrees.

Not the most alluring prospectus in the world but the
very name, Death Valley, opened the wide door of
imagination for me. I visualized whiskered old pros-
pectors wandering about with their burros, twenty-mule
teams and Conestoga wagons laden with gold ore and
borax.

I changed course and was soon bumping along a
rutted road that would have challenged the staying
power of an army jeep. The road worsened as I proceeded. At any moment I could have been stopped in my
tracks by a broken axle or cracked engine case.

But I refused to allow realism to dictate my avenue of escape, otherwise I would have retreated from this atrocious excuse for a road and headed back to Los Angeles where I could have indulged my thirst for adventure by driving up and down Wilshire Boulevard.

My first view of the valley was for me the most exciting of the many moods produced by this mysterious desert land. From the dimness of a narrow canyon, walled by high black cliffs, I emerged to find a treasure-trove of beauty and mystery. The moon was up, bathing the valley in silvery radiance. In the crystalline light, the sandy floor appeared as a tremendous field of glistening snow, dotted by thickets of mesquite and walled by majestic mountains, towering high into the sky and dominating the scene by their sheer magnificence.

The road, or trail, consisted of two deep ruts meandering like a snake up the center of the valley. The ruts were so deep that if it had not been for the many sharp curves the wheels would have held to them, eliminating the necessity for driving.

The car's performance was so silent and effortless I might have been gliding over soft snow on a toboggan— a delightful sensation. So delightful in fact, that together with the magic of the environment, the effect upon me was almost hypnotic. As I gawked at the magnificent scenery my foot got heavy on the accelerator. At fifty-to-sixty miles-an-hour, I hit curves that called for a maximum speed of twenty.

Something had to happen.

Swooping around a curve, the trail ahead hidden by a thick clump of mesquite, the car came to a jolting stop and foundered in sand up to the running boards.

I deflated the rear tires, stripped the brush from a quarter-section of desert to provide a traction mat, and dug trenches with my hands. Nothing worked. The car seemed to sink deeper and deeper.

As a last resort I tried to conjure up a twenty-mule hitch. But the ghosts weren't walking that night and I reluctantly conceded defeat; a galling decision for me to make at any time. I would have to ask help from the first passing motorist.

It was at this moment that I conceived the brilliant idea that this was the perfect spot to make camp. Too weary to bother about cooking, I dined on a cold snack, spread my tarp over a mattress of mesquite boughs, rolled up in a blanket and for the next eight hours I doubt that I so much as moved a muscle.

When I awoke the sun was up and the desert floor was flooded with a soft golden light, blending the many shades of green, brown, gray and mauve into a pastel wonderwork.

In sharp contrast, the mountains, swelling up from the shadowed tumble of rock at the bottom, soared in vividly colored temples and pyramids to the incredible blue of a cloudless sky.

The aromatic air—I thought of myrrh and frankincense—was slightly warm and very still. As far as I could see, nothing, not even a leaf, was stirring.

The silence was absolute, enhancing the impression of a great canvas of painted magnificence.

The world and Metro-Goldwyn-Mayer were very far away.

As the carnal spirit within me clamored for attention, my brief flight of poetic fancy was halted and I turned to the prosaic business of cooking breakfast.

Never had food tasted so good despite the sudden onslaught of millions of gnats. The pestiferous insects garnished my bacon and eggs, drowned themselves in my coffee, played hide-and-seek in my hair and swarmed into and about my eyes, nose and mouth. But the magnificent environment plus my lusty appetite overbalanced the annoyance.

At that moment I was allowing nothing to dampen my good spirits, not even the realization that I had blundered onto an untraveled road. It was now eight a.m. and for twelve hours I had met with no traffic. I thought it extremely unlikely that a good Samaritan would happen along now.

So what? I had plenty of food and water; I was thrilled by the majestic beauty of my surroundings. Why not stay put and enjoy myself for the rest of the day? Later in the cool of the evening, I would take off on shank's mare and hike up the valley until I found help.

In the shade of a mesquite bush I sat, comfortable enough except for the gnats, and feasted my eyes on the Eden before me. I was enamored of it. It lacked only an Eve, an apple tree, and a serpent to convince me that I was Adam incarnate.

But I soon learned that the desert had many phases. As the sun rose higher, the temperature climbed with it and by high noon the heat gave the lie to the calendar. With the sun directly overhead, the only shade was under the top of my foundered car.

Retreating to it I sat gazing morosely at the now bleak and forbidding aspect, finding it difficult to reconcile it with the magic and beauty which had enthralled me during the early morning hours. The only thing cool about me was my ardor. The honeymoon was waning.

The valley floor, so enchanting in the moonlight, now appeared flat and harsh. The mountains, too, were show-

ing their fangs. Silhouetted against the yellowish glare of
the sky, the sheer cliffs and towering peaks which I had
gazed upon with reverent admiration now appeared
merely as insurmountable barricades. This was the desert
in its savage and least attractive mood and inspired in me
a mixed feeling of awe and wonder—and claustrophobia.

I suddenly felt trapped. I had to get out of this inferno.
And fast.

I did just that. Slinging a canteen of water over my
shoulder, I hit the trail. It would have been tough going
for a camel. For me, it was purgatory. The sun, blazing
down from the sky and reflecting up from the burning
sand, seemed bent upon reducing me to a grease spot and
the odds seemed to be rigged in its favor. I was shod in
rubber-soled sneakers and wore no hat. I hadn't covered
a mile before I was gasping for breath and keeping a
desperate lookout for the little spot of shade that wasn't
there.

My horse-sense directed me to turn back and rest in
the car until after sundown. But I was running true to
form. As always, I chose the hard way. The mule in me
held sway and I continued to pick 'em up and lay 'em
down.

On and on I slogged. The trail was deeply rutted and I
stopped at intervals to shake the loose sand and pebbles
out of my sneakers. At first I kept a sharp eye out for
signs of human habitation but the drab monotony of the
unchanging landscape, seen through shimmering heat
waves, induced a narcotic effect and my movements became purely mechanical. I was a zombie walking a treadmill in a dead world. I lost all sense of time and distance.

In a semi-collapse I stopped near a clump of brush to
rest. As I sank to the ground, I was suddenly enveloped

by a delicious sense of coolness. I came awake instantly and for the first time in hours looked about me in complete awareness of my surroundings.

I had been walking for five hours. The sun was about to set. A great molten ball of fire, it was poised on the rim of the Western Range, bathing the valley floor with a soft golden light.

Sitting in my patch of blessed shade, I gazed in fascination at the transformation that had taken place. The whole picture was changing as I watched. Everything— rocks, trees and shrubs—stood out in sharp focus against the golden glow, casting shadows that, lengthening by the second, merged and formed great pools of purple shade.

The mountains no longer appeared as harsh and sinister, but had reverted to their former majesty, with the added magnificence of incredible coloring. Among the domes and minarets, I could see every conceivable shade of brown, red, yellow, purple and blue.

Below were the foothills, now as soft and inviting as great mounds of chocolate, vanilla and strawberry ice cream.

As I thrilled to the breath-taking beauty of the scene, the sun rolled over the edge and was gone. The colors, in great flaring streaks, miraculously transferred to the sky, leaving the western mountains shrouded in dark blue velvet. Spellbound, I succumbed anew to the charm of this mysterious land, thrusting aside the savage memory of the afternoon. The reconciliation was complete.

I had not meant to sleep at this time and was therefore surprised when I suddenly opened my eyes to black night. Three hours had passed. The temperature had dropped sharply and I was now shivering with cold. My muscles had stiffened and my feet were swollen and sore.

I had to force myself to rise and continue the hike. Every step was a torture to my abused feet and body. It was pitch dark; the rising moon had yet to clear the mountains. I had to feel my way to the unseen trail, weaving and stumbling like a blind man. My progress was further retarded by the fear that I might step on a rattlesnake. Knowing that in arid regions they hibernated during the heat of the day, coming out at night to feed, my mind's eye held a vivid picture of my canvas-shod foot descending upon one of the things. I could see it coil around my instep as it sank its fangs into my unprotected ankle.

There was a moment when, after I had stumbled and fallen, I was sorely tempted to lay where I was until there was light but the facts of my predicament were too grim to be ignored. The valley was a hundred and forty miles long. I didn't even know for sure that it was inhabited. Certainly the area I was in didn't appear to be. I was footsore and weary and my canteen was nearly empty. If I was to reach shelter, it must be before sunrise—or else. The notion of ending up as something for the vultures didn't appeal to me at all. It did spur me to action. The order of the night became "Damn the rattlesnakes. Full speed ahead" and I was soon up and away, letting the feet fall where they may.

I doubt I missed a hummock nor a hole in that damned trail. Stumbling constantly, I plodded on, seeing nothing and hearing nothing. The black silence was deathly.

I pondered the name   Death Valley. Perhaps without realizing it, I had died and had passed into the Beyond. Maybe this was my Heaven and I was enjoying my just reward. Never had I felt so alone. I was, after all, a lover of solitude. Could it have been ordained that I was to follow this lonesome road to eternity?

Or was this the Other Place? Certainly, my aching bones and bruised feet made every step a purgatory.

But, always logical, I rejected the idea. In the first place, I had never done anything in my life to rate it; secondly, Hell must be thickly populated. This place was empty. Finally, it was colder than Hell.

I settled for Heaven.

I was perturbed, however, that whoever or whatever had set up the deal had forgotten to equip me with wings. I resolved that if I ever achieved a position of authority in the place, there would be some changes made.

With these cheery thoughts coursing through my brain, I trudged on and on, not stopping to rest for fear that I might never get started again. For the second time I lost all sense of time and distance. I became just a perambulating bundle of aches and pains.

Suddenly, as though some celestial electrician had switched on a gigantic flood lamp, the valley was bathed in silvery brilliance. The moon had finally made it over the rim of the Armagosas.

The effect upon me was immediate and miraculous. Now that I could see, my spirits soared, my muscles limbered up and in disregard of my protesting feet my uncertain step became a purposeful stride. I became a one-man parade. I marched.

The way was long and the going tough but I really knocked off the miles until at long last I arrived at the edge of a vast expanse of salt flats, a devilishly sinister place across which the trail wound its torturous way among great hummocks of glittering salt.

On the far side was what appeared to be an oasis.

There were fruit orchards and palm trees through the foliage of which I glimpsed the sparkle of water. And on a little knoll was situated the most magnificently comfortable-appearing, man-made structure in the world.

I closed my unbelieving eyes for a long moment, then looked again. It was no mirage. There *was* a hotel there. A real hotel, with water, food and—I nearly collapsed at the thought—a bed.

In my exhuberance, I started at a half run across the flats and promptly turned an ankle.

Those last couple of miles were the longest. Hobbling, hopping and crawling, I crossed the rest of that infernal region; and finally, as the sun was rising, I crawled on my hands and knees into the lobby of the Furnace Creek Inn . . .

Later the inn's tow truck found my car twenty-nine miles down the valley and was itself stuck twice during the trip. The road was indeed impassable and had been posted to that effect both at the inn and at the highway turn-off. The turn-off had also been barricaded, a fact that made me feel pretty stupid until it was discovered that in an effort to protect his business, an unscrupulous motel operator had removed the barricade.

I bore the man no ill will. If I had met him face to face I would probably have punched him in the nose but at the same time I'd have thanked him for a rich experience. For while there were gruelling intervals which could have proven disastrous, my spirit of adventure had made it the stuff of dreams.

Several more weeks passed before the De Mille picture started shooting, weeks spent exploring California, Arizona and New Mexico. And they were wonderful weeks, the only wonderful weeks I knew during the extent of my MGM contract.

I was in Mexico City engaged in an exhaustive study of the drinking and sex habits of the natives when the clarion call came, relayed via my Hollywood hotel. I was ordered to report to Cecil B. De Mille's office at ten o'clock the following morning.

As the time element demanded that I fly back to Hollywood, I reluctantly said "Goodbye" to my Cadillac. The faithful old car had served me well. I had driven her thousands of miles in the comparatively short time since we had met and we had grown to understand and love each other. It was a melancholy farewell and on this note I boarded the plane.

The group which came together in De Mille's office consisted of De Mille, his entire staff of writers, technicians and assistants; the cast of "Dynamite," which included Conrad Nagle, Kay Johnson from the Broadway Theater, Carol Lombard who was then known, I think, as Jane Peters, Joel McCrea, then a tyro, and myself.

We were all eagerly expectant and keyed up to the importance of the occasion. "Dynamite" was to be De Mille's first talking picture. It was a very first motion-picture venture for both Kay Johnson and me. It was a new medium also for most of the sound engineers and for the camera crew.

By comparison, Conrad Nagle was the only veteran; he had already made several sound pictures for Warner Brothers.

After introductions, De Mille, very horsey that morning in riding breeches, tweed jacket and boots, conducted us into the big conference room where rows of folding chairs had been set up.

As we seated ourselves, De Mille, flanked by three scenario writers whose names I have mercifully forgotten, ascended a platform on which were his desk and throne chair.

The first assistant called for silence and De Mille began to speak. It was a masterly oration, comprising the complete history of his film career from its inception in a Vine Street barn where he had given birth to "The Squaw Man" up to the momentous present in which a panting world waited to view his first masterpiece in the new medium of sound.

Then followed a commendably short lecture on togetherness, stressing the newness of sound and the consequent necessity for working as a team.

He spoke well. The talk was interesting, constructive and at times amusing.

So far, so good.

There was a pile of scripts on the desk. Picking up one of them, he read aloud the descriptive material concerning the three leading characters and the locale of the story.

At this point my expectation was that the scripts would be passed out so that we could go ahead with a reading rehearsal, such as I was accustomed to in the theater.

But he continued to read and had progressed well into the dialogue of the first sequence when Kay Johnson blurted to me, "My God! He's not going to read the whole script to us?"

Everybody in the room heard her. There was a ripple of laughter followed by a pregnant silence as De Mille, his face reddening with anger, glared down from the dais.

I was embarrassed for Kay, expecting her to be withered by a blast of devastating sarcasm.

I needn't have been. De Mille suddenly smiled and said graciously, "I'm sorry, Miss Johnson, I didn't quite catch what you said. You have a question?"

Kay was not one to be caught with her tail up. Returning smile for smile, she said sweetly, "No, Mr. De Mille. I was just saying to Mr. Bickford that it's wonderful of you to read for us. I didn't mean to interrupt you."

"Think nothing of it," he returned blandly, and resumed his reading.

My own reaction was neutral. I'd never known a producer to read a script to the cast, but, I thought, if this is Hollywood procedure, so be it.

My complacency didn't last long.

The story began to emerge as a mish-mash of contrived situations, peopled with unreal characters and weighted down with dialogue so naïve as to be ridiculous.

De Mille's reading was no help. He had been an actor in his younger days and if one was to judge by his stilted speech and ponderous emphasis upon points, his acting must have left plenty to be desired.

But his enthusiasm was magnificent and he blithely forged ahead, pausing at intervals to note the impact of this dramatic bomb upon his captive audience.

Most of the listeners were raptly attentive. But why was I so disappointed? Months previously, when De Mille had told me the story over long distance telephone, I had judged it a mess of corn and had, nevertheless and after careful consideration, committed myself to it. Nothing had changed. By this reasoning then, my criticism must be directed at the dialogue.

Having arrived at this conclusion, I thought back to the beginning of the story and in my mind played some of the scenes, improvising the dialogue. As I became absorbed in these thoughts, De Mille's voice receded from my consciousness . . .

I was most embarrassed when I woke up. A grinning assistant director, having shaken me awake was standing be my shoulder while De Mille, smiling benignly at the delighted assemblage, said humorously, "It appears that the gentleman from the Great White Way is feeling the impact of our Hollywood night life." Then, after the resulting laugh, "Rough night, Mr. Bickford?"

"Something like that," I said contritely. "I'm sorry."

"Do you feel quite rested now?"

"Quite. Thank you."

"Sufficiently so that we may expect your attention during the remainder of this rehearsal?"

"I hope so."

"You're sure it's not too much to ask?"

"Positive."

In spite of the fact that his jocular manner had held the barb of sarcasm, I felt that he had handled the situation in true princely fashion.

He resumed reading and as this was the pre-coffee-break era, continued without interruption until the end. The reading had taken three hours. The script may not have been a good one but no one could say it wasn't a thick one.

The boys and girls gathered around the master and there was much oh-ing and ah-ing as they congratulated him for his rendition of a great script.

The only abstainer was—guess who.

Feeling singularly awkward and conspicuous, I turned to make what I hoped would be an unnoticed exit. But the lynx-eyed De Mille stopped me in my tracks. "We still have to hear from our distinguished leading man."

he said. "How about it, Mr. Bickford? Are you pleased?"

Flushed with pleasure at the enthusiastic reaction to the script, it was obvious that he sincerely believed in it himself and was expecting to hear words of praise from me.

I was embarrassed for both of us.

Arranging my face into what I hoped was a pleasant smile, I took a stab at diplomacy.

"Fine, Mr. De Mille. Just fine. Very exciting. What a story."

He beamed like a little boy being handed a lollypop. "I'm delighted. Coming from you, that's praise indeed." Then, to the others, "Mr. Bickford is a perfectionist. He's dedicated to the theater and is quite skeptical about us here in Hollywood. As a matter of fact, it took a lot of persuasion to induce him to leave his beloved Broadway. Now that he's here I hope he'll be with us for a long time to come."

Then, as the scripts were being passed out, he said, "If there are any suggestions, I'd appreciate hearing them now as there will be no time for changes after we begin shooting."

Not caring for the position of having burned my bridges, I said, "I have a few points but I'd like to discuss them in private, if you don't mind."

He was not a subtle man. The smile became fixed and his voice was edgy as he said, "We're all working together here, Mr. Bickford, and are interested in one objective—to make a great motion picture. So don't be afraid to speak up."

He stepped from the dais and as he approached me, I caught the now-familiar glint of antagonism in his eyes.

His very proximity exerted a juggernaut effect and seemed to pose the challenge—"Back up or be flattened."

My hackles began to rise.

"There is no question of my being afraid, Mr. De Mille. I just thought it might be wiser for me to speak my piece in private. I'm quite concerned about the dialogue."

"An interesting comment, particularly in view of the fact that it was written by the three highest paid writers in Hollywood."

"What you pay them is none of my business, Mr. De Mille. My concern is with the material they have turned out. In my estimation some of it is unplayable."

At this point the male member of the writing trio, highly incensed by this attack upon his work leaped to its defense. "What are you talking about? This script was tailored to your measure."

"Then you must have used a lousy yardstick."

"And just who are you to make such a judgment? This is to be your first picture, isn't it? What do you know about picture scripts?"

De Mille silenced him with a gesture. He had no intention of allowing anyone else to cut me down.

"Mr. Bickford, you're out of order. I have been producing motion pictures for many years, successful motion pictures. And I know what I'm saying when I call this an excellent script."

I was suddenly weighted down by a nascent foreboding of disaster. I was probably about to end a short and unhappy film career without having made a picture. But the die was cast. The dogs of war had been loosed and my Irish was up, way up. "Onward and upward". I forged ahead.

"Understand me, Mr. De Mille. I am not criticising the construction of this story. I don't know enough about screen writing for that. But I've been writing and acting in stage plays for many more years than you've been producing motion pictures. And this dialogue stinks."

There was complete silence in the room. This was *lèse majesté* indeed.

De Mille's eyes narrowed to slits.

"He's measuring me for the kill," I thought, and tried to think of a good exit line.

But the expected explosion did not occur. It was averted by the intervention of one of the women writers. Her voice dripped venom as she shrilled, "Mr. Bickford has a reputation for this sort of thing. He tries to rewrite everything he plays in."

He resented the intrusion. "I'm well aware of Mr. Bickford's reputation," he snapped. "That's why he's here."

By comparison, his tone was almost gentle as he turned again to me. "Pretty harsh criticism, Mr. Bickford. But if something smells that bad to you there must be a reason. I'll have to ask you to be more explicit."

"The words are completely false," I said. "Particularly to the characters of Cynthia and Hagon." (These were the roles to be played by Kay Johnson and myself.) "For instance in the bedroom sequence, the words the writers have put into their mouths are ludicrous. Those two people would not talk like that."

"You're sure of that?"

"Positive."

"I see. And just how, in your expert opinion, would you have them talk?"

Luckily I was a facile ad-libber. I picked up a script and started to read the sequence, improvising dialogue to fit the situation. It sounded pretty crude even to me and when I finished I fully expected to be blasted by sarcastic invective.

But this chameleon had changed color again. He was beaming like a benevolent Santa Claus. "That sounded pretty good. I'll really have to admit it sounded pretty good. Anyway, it's an improvement."

Turning to the three glowering writers, he asked, "Don't you agree?"

Obviously they did not agree but knowing which side of the bread the jam was on, they nodded their assent as De Mille knew they would.

He then dismissed the rehearsal, asking the writers, his secretary and me to remain for further discussion. During the ensuing couple of hours, I sympathized with the writers as, fairly oozing hatred of me, they sat and took notes while I improvised dialogue.

I dismissed the incident as of little account but distorted versions of the story soon began to reverberate from the Hollywood hills. Charlie Bickford had said "no" to Cecil De Mille. A myth was spawned . . .

A few days following the reading, "Dynamite" went into production and for months thereafter I was engaged in intensive, fascinating, and sometimes ludicrous activity. My days of carefree roving over the mountains and deserts were over.

The starting day of the picture I left my hotel at seven-thirty and with the top down drove my glittering new car to the studio. All seemed to be right with the world. Feeling very important and successful, I arrived at the gates only to have my entrance barred by an armed guard who truculently demanded to see my pass.

I had no pass.

I informed him, naïvely, that I was Charles Bickford, Cecil De Mille's new leading man from New York.

He was unimpressed and instructed me to apply at the main office for admittance.

"Look, officer," I said, "I haven't time for that. I'm the star of De Mille's new picture and they're waiting for me in there."

"It makes no difference to me who you are, Mister. You're not driving in here without a pass. Now get that car out of the way. You're holding up important people."

The important people were the occupants of several cars lined up behind mine.

I suggested that he call the De Mille office for a clearance. He impatiently answered that he had no time for that and again ordered me to get out of the way. Some of the drivers behind me were now honking their horns.

My back began to itch.

"All right, you stupid bastard," I said. "If anyone comes around asking for me, just tell them that I was here at eight o'clock and that you refused to let me in. Now, tell those important shit-heels behind me to back up and let me out of here."

By this time cars had lined up to the extent that traffic on the main boulevard was obstructed. For a couple of blocks cars were bumper-to-bumper and to a man the drivers were leaning on their horn buttons. The uproar was deafening.

As it was now impossible for me to back out, the guard ordered me to drive on through the gate and then pull over to the side.

This I refused to do, explaining with what I considered perfect logic that as he had already and in no uncertain terms informed me of the impossibility of my driving through the gate without a pass, and as the situation remained unchanged due to the fact that I still had no pass, he could not force me to do the impossible.

"Don't hand me that crap," he said furiously. "I'm telling you for the last time—pull that car out of the way."

The racket now had mounted to sheer pandemonium. Heads were popping out of office windows, drivers were yelling and two more studio guards were approaching on the run, their Forty-fives bobbing on their hips.

My back stopped itching. The situation was taking on the flavor of a Keystone comedy and I was beginning to enjoy it. I smiled sweetly at the guard.

"Listen, stupid," I said. "You got yourself into this mess. I suggest that you get yourself out of it by phoning the De Mille office. I'm going to sit right here until you do."

By now the two additional guards had arrived and the three went into a huddle while the infernal uproar increased in volume, the automobile horns having been reinforced by the scream of a police siren.

Their huddle finished, the guards split up, one of them rushing into the gate-house, the remaining two approaching me.

"Look, fella," one of them said. "Are you nuts or something?"

"That I refuse to answer on the grounds that it may incriminate me," I said grinning at him.

"Get out of that car," he growled and made a threatening gesture toward his gun.

"Not by a God-damn sight," I growled back. Then, as he reached for the door handle, "Keep your lousy meat hook away from that door."

The situation had altered its complexion and was now loaded for violence; I would certainly have resisted any attempt to pull me out of the car.

As luck would have it, however, the law took over. A city motor-cycle policeman boiled onto the scene, demanding to know what was going on. After a quick briefing by the studio cops, he dismounted from his machine and strode toward me. One glance at his steely eyes and I didn't have to wonder whose side he was on. I braced myself for the collision.

His opening line was the stereotyped, "Let-me-see-your-driver's-license."

I dutifully complied.

Having established my right to drive a passenger vehicle in the State of California, he said abruptly, "Have you been drinking?"

Throwing my head back in righteous indignation, I said severely, "Certainly not, officer. That would constitute breaking the law of this benighted land. Do I look like the sort of person who would do a thing like that?"

He didn't appreciate my humor.

"Get out of the car," he snarled and as this was the authentic voice of authority, I obeyed.

"Let me smell your breath," he ordered, and leaned forward, his nose almost in my mouth.

Regretful that I hadn't eaten kippers and limburger cheese for breakfast, I filled my lungs and favored him with the greatest blast I was capable of.

What the outcome of this little comedy drama might have been is anybody's guess. I probably would have ended up in the Culver City clink but the argument was resolved by a studio cop who had finally wised-up and had checked with the De Mille office. He came rushing from the gate-house yelling, "It's O.K. It's O.K. Go right ahead, Mr. Bickford. They're waiting for you on stage four. Sorry we held you up. Somebody goofed"

And that was just the beginning of a screwy day. A portable dressing room had been set up for me on stage four. In and around it swarmed a small army of people whom I soon discovered were there to make sure I would be ready to start acting on the stroke of nine o'clock. There were the number three assistant director, a wardrobe man, a makeup man, a—believe-it-or-not—hairdresser, a stand-in and an intellectual-appearing gent who introduced himself as the dialogue director.

Never had there been so many to do so little.

My costume consisted of a cheap, ill-fitting suit, a workman's shirt and a dilapidated pair of shoes. For makeup I needed only a dab of pancake for my cheeks and a touch of eye shadow. As for my hair—well, I never did go in for meticulous hairdos.

The help thrust upon me by these well-meaning people hampered me to the extent that to keep from flipping, I invited them all to leave, that I might put on my own pants in peace.

The actual set was a beehive of activity but mostly noise and confuison. There were at least forty workers: camera men, sound men, electricians, property men, grips, wardrobe people, makeup people, hairdressers, carpenters, painters, set dressers, extras, assistant directors, and the "green man."

The "green man"? He represented the greenery department. His function was to care for the few potted shrubs which, seen through one of the set windows, represented a garden in the background.

It was evident that the working crew was anything but understaffed. I was amazed that it required the efforts of so many people to ready a simple little set until it dawned upon me that many of these seemingly busy workers were making a big deal out of nothing. It seemed that in some departments three men were occupied in doing the work of one. Obviously the studio was in sore need of an efficiency expert.

In addition to the identifiable workers there were several nondescript individuals whom I judged to be either publicity people or studio executives as they seemed to be functioning merely as onlookers.

A few minutes before nine o'clock the stage door was flung open and the uniformed guard announced, "He's coming."

"Who's coming?" I asked of the nearest person.

"God. Who else?" was the laconic reply.

Irreverent people, those studio workers.

In spite of myself I was caught up in a kind of breathless anticipation as I awaited the Advent.

And it needed but little imagination to hear the sound of trumpets as, a moment later, the demi-god of the flickers swept through the door.

Three paces behind him and in near-military formation were his assistant director, unit manager, film cutter, script clerk, megaphone bearer, chair bearer and secretary.

As he marched across the stage in my direction, I found it difficult to decide whether I should genuflect, laugh or applaud.

These derisive thoughts were quickly overpowered by a grudging admiration for the aplomb with which he carried out his ostentation. Not even now after years of intermittent association can I say for sure whether his pomposity was dictated by a sincere belief that he was to the manner born or by a magnificent flair for showmanship.

That first working morning, for instance, I watched in fascination as he mapped out the mechanics of the first scene. Every move he made found the script clerk, chair bearer and megaphone bearer moving with him like shadows, always but an arm's length behind him. They were trained to anticipate his every wish. If he wanted his megaphone, he had merely to extend his hand and it would be immediately placed in his grasp. If he were about to sit, he didn't look to see if the chair was there. He just sat.

I, figuring that the bearer must at some time succumb to the perfectly human urge to topple authority, waited gleefully, hoping. But each time the guy virtually thrust the devil behind him. The chair was always there.

The first scene was one in which I, about to be executed for a murder which I did not commit, say "Goodbye" to my nine-year-old sister. Needless to say, Sis and I love each other very, very much and the scene as written was pretty mawkish stuff. What happened next I wouldn't believe except that it happened to me.

I was in my dressing room awaiting the call to rehearse when suddenly all activity on the set abruptly ceased. I heard the first assistant call for, and get, utter silence. From somewhere came the sound of music—soft music, and played with consummate feeling. A spinet player and a fiddler were pulling out all the stops as they played that tried-and-true old tear-jerker, *Hearts and Flowers.*

A minute later an assistant director rapped discreetly on my door and in hushed tones said, "We're ready for you, Mr. Bickford."

Responding immediately, I blithely walked onto the set where everyone, including the crew, stood with doleful expressions and bowed heads. Putting two and two together, I jumped to the conclusion that a gag was being pulled on me because of the sentimentality of the scene I was about to play. And, I thought, a very funny gag.

Going along with the joke I struck a pose and began to declaim, "Friends, Romans, countrymen, lend me your ears. I come to bury Caesar . . ." but stopped abruptly as I caught the shocked look of disapproval on De Mille's face.

Instantly contrite, thinking I had inadvertently been flippant at the expense of some memorial rite, I attempted to make amends. "Oh. I'm sorry," I said. "I didn't realize. *Has* someone died?"

From the resulting roar of laughter from the listening group, I realized even before the flush of anger crept up and over his high forehead, that I had made a *faux pas* and had only succeeded in shoving my foot farther down my throat. He was really concerned at my flippancy and explained in solemn tones that the music—and I swear by the beard of my sainted grandfather that I'm telling it straight—was necessary in order to create in me the proper degree of emotional intensity demanded by the scene.

Coming from the top producer-director of his time and delivered to an actor of my experience and standing, his statement was hardly to be taken seriously. Once again I suspected a rib. "You have to be kidding," I said.

Once again I was wrong. He was painfully serious. "I never joke where my work is concerned, Mr. Bickford. And that's what we're here for, to work. I have found that music is of material help in creating a mood."

Since to some extent we all use individual methods to obtain results and as this musical gimmick appeared to have worked for him, I was bound to respect it. On the other hand it could not possibly work for me, inspiring in me as it did nothing but derisive mirth. As I did not wish to be rude, insulting, or even mildly disrespectful, it was up to me to come up with an intelligent refute.

I was handed the key when my eye rested upon the megaphone bearer. The ensuing dialogue went something like this—

"It occurs to me, Mr. De Mille, that most of the actors you have directed during your long and illustrious career were silent screen actors. Right?"

"That's correct. Although I've worked with many stage actors."

"You were once an actor on the legitimate stage, weren't you?"

"I was."

"Then perhaps you'll agree that we of the stage have a different approach to acting than the people of the silent screen."

"I don't follow you."

"To put it bluntly: if the time ever comes when I need this type of stimulus to make me act, I'll go back to swinging a pick for a living."

This brought forth a general laugh in which he joined. He was sporting enough to concede my point. The musicians were dismissed and we settled down to the business of making the picture.

This little brush with De Mille and the incident at the gate were of no importance to me but within hours both had become common gossip in the studio, adding of course to a rapidly growing myth of Bickford, stormy petrel of Hollywood.

At that time I was unaware of the extensive system of espionage that spread its tentacles into every department of the studio.

Because of their proneness to shoot off their mouths, actors are fair game and the hairdressing and makeup departments were happy hunting grounds for the stoolies employed there. Every action or word that could be construed as disloyal was reported to the front office.

Particularly malevolent were the spies in the publicity department. The practice was for a spy to be assigned to a specific star, with orders to ingratiate himself. And after gaining the confidence of the unconscious victim, the spy would keep his superiors informed as to any untoward actions or statements.

One of the most efficient of these creeps, a female, was known to be a drug addict and sex pervert. This did not prevent her assignment to one of the youngest and brightest stars in the MGM galaxy. The two became constant companions in and out of the studio with the result that in a comparatively short space of time the talented and lovely young star had been converted into a sex-driven, drug-crazed wreck.

A personable young male flack was one of the most proficient stool pigeons on the lot. A seducer *par excellence*, he was very popular with the more ambitious starlets, and, being a smart fellow, he seized opportunity by the forelock and brought himself to the attention of the higher ups by adding a bit of specialized pandering to his talent for espionage. He also exhibited a flair for hatchet wielding and could be depended upon to accomplish a thorough job of character assassination whenever his bosses wanted to ruin an actor. Naturally, he became a confidante of L. B. Mayer's. Naturally, also, he became a very big man in the department.

During the early shooting of "Dynamite," I was not of sufficient interest to the studio heads to have one of these leeches attached to me. Their policy was one of watchful waiting.

But as work on the picture progressed, word began to circulate that I would be sensational in the picture and as inquiries poured in from magazine editors, columnists and others, I was approached more and more frequently by studio publicity people. Usually when one of them appeared on the set there would be an interviewer in tow, often a fan magazine writer. I soon found that writers seemed interested chiefly in two subjects concerning me. First, my battles with Cecil De Mille, which seemed to indicate that I was a "He-man," and second, my personal life.

I refused to admit that there had been any battles with De Mille, insisting that we were in perfect accord.

Their questions about my personal life were so vapid that I soon quit trying to sustain intelligent conversation and invented some quite outlandish stories. One was to the effect that I was descended from a famous family of eunuchs and that since the age of twenty-one, at which time I came into my heritage, I had known no sex life.

The character I told that one to thought she had stumbled on one hell of a scoop and was wildly excited until a studio flack set her straight.

To another I confided that I had been a notorious rumrunner known as Big Mike. His hair started to curl as I told him of ferocious shoot-out battles with hijackers and prohibition agents.

One of my prize stories, and I was really proud of this one, was, as I told the lady interviewer, the true story of my childhood. I had been born in Sweden. Garbo and I had been schoolmates and childhood sweethearts. She had come to America only because I was here and eventually we were to be married.

Needless to say, the publicity department was not too fond of me. I'm sure they considered me a trouble-making ego-maniac. And I couldn't have cared less.

De Mille's deal with MGM was one which allowed him to make pictures under his own creative control. No one, not even L.B. Mayer, had access to any of his film except at his invitation. Consequently, the studio executives knew nothing of my film work except by hearsay.

"Dynamite" had been in active production six weeks when De Mille told me one morning that at Mr. Mayer's request he had arranged to have me meet some of the executives at his bungalow for a luncheon that very day.

The executives were Louis B. Mayer, Harry Rapf and Irving Thalberg. As none of them had so far yet shown me the courtesy of acknowledging my presence at the studio, I deduced that something important was brewing.

I knew of these three men, of course, but of their backgrounds I was completely ignorant. Therefore I was surprised to recognize in Mayer a man I had met some years before in Boston. I remembered him as a hard-faced, badly-spoken and crass little man.

The image hadn't changed much. He was older of course, heavier, wore a two-hundred-and-fifty-dollar suit, had the glibness of a self-taught evangelist and was mantled in the arrogance of success.

Harry Rapf, a shrewd-eyed man with an enormous nose, appeared to be present only as an observer. So silent was he, in fact, that I thought of him as the little man who wasn't there. I had an uneasy feeling that hidden somewhere on his person was a stiletto.

Irving Thalberg seemed a bit out of place in this company. He impressed me as a personable young man who had somehow fallen in with bad companions. Frail, unhealthy-looking (his skin had a bluish tinge), his eyes revealed intelligence and sensitivity. I liked him on sight and tabbed him as someone I could probably talk to on my own level.

I was amused and gratified as De Mille performed the introductions. He was very proprietary; the personification of the master showman proudly introducing his new discovery to the money men. He stressed my cooperation on the set, spoke highly of me as a person and eulogized my acting ability. So thickly did he lay it on that I began to see myself as God's gift to the motion-picture industry. When he finally put down the shovel, Mayer picked it up.

Mayer was a pitchman from way back. A born show off, he never passed up an opportunity to make a speech and on this day he was in fine fettle. I giggled inwardly as, ignoring the fact that I had been on the scene for months, he welcomed me to Hollywood. He splattered me with flattery, referring to me as one of the great actors of the age, or any other age. He assured me that it was with great pride that he could now number such an illustrious actor in the MGM family.

When he paused for breath I seized the opportunity to accept the accolade—with proper humility of course.

Hardly noting the interruption he went on to say that although he hadn't seen the "Dynamite" rushes, Mr. De Mille had assured him that my performance in the picture was fully up to expectations and that I was bound to make a big impression on the public.

"I am planning big things for you," he said. "I have alerted the story department to search for stories, big stories, that will carry you right to the top."

Again I expressed my appreciation, and with the sincere desire to be constructive suggested that my last Broadway play, "Gods of The Lightning," would make a fine vehicle for me.

"What's it about?" he asked.

Thalberg, speaking for the first time since Mayer had begun his oration, answered the question. "It was based on the story of Sacco and Vanzetti. I saw it on opening night. You were magnificent, Mr. Bickford."

Mayer exploded. "Sacco and Vanzetti! A play about a couple of Bolsheviks? How could an actor of your standing lend himself to that kind of propaganda?"

This was but the start of a long harangue on the subject of clean pictures. He thanked God that he had never made anything but clean pictures—pictures he was proud to show to his wife and his two little innocent daughters. He was proud of being an American. He was proud that his pictures had never shown anything but the good, clean, moral phase of American life. He worked himself up to the verge of tears and ended up by vowing that as long as the good God spared him to be the head of MGM, he would never make a picture to glorify a couple of Bolsheviks. Besides, that play was a flop.

Then he blew his nose. On his napkin.

I came away from that luncheon with a pretty clear image of Louis B. Mayer.

On the set that afternoon, De Mille told me in confidence that Mayer and Thalberg had been very favorably impressed by me and had decided to co-star me with Greta Garbo in a film version of "Anna Christie."

I was not a Garbo fan, but she was a big star and the idea of being teamed with her was certainly to my advantage as a newcomer. On the other hand, I was bothered about the vehicle. I knew the play; the role of Matt was about as thankless as a leading part could be. I did not want to play it. But as I was not supposed to know anything of the project, I held my peace until such time as I would be officially assigned to it.

Shooting on "Dynamite" continued for several weeks. In spite of the constant rumors of pitched battles between us, De Mille and I had achieved a genuine respect for each other's abilities and were working smoothly together. We had even progressed to the point of addressing each other as "Charlie" and "C.B." Occasionally we had differences of opinion, differences which were promptly solved and promptly forgotten as being all in the day's work. But each unimportant incident, however, was distorted and inflated by the sensation-hungry journalistic leeches that were feeding on Hollywood's life blood, and each became part and parcel of a kind of Bickford myth.

There were a couple of serio-comic incidents that are worthy of note; at least, they still amuse me.

One day, for instance, Kay Johnson and I were working out a scene in which she was supposed to smash a bottle over my head. I, as a rough and virile character, disregard the blow, pick her up and carry her into a bedroom. During rehearsals Kay was worried about the bottle business until De Mille, to reassure her that there was no danger of harming me, showed her one of the prop bottles. They were break-a-ways and made of transparent candy.

But Kay remained skeptical so De Mille, bottle in hand, smilingly turned on me.

"How about it, Charlie—do you mind?"

"Be my guest, C.B.," I answered, trustingly.

"Now, watch carefully, Kay. I'm going to hit him as hard as I can."

So saying, he hauled off and let me have it.

No glass bottle could have been more lethal than that candy one. The property department personnel were realists. It didn't break.

When I came to, my prone figure was surrounded by worried people frantically striving to bring me back to the land of the living.

Kay, hysterical with laughter, was being helped to her dressing room.

There were a few malicious wags around the studio who insisted that De Mille had deliberately planned to do away with me . . .

In those early days of sound, the recording equipment was installed in sound-proof booths built into walls overlooking the sound stages. It was the practice for a director, after rehearsing a scene to his satisfaction, to retire to the booth where he could listen to the recorded dialogue during a final rehearsal.

On one occasion Kay Johnson and I were rehearsing a scene which she was having difficulty in playing to De Mille's satisfaction. The situation called for her to deliver a blistering tongue-lashing and De Mille felt she was not sufficiently virulent. We went through the scene several times with De Mille growing more impatient by the minute. Finally, he felt that the scene was ready to shoot and retired to the sound booth to listen to a final rehearsal.

Everything was proceeding splendidly when Kay suddenly fluffed a line. We stopped. Kay apologized and then De Mille, his voice booming over the loud speaker, waxed gently sarcastic. "That's all right, Miss Johnson. Don't let it bother you. Our production cost is only fif-

teen thousand dollars a day. Now, would you like a few
hours out to study your lines or shall we try a take?"

Kay, of course, was badly flustered, but good trouper
that she was laughed it off and answered to the effect that
she would like to try a take.

Everything was readied, the camera rolled and we
started the take. The scene played beautifully up to the
same line Kay had fluffed before. Then, as I was speaking
her cue, I saw the panic rise in her eyes and knew she
was going to blow it again. And she did. She sounded as
though she had a hot potato in her mouth.

There was a moment of deathly silence. Then the
master spoke. Through the speaker came a blast of sarcasm, biting sarcasm—belittling, humiliating and un-
called-for.

Kay was hurt and slightly bewildered. Her eyes filled
with tears.

I was angry for her. "Why do you take it?" I demanded.

"What else can I do?"

"Tell him off, for Pete's sake! Get mad. Tell the son-of-
a-bitch to go to hell."

She didn't answer and for a long moment the big stage
was as silent as a tomb.

De Mille broke the silence, his voice rasping through
the speaker. "Miss Johnson . . ."

"Yes, Mr. De Mille."

"You're holding us up."

If Kay had hackles, I'm sure they were rising at this
point. Her voice had the flavor of Tarragon vinegar. "I
don't know what you're talking about, Mr. De Mille.
What do you mean by that? I'm right here, ready and
waiting. I haven't left this set for one moment."

"I'm aware of that, Miss Johnson. I can see you very plainly. I can also hear you. Both of your voices register very clearly. I'm waiting in case you care to follow Mr. Bickford's kindly advice."

This revelation of microphonic eavesdropping wowed the crew. I didn't think it was quite that funny. Neither did Kay. She was getting madder by the second.

De Mille supplied the last straw. His tone was now benign. "I'm still waiting, Miss Johnson."

Kay, stout lass, picked up the gauntlet. Her voice trembled with emotion. "You don't have to wait any longer, Mr. De Mille. You can start any time. You go to hell."

Surprisingly enough, no one laughed. The men on the set had the sensitivity to realize that Kay might be in for a most unpleasant time and their sympathies were with her.

I placed my arm around her and waited for the bolt to fall.

It didn't. Instead, the first assistant called for a take and the camera began to roll.

Kay didn't fluff this take. She was magnificent. All the wrath she had built up against De Mille was loosed upon me during the scene, with gratifying results. The scene was perfection. The crew favored us with a round of applause.

Afterwards, De Mille descended from his aerie and in his most masterful fashion, came striding onto the set where Kay and I waited for the battle to join.

But this remarkable man was not in a war-like mood. Quite to the contrary. His eyes were twinkling with good humor and his grin was cherubic as he approached us, his arms out-stretched to clasp Kay in an embrace.

"Kay, darling, you hit it right on the button," he said. "That was a beautiful scene, just beautiful. You were both great."

Then, taking from his pocket two twenty-dollar gold pieces he handed one to each of us, saying impressively, "Those are De Mille medals. They are only awarded for what I consider magnificent performances."

And the crew came through with a round of applause.

He turned to me and said, "My double thanks to you Charlie, for your psychological assistance. I assume, of course, that you *were* being constructive."

"Of course, C.B., of course," I answered hypocritically, "and my thanks to you for your understanding appreciation."

And so the incident came to a happy conclusion, effectively giving the lie, I think, to those who insist that Cecil De Mille lacked a sense of humor.

"Dynamite" was in its last week of production before I met Greta Garbo. While rehearsing a scene I noticed a stranger on the stage, a woman. She was watching from the shadows well back from the camera. My curiosity was aroused because of a vague impression that she resembled Garbo.

After finishing the scene I looked again, only to glimpse her as she was disappearing through the stage door. I quickly followed. By the time I was outside she was already half a block away and walking fast. She really could cover the ground but I was faster and soon overtook her. She greeted me with a cold stare.

I apologized immediately. I said, "I'm sorry for chasing you like that. My mistake. I thought you were a rabbit."

She went into peals of laughter. I took the rabbit by the ears and assumed the offensive.

"What were you doing on my set, Miss Garbo?"

"I wanted to see you act."

"That's very flattering. Did you like what you saw?"

"Very much."

"Thank you. Why did you run away?"

"I was embarrassed to have you see me there."

It dawned upon me that I was talking to a delightfully honest and unassuming human being. I was charmed.

We walked together to her dressing room which was situated directly over mine at the front end of the lot. There we discussed many things; one of the early subjects being the play "Anna Christie." I told her that although I thought it a terrific vehicle for her, I felt it a bad one for me. I told her honestly that I considered the character of Matt a mere human prop for Anna to play against.

We found we had a mutual liking for many things, however—hiking, swimming, tennis, Scotch whiskey and money.

So en rapport did we find ourselves that I lost track of time; I completely forgot that De Mille and my fellow players were waiting for me to resume work on the set.

I learned subsequently that I hadn't been in Garbo's dressing room five minutes before the front office, via studio espionage knew all about it. The reason I had not been called back to my set was that they had reached De Mille and requested that the situation be left undisturbed.

On the following day I was invited to lunch with Irving Thalberg and was pleased to discover that my first impression of him endured. We were quite compatible.

He confessed his predilection for actors and seemed to have a sympathetic understanding of our problems. This was due in some part, he said, to the fact that he was married to an actress—Norma Shearer.

After a few minutes of agreeable chatter, he brought up the subject of "Anna Christie," revealing that he was personally to supervise the production and expressing his delight that he was to have me in the role of Matt.

Reluctantly, as I hated to disturb this new-born and affable relationship, I expressed my lack of enthusiasm for the project.

He was genuinely surprised by my attitude. It appeared to be his understanding that in discussing the matter with Miss Garbo, I had committed myself to playing the role.

I didn't argue the point. Nor did I ask the source of his information. I had to admit to myself that while I had no remembrance of any such commitment, it was entirely possible that Garbo's charm could have aroused a momentary enthusiasm which induced me to say things I did not mean.

Nor did Thalberg press the point. He was too clever for that. Instead, he readily admitted that the role was a supporting one; then proceeded quietly to brief me on the importance of the picture to MGM—the eminence of Garbo as a star, the extensive advertising campaign planned to exploit the world-shaking revelation that Garbo could talk, and finally, the undeniable fact that the picture would expose me to millions of Garbo fans throughout the world thereby materially aiding the studio to create the following necessary before I could be rated as an important motion-picture star.

So persuasive was he that by the time luncheon was

over, it had been firmly established, I thought, that following "Dynamite," my next picture under the MGM banner would be "Anna Christie."

And now that "Dynamite" was finished, I planned a seven-day camping trip to the Arizona desert, thinking that my time was my own until "Anna Christie" started production, some three months away.

But I was reckoning without the MGM publicity department. On the day before I was to take off, I was called on the phone and notified that an interview had been set up for twelve noon on the following day. I was to report at the studio commissary and lunch with a fan-magazine writer and a studio publicity person.

I expressed my thanks and regrets and requested that the interview be postponed as I had planned to leave town early the next morning.

Ten minutes later I was called by a character, the studio casting director, who gave me the following lesson in "How to incite talent to rebellion."

In smug and oily tones he suggested that I take a good look at my contract. He informed me that according to clause number sixteen thousand, two hundred and fourteen, on page three hundred and nine, in book number seven of my contract, I agreed to comply promptly and faithfully with all requirements, duties and requests and with all rules and regulations made by MGM in connection with the conduct of its business. I further agreed to act, pose, sing, speak, play such musical instruments as I may be capable of playing, to render services conscientiously and to the full extent of my ability in connection with publicity interviews, poster art, still photographs, electrical transcriptions, films, trailers and similar matters, for the purpose of advertising and exploiting the films in which I appear.

The pompous ass really did read off that clause to me and concluded by giving me official notice that I was to report for the interview, as requested.

My reaction was like that of a bull with a horse-fly up his nostril. After telling him that his vocal delivery indicated a severe diarrheal condition of a misdirected bowel, I suggested that he shove the aforementioned clause where it would do the most good. Then, as I didn't relish the thought of being splattered with more of the same, I hung up on him.

A half hour later, a message was delivered to me via Western Union. It contained a terse order for me to report to the publicity department at twelve o'clock on the following day.

At eight a.m. the next day, I was loading camping gear into my car. Rocky, a recently acquired friend, was helping me.

The word, friend, is one which I do not apply loosely. In my lifetime there has been a surfeit of acquaintances, human relationships which have very often ended in mutual disregard. But I have never met a dog which I referred to as a son-of-a-bitch. Rocky was a magnificent Springer spaniel and we were friends. We loved each other.

And by twelve o'clock noon Rocky and I were well on our way to that wondrous plateau of spectacular beauty known as the Painted Desert of Arizona.

Camping in spots well away from the beaten track, we had this colorful garden of rock and sand all to ourselves, excepting of course, spiders, snakes, lizards, coyotes, and the Indians, who ignored the fact of our existence.

For several glorious days we lived a more primitive life than the Indians themselves; we had no cookstove, refrigerator nor bed. No hogan to shelter us nor any water to bathe in.

The red dust turned Rocky's glossy black coat to a dull, red brown. I, having started with a red head and white skin, turned red all over. We smelled a bit on the gamey side, too, but as each counteracted the other, there were no complaints.

Rocky wasn't much of a conversationalist and I found this great solitude very conducive to introspection, particularly during the long evenings. I cast an appraising eye at myself; my status as an actor and my future prospects in the films and what I saw dispelled any lingering doubts as to my wisdom in coming to Hollywood. My future as a motion-picture star was, I thought, assured and it was while there, on that flaming desert, that I made the decision to thrust my roots deep into the soil of California.

On the morning of our sixth day in the desert, I awakened just before dawn, which was nothing unusual except that ordinarily I would have turned over and gone right back to sleep. This time I was too wide awake for that. I seemed to be listening for something. I had a vague feeling that something was wrong. I sat up and lit a cigarette. Then, suddenly, I got it. Rocky. Something had happened to Rocky.

He always slept with one eye open, instantly aware of any movement on my part, however slight. Mornings, for instance, he always knew when I was ready to get up and was instantly at my side to greet me with a big sloppy kiss.

I called and whistled with no result. The stars had

paled and in the pre-dawn darkness I could see nothing. Flashlight in hand, I searched, walking in widening circles around the camp, but I saw no sign of him.

Sick with apprehension, I returned to the camp. There was nothing more I could do. When it was light I would take the car and search some more. He had to be somewhere in the vicinity.

I built a fire and was sitting by it, waiting for a pot of coffee to make when I heard Rocky whine—so feebly as to be almost inaudible. He was in the one place I had stupidly neglected to look—under the car. He was stretched out on his side and when I crawled in to him, he tried to lift his head in greeting but couldn't make it. The best he could manage was an almost imperceptible wag of his tail.

His right fore-leg was swollen to nearly twice its normal size and as I examined him my heart sank. There was no indication of a break. He had been bitten by something, probably a rattlesnake, and it was odds-on that I was going to lose him.

I placed him by the fire and searched for the wound. It was there. Two tiny punctures.

With scissors from my toilet kit, I cut away the hair and slashed the wound with a razor blade. Then, using my blankets, I made a soft bed for him in the car, placed him in it, and took off like a frightened rabbit.

There was an Indian village about fifteen miles distant and I headed for it, reasoning that if anybody could save Rocky, it would be the Indians. They would know more about treating snakebite than any vet in the country.

That primitive community probably never had a more startling awakening. As I roared into it, a dozen emaciated dogs converged on the car, frantically barking their defiance. Several roosters, evidently under the impression that they had overslept, crowed lustily to make up for lost time and the resulting racket awakened just about everybody in the place.

Even so, not a light showed and no one appeared. Adding to the uproar, I tooted my horn. No one showed. Exasperated, I yelled, "I need help. Does anybody here speak English? Do you hear me? I need help." No one answered.

Taking my thirty-eight from the glove compartment, I fired three shots into the air. Seemingly the only result was to frighten away some of the dogs. I was about to start for the nearest town, some forty miles away, when a cassocked priest appeared from behind the little stone church. In halting English, he angrily demanded to know what I wanted. After hearing my story and seeing Rocky, he became instantly sympathetic. Instructing me to wait, he disappeared into one of the Indian dwellings.

Five minutes later he reappeared, accompanied by an elderly Indian who, after one expressionless glance at me, never deigned to look at me again. Evidently a tribal doctor, he briefly examined Rocky then spoke to the priest. The priest translated. Rocky had been bitten by a rattlesnake. In two hours he would be swollen like a balloon and would die.

As the Indian started to walk away, I begged the priest to stop him. "Ask him, please, to *try* and save the dog," I said, "I'll pay him anything he asks. All I ask is that he *try.*"

There ensued a brief exchange of staccato Indian tongue, after which the Indian took Rocky in his arms and started for his hogan. I knew from the gentle way he handled Rocky that the dog was in good hands.

I started to follow but was stopped by the priest and told that I must go. "Come back tomorrow," he said. "In the meantime you must pray. If it is God's will, your dog will be returned to you."

I thanked him and then, as though I were a little boy, he patted me on the shoulder, turned and went back to his church.

Maybe I'm a corn-ball at heart, or perhaps I'm more religious than I realize. Anyway, I did pray for my friend, and I'm willing to concede that the prayer may have had something to do with the fact that three days later, Rocky, painfully thin and weak but wriggling with delight at seeing me, was delivered to me by the broadly smiling priest.

The Indian doctor's fee was two dollars. I gave him a hundred. And to the priest I wrote a check for a thousand dollars to help in equipping a little manual-training school he was setting up for the Indian children.

As it was now three days past my planned time away, I headed back for Hollywood, stopping overnight in the first city I came to for the luxury of a hot bath. The Los Angeles newspapers were available here and it was while reading one of them that the cloud appeared. A little one to be sure, no bigger than a man's hand, but dark enough for me to question MGM's intentions toward me.

The banner line of one of the columns read, "Bickford to Universal." It said I had been farmed out to co-star with a beautiful young lady of doubtful talent, whose theatrical experience consisted of a few seasons as a New York show girl.

I recognized the film story. It was based upon a flop Broadway play of a few seasons back. Not only was it a bad play, it was also the woman's vehicle.

This all added up to the alleged fact that MGM had loaned me to Universal to work in support of an unimportant girl in a picture that no studio would allow one of its major stars to appear in.

The following afternoon found me cooling my heels in Thalberg's outer office. My stormy mood was not eased by a two-hour wait and when my turn to enter the sanctum came, I ignored his genial greeting and got right to the point. "What are you people trying to do to me?"

He seemed genuinely perplexed. "What do you mean?"

"I mean that load of crap at Universal. What in hell gave you the idea I'd stand still for it?"

Perplexed and slightly riled, he said, "Now wait a minute. I haven't the slightest idea what you're talking about."

I told him of the newspaper item and my reaction to it, outlining my objections.

After hearing me out, he said thoughtfully, "So that's what's eating you. I don't blame you for feeling sore. I didn't know anything about this, Charlie. I'll look into it. Come back in the morning and we'll talk about it."

That night, I did a bit of sleuthing on my own and learned that the girl in question was the current lady-love of a major studio executive. This bit of information further aggravated my itching back and I showed up in Thalberg's office at ten of the next morning, ready to take on the studio bosses, one by one or en masse.

I saw instantly that Thalberg's attitude had changed. There was no genial greeting, nor did he ask me to sit down. He remained seated at his desk and his manner was that of a stern executive whose unpleasant duty it was to keep a recalcitrant employee in line.

He began by telling me that I was mistaken about the

Universal picture. "It's to be one of their features," he said, "and they have great hopes for the girl. They intend to put her over in a big way."

"Not at my expense," was my terse reply.

"I'm sorry you have this attitude," he said. "But there is nothing I can do about it."

"You said yesterday that you didn't blame me for my attitude."

"I didn't know the details of the deal. Don't forget that this studio has a considerable financial stake in you. We carried you for a good many weeks before "Dynamite" went into production. This deal will recoup some of that outlay."

"I'm sorry," I said, "but I can't swallow that. I don't believe the studio is willing to sell me down the river just to get back a few lousy bucks. Who set up this deal?"

"What's that got to do with it?"

"Plenty, I should think. Considering the fact that the girl is sleeping with an MGM executive, it might have a hell of a lot to do with it."

"Well, you're wrong. We don't do business that way."

"I'm glad to hear it," I said, "but wrong or right, I didn't come to Hollywood to be a stooge. It's bad enough to play second fiddle to Garbo, but asking me to support this dame is just too much. I won't do it."

No important executive could be expected to accept this brand of positive defiance sitting down and Thalberg rose to the occasion. He didn't speak, he yelled; and his voice was strident with anger. "Where do you get off coming in here and telling me what you will or will not do. You're under contract to this studio and you'll do as you're told."

I out-roared him. "The hell I will!" And I was about to

tell him what he could do with the contract, the studio and the motion-picture business when the situation, and probably my film career, was rescued by his secretary who, at this critical moment, opened the door and announced that Mr. Mannix was waiting.

"Have him come in," snapped Thalberg.

This was to be my first meeting with Eddie Mannix. I never did know his official title, but there was no question of his being one of the powerful group of men who ran the studio. He was of stocky build and rough-hewn features; had he been an actor, he could have been perfectly cast as an ex-fighter, baseball player, or gangster.

As he approached me, hand extended in greeting, his twinkling eyes and friendly grin gave him the aspect of an amiable bulldog and as I am partial to dogs, I formed an instant liking for him—with reservations.

"Here," I said to myself, "is a truthful man. If he were to tell me that he was about to slit my throat, I'd believe him." I doubt that he was a shiv man, however. I had the feeling that if I frisked him, I'd find brass knuckles.

"Hello, Charlie," he said. "I'm Eddie Mannix."

I returned his grin. "Glad to see you, Eddie."

He got right down to business. "Irving tells me you don't like the idea of going over to Universal."

"He told you right."

"Well, maybe I can put you straight on this. I think we speak the same language. I can talk turkey to you, right?"

"Could be."

Then, turning to Thalberg, he said, "O.K. Irving?"

"Good luck," said Thalberg. Then, his anger strangely dissipated, he grinned at me.

Mannix continued. "First off, let me tell you that we consider you a pretty valuable piece of property."

"Perhaps that's the trouble. I'd much prefer being considered an intelligent human being."

Again Thalberg smiled.

Mannix, still the soul of affability, continued. "Naturally. That goes without saying. If you weren't a human being and a good actor to boot, we wouldn't bother with you. That being the case, we'd certainly be damn fools if we deliberately did anything to hurt you. Right?"

I had to agree with him.

"We're out to build you up, not tear you down. As I understand it, your objection to the Universal deal is that the girl is unknown. Right?"

"That's partly my objection. Yes."

"All right. Who do you think *you* are? In the picture business, I mean."

"Nobody, if you want to put it that way. But not quite the same kind of a nobody. At least, *I'm* a known quantity."

"Sure, a few people have seen you act on Broadway, but so far as picture audiences go, you don't mean a damn thing more than she does. Do I make sense to you?"

"No. You see, Eddie, that's my problem. I have no sense at all. That's why I'm giving you the same answer I gave Irving Thalberg. I will *not* play in that picture."

His affability vanished and as he set his jaw, I noticed that it was slightly undershot. "Just like that, huh? You *won't.* I don't remember any clause in your contract that gives you the right to refuse."

"Screw the contract," I said, in my most picaresque fashion.

For a moment he eyed me as though he questioned his own eyesight. Then he turned to Thalberg, who smiled quizzically and said quietly, "As I said before—good luck."

"I see what you mean," said Eddie, his good humor seemingly restored. "I like a guy that speaks his mind. But don't push us too far, Charlie. We can be tough too, you know."

"I'm not doing the pushing, Eddie, and if I were being tough, I wouldn't bother to argue the point. I'd just walk out and go back to New York."

It's quite probable that he was about to invite me to do just that, but as he opened his mouth to speak, Thalberg intervened. "There's no occasion for anyone to get tough," he said, sharply. "Look Charlie, I don't think you quite understand our position. You *are* under contract here and the studio has seen fit to loan you to Universal for a picture. If I had known about it, I would have been against it. But I didn't, and the deal was made and we're on a spot. Now we're not going to force you into that picture. Right, Eddie?"

Eddie, a bit baffled, as was I, acceded. "Sure."

Thalberg continued. "But we are committed, and I'm going to ask you to help us get off the hook. All I'm asking you to do is to have lunch with Junior Laemmle at Universal studio. You don't have to commit yourself to anything, but just lunch with him. Will you do that?"

"Certainly," I said. "When?"

"Today. I'll arrange it."

I left Thalberg's office feeling that I had scored some sort of victory. Yet, as I had detected the faint effluvium of hostility between those two men, I wondered if I had unwittingly become a pawn in some sort of intra-studio struggle for power, a feeling that has persisted even up to today. It was very difficult to figure out just who was doing what to me.

Nepotism was, and is, rampant in the motion-picture industry, and Carl Laemmle, Senior, head of Universal Pictures Corporation, was probably the greatest nepotist of the time. Working in the studio in addition to Junior were innumerable relatives who had been brought over from Germany and given positions of varying importance.

Laemmle's heir-apparent, Junior, was being groomed to take over the reins at such time when Senior stepped down.

Being aware of this situation I expected Junior to be cut from the usual pattern and was prepared to meet a young man of little or no ability, inadequate education, probably bloated with self-importance, and bursting with arrogance. I was predisposed to dislike him.

The first thought that came to mind when I was ushered into his office was "Why isn't this kid in school?"

A frail little man, he seemed much too young to bear the responsibility entailed in the production of motion pictures. But as we talked, my respect for him grew. He evidenced a keen interest in the theater, which we discussed at length. And to my greater surprise, he had actually read a book.

I had been given to understand that excepting Thalberg, and possibly one or two others, Hollywood producers didn't take time out to read books. A few of the professed intellectuals among them did read reviews—of the best sellers, that is—from which they gleaned sufficient background information to enable them to hold their own in superficial discussion.

I knew of one guy who didn't even read the scripts of the pictures he produced. He didn't read anything. He judged material after hearing his secretary read aloud from synopses prepared by his sixty-seven dollar a week reader.

Junior and I talked for two full hours, during which time no mention was made of the project I had refused. It was not until I was about to leave that he handed me a script, saying, "I wish you'd read this, Charlie. I think it has great possibilities. If you like it, maybe we can get together on it. I'd like to do a picture with you."

That was all. No pressure, no recriminations, no blandishments. There had been no hint of self-importance, nor arrogance. To the contrary, he was refreshingly natural and modest to a fault.

The script proved to be a revised version of a hit silent picture made by Universal a few years previously. At first blush the story struck me as being ridiculously sentimental; the dialogue was atrociously bad and the script, as written, called for the leading character to be played by a juvenile leading man, which I was not.

Basically, however, the plot was sound theater. It occurred to me that if rewritten with me in mind, a stark, brutal quality could be blended with the tear-jerking hokum the story already contained. It might thus achieve a potency which the script in its present form was sadly lacking.

My subconscious must have worked overtime for when I awakened in the morning, my mind held a detailed and workable outline for the new screen play. Over the phone I outlined my ideas to Junior Laemmle who expressed great enthusiasm and agreed wholeheartedly to the proposed rewrite.

Later that day I sat in conference with Junior, a writer, and a man from the studio production department. Again I expressed my ideas and although there was some discussion concerning story points, there was no argument and the meeting ended in harmonious agreement. The rewrite was to be accomplished and the picture was to begin shooting in four weeks. My commitment was of course subject to MGM's approval.

The deal was consummated and everyone concerned was pleased, particularly Junior Laemmle. He had acquired a star for his picture who had just completed a Cecil De Mille feature and who was soon to play opposite the great Garbo in her first talking picture.

And although the reason was then obscure to me, the boys at MGM were pleased because, as of that day and for a period of ten weeks, they had transferred a carcass to the Universal Studio payroll.

At the end of that time I, presumably still sound in mind and limb, was to be returned PDQ to Culver City where I was scheduled to start work on "Anna Christie."

I was pleased because I had developed great enthusiasm for the project, not realizing that in my abysmal ignorance of the business, I had fallen into a trap that was almost identical to the one I had just fought to escape.

At that time, motion pictures were to me just that— motion pictures. Some were excellent, some were good and others were bad. But I was stupidly unaware that the major studios classified their pictures according to the amounts of money to be spent on them. For instance, a studio's yearly production schedule might list eight big feature pictures and forty program pictures. The features were made with the advantage of star names, top directors and big budgets. The programmers were cast with lesser or no names, directed by any relation who happened to be handy, and made for as little expenditure as possible.

The picture I was about to make was in the latter category. If I'd had the slightest inkling of what I was letting myself in for, I would have run like hell away from it.

And if my agent of that day had been worthy of the title, he would have been right behind me, goosing me. But he, I suspect, was one of the boys.

I was remiss in that I did not stick around to keep a supervisory eye on the rewrite. Instead, Rocky and I went gallivanting off on another camping trip, this time to the ruggedly beautiful Trinity Alps, in northern California; an area I can wholeheartedly recommend to any vacationer who appreciates magnificent scenery and great fishing.

For twenty-four days, Rocky and I camped beside a mountain stream that was a veritable fisherman's paradise. I fished merely to supplement our food supply, filet of trout being the main course of at least one meal every day. At no time did it take more than ten minutes to catch a meal.

Also appealing to me was the solitude. The mobs hadn't discovered the area and during the entire time we were there we encountered only one human being, a professional hunter by the name of Bill Leacock. Bill was fifty-nine years old, stood six feet, three inches tall, was lantern-jawed, wall-eyed, and altogether just about as unpretty a man as I've ever seen.

Employed by the state, his current job was the extermination of mountain lions, which had "et up too durn many deer last year so we got to thin out the varmints."

He stayed with us for three days and stopped talking only when he was snoring. I was happy to see him go but Rocky adored him, probably because Bill exuded an aroma reminiscent of an old dog who had rolled in something very dead.

Brimming with energy and rearin' to get started on the new picture, I arrived back in Hollywood on the eve of the starting day. The company had already left for a Mohave Desert location, leaving instructions for me to join them there on the following morning.

I doubt that I have ever approached a film project with more enthusiasm, probably because it was in part my baby. My first act after reaching the location was to grab the new script, eagerly curious to see how the revision had been treated. By the time I had read ten pages, I knew it was not my baby; it wasn't a baby at all. If anything, it was a miscarriage.

Excepting a few minor changes, it was identical with the script I had refused. The dialogue was unspeakable. The writer had surely been under the delusion that a talking picture was simply a silent with spoken titles.

My enthusiasm was replaced by anger. Anger, directed not only against MGM and Universal but against myself for being such a jackass as to fall into the trap.

Resisting the impulse to get into my car and head for New York, I forced myself to calm down and analyze my position. I decided it was too late to do anything but make the best of a bad situation. I would do my own rewrite, working on each sequence as we came to it. I would, of course, require the co-operation of the director.

Ah, yes! The director . . .

Even though his image is graven on my memory, I find it difficult to describe him. He was, I believe, one of the numerous members of the Laemmle tribe. His credits consisted of a few silent Western quickies and the present assignment was to be his first experience with sound.

My first sight of the man was slightly disconcerting, but having learned long before that appearances can be deceitful, I gave him the benefit of the doubt. It wasn't the costume that threw me; people wear all sorts of strange garments in the desert. Even British Army Officers can appear incongrous when clad only in khaki shorts and a topi. Supplemented by a pair of cowboy boots and placed upon a short tubby guy, the effect can be ludicrous, particularly when the tropical helmet emphasizes a featureless face, split by a vacuous grin.

It wasn't until after I had stated my position, emphasizing Junior Laemmle's acceptance of my rewrite demands, that I began to wonder what I was up against. He gave no evidence at all that I'd gotten through to him but sat like a lump, his eyes vacant and his jaw slack.

I continued to talk, calmly outlining the story as I saw it, but still failed to strike a spark. He seemed to be lost in contemplation of some fantastic world of his own. It suddenly occurred to me that I might be undergoing a rare experience. This wasn't a man. It had to be a golem.

It wasn't though, because all of a sudden half of a little finger disappeared up its nose. I had to concede that it was human after all. Damned stupid, but human. I'd never heard of a golem picking its nose.

Soon he began to make noises. After a few seconds I realized that he was talking—inarticulately, but talking nevertheless. In halting fashion, he professed to know nothing of my agreement with Junior Laemmle. The script was, in his opinion, a great one. My idea of changing the protagonist from hero to villain was against all established formula for this type of story and he was flatly against it.

Plainly there was to be no co-operation from this quarter. And as I could see no percentage in further discussion, I made it clear to the little man that if the picture was to be made with me, it would have to be made my way. The ultimatum was terse, unequivocal and uncompromising.

In my view, my action was not unethical nor was it open to criticism. I had simply done what came naturally to me—an agreement with me had been broken and I refused to stand still for it. I saw no problem. If there was one, it was Universal's, and of their own making. To solve it, they had merely to replace me with another actor. The case was that simple. Simple to me, that is.

It was therefore, with considerable surprise and some amusement that from the shelter of my portable dressing room, I watched the commotion as the assistant directors, the script clerk and the production manager converged upon the golem. (To this day my mind refers to him as the golem.) After a few minutes of excited palaver, the production manager took off in a standby car. I sensed that he was headed for the nearest telephone situated thirty miles away. The studio heads must be notified at once of this unprecedented act of rebellion.

Someone in authority, probably Junior Laemmle, tipped the scales in my favor and that afternoon we shot the first sequence.

Seldom has a picture been made under less favorable circumstances. A truly crummy script, doctored piecemeal by an inexperienced writer (me), a cast of silent screen actors, an inexperienced sound crew, desert temperatures ranging from ninety to well over a hundred degrees, and—the golem.

By the end of the second week the studio had sent up a trouble-shooter to find out why we were two weeks behind schedule.

The reason was obvious. The golem. He had one positive talent, procrastination, and time after time, the company was forced to wait in the broiling sun while he paced up and down, sometimes for hours, trying to decide where the camera should be set up.

After the camera was set up and the scene shot, he would order take after take of the same scene, and for no apparent reason. Or if there was a reason, he was too inarticulate to explain. One could only conclude that the guy didn't know his stuff and hope that out of thirty or forty takes, the cutter might find one that could be used.

Although all this was vastly irritating, I submitted to it because I had resolved not to interfere with his directorial functions, or malfunctions, beyond doctoring the script.

The trouble-shooter, perhaps because he suffered from astigmatism or more probably because he too was a golem,—the studio was lousy with them—placed the responsibility for delay upon me. The proof was a telegram that I received from Louis B. Mayer ordering me to stop making trouble and causing delays on the Universal location.

Across the offending telegram I wrote a message, inviting Mayer to do something to himself which even a contortionist would have found extremely difficult to accomplish. Slipping it into an envelope, I mailed it back to him.

Not too clever of me, I must admit, but the provocation was great. He had added insult to injury. And I was in the mood to do battle with anybody, regardless of odds or consequences.

So for the trouble-shooter, I evened the score with him. I bribed a Mexican waitress to dose his coffee with jalap for three consecutive mornings. Brother, did he have a run for it! After a couple of days he had run himself clear out of sight. Could be he's running yet. I hope so.

In spite of the miserable conditions, I was sustained by the feeling that I was really accomplishing something. Bad though the picture might be otherwise, I knew that I was suffusing it with the incisively savage quality I had fought to achieve, and when finally the desert sequences were finished, I had no regrets.

However, we were hopelessly behind schedule and had still to shoot the interior sequences at the Universal studio. Handicapped by the ineptness of the golem, it was evident that we could not finish before the deadline set for my return to MGM.

Laemmle petitioned MGM for an extension of my contract and was refused. I was served notice by MGM and on the given day picked up my hat and drawers and departed Universal. I knew I would be engaged on the "Anna Christie" production for at least twelve weeks to come. In the meanwhile, Junior Laemmle would be sitting with an unfinished picture on his hands. He was understandably frantic.

Motivated by the fact that his picture had again become my baby—I no longer had any sympathy for Laemmle—I called him and volunteered to go after finishing work at MGM each day to his studio from eight to twelve p.m. I also offered him my Sundays from nine a.m. to six p.m., suggesting that the arrangement be kept strictly *entre nous.*

He was grateful for the offer, but being a cautious gent took the advice of his legal department and asked MGM to authorize the deal. He was turned down, flat. MGM wasn't about to jeopardize its own production by allowing me to tire myself out working on two pictures at the same time.

As for my associates during the "Anna Christie" engagement, I couldn't have asked for a more compatible group. Garbo was consistently charming. Those two old pros, Marie Dressler and George Marion were a delight to work with. The director, Clarence Brown, was an amiable gent. Frances Marion, who adapted the play for the screen, was intelligent and a charming woman. Irving Thalberg, personally supervising the production, was at all times constructively critical and consistently agreeable.

Complete harmony is rare on a movie set and had it not been for my lack of enthusiasm for the play and for my role, it would have been a perfect engagement.

After we had been shooting a week, my plan to finish the Universal picture was put into effect, unknown to MGM. How it was arranged will have to remain my secret. Suffice it to say that I finished the picture on my own time and that in no manner did it interfere with my work on "Anna Christie."

Scarcely was "Anna Christie" in the can when I received an invitation to spend a long week end at San Simeon—William Raldolph Hearst's barony in northern California. I knew, of course, that Hearst was producing pictures in association with MGM but never having met him, I presumed that the invitation was merely a courtesy extended to me as a Metro-Goldwyn-Mayer star. Having no interest in Mr. Hearst, nor in his castle on the mountain, I declined the invitation with thanks.

But one does not refuse a Royal Command with impunity. Within minutes of talking with Mr. Hearst's secretary, I was called by Irving Thalberg who requested that I come to his office immediately. Sensing that the summons had to do with Hearst's invitation, I walked into Thalberg's office, hackles standing straight up. He, sensitive soul, knew at once that I had guessed the reason for his call and beat me to the punch, telling me straight-off that nobody had any intention of pressuring me to accept the Hearst invite.

Having thus flattened my short hairs, he proceeded to apply pressure; gentle, I must admit, but nonetheless pressure. He explained that because of the studio's association with Mr. Hearst, it held a tremendous edge over competition in regard to space in the Hearst publications. And as Mr. Hearst was a very demanding individual, the studio leaned over backwards to keep him happy. Nothing within reason was denied him. "Believe me, Charlie," he said, "he's a good man to have on your side."

"That sounds like a warning," I said. "I don't get it. Why should a man like Hearst care a damn about my showing at his party? I don't know him. I haven't even met Marion Davies."

"You've put your finger on it. Mr. Hearst is interested in you for Marion's next picture and he wants to talk to you about it."

"What's wrong with talking in his office?"

Thalberg's temper flared. "Oh, for Christ sake, Charlie! Why do you have to be so difficult? It happens to be the way Hearst operates. And its a pleasant way of doing business. It's a fabulous place up there. Most people would jump at the chance to visit it. You act as though you'd been insulted."

"Not at all, Irving. I resent being treated like a sack of potatoes, that's all."

"I won't take the trouble to answer that. You're being deliberately obtuse. All right, let's put it this way. I personally would like you to go up there. I'll go further than that. I'd consider it a personal favor if you'll reconsider. I'm not asking you to commit yourself to Hearst. Just listen to what he has to say. That's all I ask. Will you do it?"

I agreed to do it.

The studio provided a chauffeur-driven limousine and in the early afternoon of the following Friday, I was rolling north on the Pacific Coast Highway. I was scheduled to dine at San Simeon at seven-thirty, but at Santa Maria, a town about half way to my destination, I was inadvertently delayed.

Stopping in at the excellent Santa Maria hotel, I fell into conversation with three lumbermen from Oregon. Upon discovery that we spoke the same language, we retired to their suite. They were carrying a suitcase full of excellent pre-war liquor. One drink led to another until for me time had no meaning.

I forgot my dinner engagement at San Simeon and was only reminded of it when at seven p.m. my driver came to me and asked permission to have his dinner.

I remembered my manners to the extent of phoning San Simeon and asking the major-domo to extend my regrets to Mr. Hearst.

Then the five of us—the three Oregonians, the driver and I—drank dinner together. Three hours later, my pal the driver and I said "Goodbye" to the semi-conscious Oregonians and hit the road.

Some fifteen minutes later as we were rolling through a small town, I thought I recognized it as one we had passed through on our way north. "Are you sure you're headed in the right direction?" I asked my pal.

He was highly amused. Leering at me over his shoulder, he said, "You mush be kiddin', Misha Victor. Hell, I been drivin' thish pike for over fifteen years."

Just then, to my horror, I saw two elderly women start to cross the road, less than two hundred feet ahead. I yelled, "Keep your eyes on the road, God-damn it."

He jammed on the brakes and the car came to a shuddering stop, barely missing the two women who, clucking like a pair of indignant biddies, scuttled to safety.

That did it. I came to the belated realization that my erstwhile pal was stewed to the gills. I ordered him to pull over to the side of the road where, disregarding his almost tearful protests, I forced him to change places with me.

At the next gas station I learned, to the driver's chagrin, that we had indeed been traveling south.

So at two a.m. I pulled up before the guard house at the foot of Hearst's mountain. From here, a private road, barred to the public by a high gate, wound its way up the mountain to the castle at the summit.

I was expected. The guard, after a glance at the drunk on the back seat, asked, "Charles Bickford?"

I nodded.

"Fried?" he asked.

"Plastered," I answered truthfully.

"We've been expecting you all evening."

"Yeah. I had a little carburetor trouble."

He then gave me specific instructions. I was to drive carefully and keep a sharp watch for Mr. Hearst's animals. I gathered that there were wild beasts running loose on the estate. Also, at two places the road was barred by gates which I would have to open and then close after I had driven through. This was important because if I failed to close the gates after me, the bears might get at the zebras and the mountain lions would massacre the deer and Hearst would massacre everybody concerned.

Upon the conclusion of the briefing, he opened the gate and I drove on, keeping a sharp eye out for animals. Neither hide nor hair of one did I see, however.

After passing the first barrier, I shook the driver awake. He was still pretty groggy but I got over to him that to protect his job, he must pull himself together and drive the rest of the way. So, in seemly and dignified fashion, I arrived at the portals of *La Casa Grande*.

A Filipino boy was waiting and I was shown to my quarters, The Josephine Suite, I believe it was called. Never before had I seen such magnificent appointments—French Empire, authentically antique and unmistakeably priceless. The only jarring note was too much of a muchness. It was like walking into an overstocked museum.

While preparing for bed I heard something that sounded suspiciously like sounds of revelry. I listened intently but the sounds came only occasionally and were so faint I couldn't place the source. I wasn't at all sleepy and decided to investigate. I thought it might be interesting to meet some of my fellow guests while they had their hair down.

Like a character in a mystery movie, I slipped out of

my suite and silently crept along the hall and down the stairs to the enormous living room. In the darkness I could see nothing, but my imagination pictured the great banquet hall of some medieval castle.

Standing at the foot of the stairs, I peered into the spooky gloom and listened for the sounds to recur. But the silence remained unbroken and as the moments passed, I began to feel like the village idiot.

Then I saw something. At the far side of the room a tiny blob of white appeared to be moving in my direction, growing larger as it approached. "Cripes," I thought, "the joint is haunted."

I was about to bolt up the stairs when it materialized and spoke. "Mr. Bickford," it said. "You're looking for the other people? They are in the kitchen. This way, please."

And the white-coated house boy led the way across the room and through an archway into a long dining hall at the far end of which was showing a glimmer of light from beneath swing doors.

As there were over twenty guests at San Simeon that week-end, I suppose the group I found in the kitchen could be called a splinter party of six: three of Hearst's editors; Marion Davies' father who was, I think, a New York City Magistrate; Louella Parsons, *Los Angeles Examiner* columnist; and Frances Marion, the charming writer whom I had just worked with on "Anna Christie."

It was a merry group gathered there at two thirty a.m. to discuss cabbages and kings over a few drinks.

Why in the kitchen? Well, I gathered that Mr. Hearst frowned upon excessive drinking. That is, anything over and above two highballs after dinner. At a prescribed time the liquor was locked away, thereby preserving the decorum and the morality of his guests.

Someone in this group—I suspect Marion's father—knew where the booze was stashed and how to get to it. Thus the deliciously surreptitious flavor of this little gathering.

It had been about to disperse but my arrival added interest enough to provide another hour of good talk. And, I must give the devil his due, Hearst's booze was the real McCoy . . .

At ten a.m. I was awake and a half-hour later, full of bounce and ravenously hungry, having missed my dinner the night before, I walked into the dining hall—a tremendous room, oblong in shape, the walls panelled in what appeared to be weathered oak and hung with priceless tapestries. In the center was the longest table I had ever seen, heavily built of oaken planks. An incongruous touch was a rack, built into the center of it and almost as long as the table itself. It contained such mundane things as salt, pepper, vinegar, olive oil, mayonnaise, catsup and just about every other relish and condiment on the market. And stacks of paper napkins.

In solitary grandeur I sat at this table and waited. No one appeared. Hearing sounds of activity in the kitchen, I called. A man wearing an apron and chef's cap appeared at the swing doors. I asked if I could have breakfast. The answer was "No."

I was amazed to hear that Mr. Hearst was very strict about guests being on time for meals. Having missed breakfast at nine o'clock, I must now wait until luncheon was served at twelve thirty.

I didn't argue with the man, nor did I even attempt to wheedle him out of a cup of coffee. I couldn't. I had been rendered speechless.

Mr. Hearst had never stood very high in my opinion but at that moment his rating dropped to several degrees lower than zero. "But," I reasoned, "this is his spread and its his right to dictate the rules. If it suits his pleasure to treat his guests as inmates of an institution, so be it. I'll get the hell out of here and have breakfast at the nearest public restaurant."

There was a house boy on duty in the living room and after requesting that he notify my driver to bring the car around, I went outside and waited on the veranda.

He had hardly disappeared when Marion Davies, in tennis costume and carrying a racquet, was at my side. She was quite perturbed. "What's this about your leaving, Mr. Bickford?" she asked.

"News travels fast in these parts," I laughed. "I'm not leaving, Miss Davies. I'm going out to breakfast, that's all."

She was genuinely distressed. "Oh, my heavens! They should have known better." Grabbing my hand, she rushed me back into the house, through the living room to the dining room where after pushing me into a chair, she demanded, "Name it."

"Lambs fries," I said.

"Lambs fries? What are those?"

"Balls," I said.

We became friends.

And lambs fries I had, with bacon and all the fixings. Marion sat with me and chattered while I ate. It was a delicious breakfast.

A picnic was the main attraction scheduled for that day. Directly after luncheon, Mr. Hearst, Marion, and about a dozen of the guests mounted horses and set out for a selected spot about three miles away. While the location was delightful, it could have been duplicated within a hundred yards of the palace. But, you see, Mr. Hearst was very fond of "roughing it."

A troop of cowboys acted as escort and a string of pack ponies carried the mattresses, pillows, sun umbrellas, food hampers, buckets of iced caviar, baskets of champagne and pails of iced beer.

On reaching the camp site, the cowboys unloaded the gear, built a camp fire, arranged the mattresses and cushions around the fire and served the refreshments. Then to the accompaniment of a guitar, they sang cowboy songs while the folks roughed it. The big deal was the marshmallow toast. Long pointed sticks were provided and those who weren't too tired stuck marshmallows on the ends of them and toasted them over the fire. Exciting—what?

That evening, at dinner, I was astonished to find myself seated as the guest of honor. Contrary to convention, Hearst's throne chair (Oh, yes—it was very definitely a throne chair and the only one in the room) was placed at mid-table. Marion was seated directly opposite and I was placed at her right. The remaining guests were seated according to their importance in Hearst's eyes, descending to secretaries and such at the ends of the table.

There were several important newspaper men present and the conversation soon turned toward politics, national and international. As the talk was mostly beyond my understanding, I kept a discreet silence except at such times, which were rare, as my opinion was solicited. And as I disagreed with most of the views expressed, my meager contribution to the conversation was deceitful. It was the wrong time to say the right things.

Mr. Hearst dominated, and to a great extent, monopolized the conversation, pontificating in a peculiarly moistureless voice upon world affairs.

From my vantage point across the table, I was able to

study this man at close range. My impressions of him were anything but flattering.

He was a big man. In size, that is. My impression was that self-indulgence and sedentary habits had allowed an impressive bone structure to become over-padded with lard; the whole sheathed in skin that resembled the underbelly of a toad.

As I listened to the pomposities uttered by him I felt he was more to be pitied than scorned. He seemed afflicted with megalomania to the extent that he was unable to differentiate between himself and the Almighty.

Bored to distraction by this exposition of self-grandeur, I was mightily relieved when, after an hour and a half, Mr. Hearst signalled, by rising, that the ordeal was over. It was tacitly understood that no one left the table until Mr. Hearst so signified.

A few minutes later, the major-domo notified me that Mr. Hearst requested my presence in his bungalow. This was a comparatively modest structure, constructed of marble, I think, and situated a couple of hundred feet from the castle. Those in the know referred to it as the *sanctum-sanctorum*.

Only Marion and Hearst were present and after a gracious welcome, I was comfortably placed in a big chair by the side of which was a small table bearing a bowl of ice cubes, a siphon of soda water and a bottle of scotch. By this mark of especial esteem, I knew I was being courted.

After a few minutes of small talk, mostly of the Broadway theater, Hearst came to the point. He was anxious, he said, to have my honest opinion of a story he was about to tell.

I expressed my gratification to be so flattered and promised to give him my candid appraisal.

Then he talked.

I listened.

For a full hour, I listened.

Luckily, I had the scotch to sustain me and by the time he had droned to the fade-out, I had killed half the bottle.

He then asked for my honest opinion. Because of his very evident enthusiasm, I hesitated to say that I considered it a mess of extremely vapid tripe, that the story was contrived and badly constructed, that the characters were unbelievably wooden and that any producer who would even consider placing it into production should have his head examined.

But with the pair of them gazing at me expectantly, I had to come up with something. Nodding my head sagely, I said, "Interesting."

His disappointment was manifest. "That's all?" he asked. "Just interesting?"

He didn't care to hear any more. The interview was over. With the frigid dignity of a sick oyster he lumbered to his feet. "Thank you for coming," he said tartly, and left the room.

Turning to my embarrassed hostess, I said, "I'm sorry, Marion. Goodnight."

"Goodnight," she whispered.

The following evening at dinner I found myself placed at the extreme end of the table.

A few days after the festive weekend at San Simeon, it was announced in the columns that I was slated to co-star with Lenore Ulric in a little number called "South Sea Rose." The Fox studio was borrowing me from MGM for this engagement.

The prospect of doing a picture with Miss Ulric was

not unpleasing. I knew her as a fine actress and person. But the title, "South Sea Rose" seemed to spell trash. If so, I wanted no part of it but held my peace until after I had been delivered a script.

My hunch had been right. Crud it was, and spelled with a capital S.

L. B. Mayer was supposed to be running the MGM studio but again I took my beef to Thalberg. I gravitated to him partly, I think, because I liked him but mostly because of his own seeming dedication to the making of worth-while pictures. I believe he credited me with some integrity and understood that my frequent eruptions were not mere manifestations of over-sized ego.

I stormed into his office and plunked the offending script down on his desk. "Will you please read this thing?" I asked, and turned to go.

"Wait a minute," he said. "What's this all about?"

"Don't tell me you don't know about this one. It's another indication of this studio's good intentions in regard to me. Read it."

He grinned at me, then picked up the script. " 'South Sea Rose'. Colorful title."

"Shit," I said, with feeling.

"They specialize in it over there," he said, and laughed heartily.

"God-damn it, Irving. It's no laughing matter. I left Broadway because it was knee-deep in crap and I don't intend to drown in it here. Read that thing—and when you finish puking, give me a ring." Again I started for the door and again he stopped me.

"Charlie! Why did you bring this script to me?"

"Because I want you to understand my refusal to play it."

"That's not what I mean. You feel that I'm on your side. Isn't that right?"

"I suppose so. Yes."

"Well, I am, believe me. Now look, I don't have to wade through this. You say it's crap. All right, I'll take your word for it. But believe me when I tell you that no matter how bad it is, it can't do you any harm. You've got two big pictures coming out and you'll be a smash in both of them. I hear also that you were able to make something pretty good out of the thing you did at Universal. They're very high on it over there."

"Screw them."

"No thanks. Now, will you for Christ's sake give me credit for knowing what I'm talking about?"

He was a very persuasive little guy.

Before the start of "South Sea Rose," I was called in to make a Swedish version of "Anna Christie." Garbo spoke in her native tongue and the rest of us spoke in what you might term phonetic Swedish. I'd venture to say that Garbo laughed more in those two weeks than during her entire life, mostly at me.

Try doing an Irish brogue in Swedish some time and you'll understand why. And why, when the picture opened in Stockholm, the audience rocked with laughter every time I opened my mouth.

"South Sea Rose" was a very dull seven-week chore. The only redeeming feature was Lenore Ulric. She was beautiful, charming and a real pro. I considered it a crying shame that she should be wasted in such junk.

I had been in Hollywood slightly more than a year when, during the same week, "Dynamite" and the Universal picture opened in New York. They played in theatres but a few blocks away from each other, both on

Broadway, and both scoring as hits. "Dynamite" hit with the public and the other hit with the critics.

Ironically, most of the kudos received were for its direction. And because of the "harsh, brutal honesty" of his direction, the golem was started on a long and lucrative career.

I was not neglected, however, and my notices for both performances were gratifying enough. I was hailed universally as a great new film personality.

Close on the heels of those two rewarding openings came the widely-heralded world premiere of "Anna Christie." It was not only a smashing success, it made motion picture history.

My future as a film star was secure—I thought.

Incidentally, "Anna Christie," which gained a place as one of the greatest motion pictures of all time—a motion picture classic—was, and in my opinion still is, vastly over-rated.

The critics raved and the public swamped the box-offices to see a picture that was indifferently produced, directed, and badly acted by the entire cast, not excepting myself. And if this be heresy, make the most of it.

It was principally because of Metro-Goldwyn-Mayer's publicity department that I came to the disheartening realization that the little cloud, which months before I had spotted over the Arizona desert, had grown to alarming proportions. In the campaign to put "Anna Christie" over, ninety-nine and nine-tenths percent of all advertising and publicity was focused on *Garbo*. I'm not criticizing the job they did. To the contrary, it was a magnificent job of exploiting *Garbo*.

As far as publicity was concerned, the rest of us might as well have stayed in bed. In spite of the department's neglect, however, both Marie Dressler and I scored heavily with the public.

If MGM really had planned to build me, this engagement with their biggest box office star afforded a perfect opportunity to do so. But, I was ignored.

I would have been idiotic had I disregarded the implications. This brushoff, added to the ignominious loan-outs to Universal and Fox clearly indicated that MGM and I did not see eye-to-eye on my status. And if further evidence was needed, they began to cast me in unsuitable roles; roles that cried for the Buddy Rogers type, and in program pictures. During a span of six weeks I refused to play in four of these turkeys.

The Bickford myth was growing fat. Columnists and fan magazine writers were now referring to me as "Hollywood Rebel," "Bickford, The No Man," "Hollywood Stormy Petrel," "Hollywood's Bad Boy." L.B. Mayer referred to me as "That God-damned red-headed Bolshevic."

I was sadly puzzled. There was something in the situation that didn't meet the eye. I was about as "hot" at this time as an actor could be. Every studio was trying to borrow me to play starring roles in big-budget pictures, and significantly at this time, being refused. One instance was when RKO tried to borrow me to star in "Cimmaron." This was one I wanted to play. I went to Thalberg and requested that I be allowed to do it. I was refused.

And yet one week following this epiosde, I was cast in a dreadful piece of clap-trap, entitled "The Passion Flower." This little dilly was to be produced by Thalberg, directed by William De Mille, Cecil's brother, and was to co-star Kay Johnson, Kay Francis and myself.

After reading the script, I screamed my protests to Thalberg. I threatened to walk out of the studio rather than play in the thing. He pleaded with me to calm down and trust him. Mr. Mayer, it seemed, had his heart set on my playing this one, and I mustn't jeopardize the big plans that were being made for me by refusing to do it.

I should have told him to shove the big plans, and walked. But my trust in Thalberg prevailed and once again I was outsmarted.

Of all the bad pictures I have appeared in, and there were many, "The Passion Flower" takes the cake. As I had warned Thalberg, it had exactly nothing to commend it and turned out to be the big daddy of all stinkeroos. It was but one of the Thalberg productions that you never hear about.

I had scarcely finished the horrific "Passion Flower" when Warner Brothers studio requested the loan of my services to play the starring role in "River's End." MGM, contrary to its previous high-handed treatment of me, submitted the script for my approval. I was intrigued by the story which called for me to play a dual role—a Canadian Mountie chasing himself as a fugitive. After a story conference with Darryl Zanuck, Warner's production head, I agreed to play the part.

The director, a character from somewhere in the Balkans, had evidently been made a director because of his great talent as a weight lifter. He was an insecure man, burdened with a terrific inferiority which he manifested by screaming gratuitous insults at little people who were in no position to fight back. I found him highly amusing, but only because of his abominable English which he murdered anew every time he spoke.

Zanuck was something else again. Dynamic, articulate, possessed of a sound story mind and arrogantly sure of himself, I tabbed him as probably the most capable executive producer in Hollywood. He was also a man of quick decisions. In the eight weeks I was engaged with the picture, he visited the set just once that I knew of. It was during a set up and I was in my dressing room reading a book. I set it aside as he entered. Glancing at the title, he asked, "New book?"

"Yes," I said. "Just out."

"Interesting?"

"Great. It would make an exciting picture."

"For you?"

"Could be."

"If we bought it, would you come over and play it for us?"

"I'd be delighted."

Within the next week "The Maltese Falcon" became the property of Warner Brothers studio. I did not get to play it, however. But that's beside the point; there were a lot of roles I didn't get to play.

During the shooting of "River's End" there was just one incident worthy of particular note. The scene was an arctic wasteland. A blizzard was raging. I, as the fugitive, was mushing through the storm, urging my six-dog team to its utmost effort. The Mountie was close on my trail and I was desperate. Suddenly the embankment along which I was speeding collapsed, tumbling the sledge, the dogs and myself into a struggling heap at the bottom.

I was dressed in parka and fur boots. The boots were made of rabbit pelts. The dogs were partial to rabbit meat. Suddenly aware that here, under their very noses, were two prime specimens of the genus hara, both very much alive and kicking, they went all out for the kill and I was fighting for my life.

It required the combined efforts of the dog handlers and the entire crew to get me away from them.

The sadistic weight lifter thought it was all very funny. I didn't. It took fourteen stitches to close up the gashes in my hide.

After completion of the picture, I saw it in rough cut and was pleased. Although no blockbuster, it was better than average, sometimes exciting, and in general, a solid piece of entertainment.

Before departing the Warner Brothers studio, I had an interesting chat with Darryl Zanuck. He quizzed me on my running battle with MGM and stated that if, by any chance, I became available, he would be very happy to negotiate a deal with me. I thanked him for his interest, saying that while it was true that I was very unhappy at MGM, Thalberg had assured me that everything would be worked out to my satisfaction.

I had no way of knowing, of course, that at the very moment, MGM was preparing to deal me another kick in the teeth.

Within the week it was announced in the columns that I, heading a cast including Raquel Torres, Nils Asther, John Miljan and George Marion, was about to leave for Mazatlan, Mexico, where we would start production on an MGM picture entitled, "The Sea Bat." The setup had a "programmer" smell to it.

Holding back my screams until I knew for certain I was hurt, I rushed to the studio, secured a script and read it in the seclusion of my dressing room.

My worst fears were realized. It was a programmer, all right—a rootin'–tootin', rip–snortin' stinkaroo from way back.

With blood in my eye, I crashed into Thalberg's office, only to be immediately disarmed by his appearance. In the two-month interval since I had seen him, he had lost considerable weight, his color was ghastly and he looked very tired. My anger melted into concern. I apologized for adding my comparably petty troubles to his already top-heavy burden of responsibilities. With a wan smile he brushed away my concern.

"It's all in a day's work, Charlie," he said. "Sit down. Tell me, how did "River's End" turn out?"

"Not badly. It's no world beater but it could be a hell of a lot worse."

"Good. Now, what's on your mind?"

"You don't really have to ask, do you, Irving?"

" 'The Sea Bat,' I suppose."

"Smart fella. I just read it. It stinks to high heaven."

"I agree with you."

"Then why, Irving? What in hell is going on? Or is this supposed to be one of those important productions you promised me?"

The climate changed. "Don't get sarcastic with me, Charlie. I only work here, too, you know." His anger was almost plaintive as his voice rose. "What do you want from me?"

My own temper flared. "Not a thing, Irving. I guess it's my error. I didn't stop to think you might be just as tired of my crying on your shoulder as I am to do it. I'm sorry to have bothered you. Thanks for nothing."

I'd almost reached the door when his voice stopped me. "Will you, for Christ's sake, stop acting like a spoiled child and listen to me? There's nothing I can do about 'The Sea Bat.' It has already been sold on next year's program and we have to make it."

"That's simple. Put somebody else in it."

"It can't be done. It was sold with you."

"O.K. I refuse to do it. What are you going to do about that?"

"Me? Nothing. But I'm afraid the company might do plenty."

"For instance?"

"You've got a contract. Read it."

"I have. I know it by heart and apropos of that contract, there's such a thing as moral responsibility. MGM agreed orally that if I was a success in 'Dynamite,' it would grant me reasonable approval of scripts. Now, is there any argument as to my success in 'Dynamite'?"

"New York claims they made you no such concession."

"Then they're lying. We argued about it for weeks. It was even the deciding factor in my decision to sign the contract. My New York attorneys, O'Brien, Melivinsky and Driscoll, can testify to that. And I expect the company to live up to its agreement. I'm only asking for what's owing to me, Irving, and if I don't get it, I won't play. I refuse to be relegated to supporting roles, or to leads in your stinking second features. I don't want any part of it. I'll go back to New York."

"And do what?"

"Broadway plays, of course. What else?"

"Not if they enjoin you."

"They can't."

"They can, and will. They can secure an injunction that would tie you up, but good. You wouldn't be able to function in any entertainment medium until you had fulfilled the terms of the MGM contract. I'd hate to see that happen, Charlie."

"I'd fight the bastards to a finish."

"I'm sure you would and they'd beat your brains out. Now will you please listen to me?"

"I've been listening to you ever since I came into the joint. Where's it gotten me?"

"I can only repeat what I've said before. Everything will work out all right if you'll have a little patience. Don't make an issue of the The Sea Bat. It can't do you any harm, believe me, and if you refuse to do it, they'll crucify you."

"You keep saying, 'they,' Irving. Does that mean you consider yourself apart from them?"

"So far as you are concerned, yes. Frankly, I think you're great. I think you can be one of the biggest stars on the screen. Just have a little faith in me."

Once again I allowed the Thalberg charm to overcome my own judgment.

Three weeks later I was on location in Mazatlan, Mexico, striving against unbeatable odds to transform one hundred and fifty pages of unbelievably inept material into a screenable motion picture.

The project was doomed from the start.

The director, Wesley Ruggles, was thoroughly aware that the script was a stinker. "Garbage," was his word for it. "But," he said, "I've been ordered to shoot it as is. They are afraid you might insist upon rewriting and cause a lot of delay. So, what the hell—why worry about it?"

To my leading lady, Raquel Torres, a personable young lady of Latin extraction, a script was a script. Good or bad, I doubt that she knew the difference.

Nils Asther, who as a featured leading man certainly rated better treatment, was cast in an unimportant bit part. MGM was not picking up his next option, you see, and as was the practice was lessening his future value to rival producers. Naturally, therefore, Nils couldn't be expected to exhibit overwhelming enthusiasm for the project.

The weather, too, was against us. Every clear day was matched by a foggy one and we were soon hopelessly behind schedule.

On the plus side were those two pros, John Miljan and George Marion, both of whom could be counted upon to do their best under any circumstances.

As villain and hero, respectively, John and I were burdened with most of the action and no two actors ever worked harder to breathe life into utterly unbelievable situations. Not that we deserved special commendation. It's the way of all really good actors that no matter how hopeless the material, once they are on, they do their damndest to put it over, sometimes risking serious injury and even death.

For instance, after an unusually violent fight sequence, during which Miljan and three of his henchmen subdue me—Miljan and I did our own fighting—I am bound hand and foot and placed in the bow of a small sail boat. Miljan navigates it across a wide stretch of ocean with the intent of delivering me back to the dreaded island prison from which I had escaped. We encounter a giant Sea Bat, which for some reason known only to the writers, attacks the boat.

Miljan, armed with a spear, fights desperately to drive the thing away but his efforts are futile. When it appears certain that we are both doomed he, to save his own worthless hide, cuts my bonds that I may join in the battle.

Because I am a brave man, a hero, I fight valiantly,

but the giant creature is invincible and capsizes the boat.

Miljan and I, unarmed and helpless in the water, which evidently in sympathy with the Sea Bat is suddenly erupting in giant waves, are faced with certain death.

But the ferocious Sea Bat, for some inexplicable reason—the most plausible being that he hears the mating call—suddenly takes off.

All is still not well, however, because Miljan, out of condition because of his intemperate living, starts to founder in the raging tide. I of course am in the pink—heroes do not indulge in riotous living—and, jeopardizing my own chance of survival, go to his assistance. After knocking him out I put forth a Herculean effort and tow him some ten miles through the storm-tossed sea to safety.

Exciting?

All of the water sequences were done under the supervision of a technical director, supposedly an accredited marine expert. The scenes in the sail boat were actually shot at sea, about three miles off shore. A heavy spar had been lashed across the stern deck of a tug boat. A rope was suspended from the end of this spar and attached to the bow of the sail boat. The idea being that the tug, steaming at eight knots and towing the sail boat, would create the illusion that the small boat was sailing along at a fast clip.

There would have been nothing wrong with the idea had the camera been set up on the tug, but to facilitate photographing the closeups, they built a platform over the stern of the small boat. And the platform was designed to hold the heavy camera, three camera men, plus one director.

The heavy weight, of course, brought the small boat dangerously down by the stern, and it appeared obvious to me that when the tug got under way, the stern of our little craft would immediately go under.

I brought this to the attention of the director who, backed up by the technical man, scoffed at my fears.

"My God, Charlie," he jeered. "You're not going yellow on us. Not you."

"Hell, no," I said. "However, I don't care what the rest of you bastards are going to do. I'm going to be ready to swim."

I called the property man and ordered him to untie the ropes binding my hands and feet. I had him lay them across my wrists and ankles with the ends tucked out of sight.

Orders were given to roll the camera. As the tug got under way the bow of our little boat went up, the stern went down and we were all in the drink. The camera was irretrievably lost and one of the camera boys nearly drowned. And if I had not untied the ropes, it is likely I would have drowned.

There was another episode during a sequence in which I worked in close physical contact with a group of local extras. There were about a hundred of them; all dirty, unhealthy-looking and lousy, I'm sure. I noticed one whose face was nearly masked by silvery-white, scaly scabs. Thus alerted, I looked further and found another one whose nose was partly eaten away.

Revolted and scared, I pointed them out to the director and insisted that a qualified doctor be sent for to examine the men and diagnose the disease.

My hunch was right. Both men were lepers. The doctor also designated two others. He insisted that there was nothing to be alarmed about, that the disease was un-communicable except by long and close contact. He could have saved his breath, however. I insisted that the poor devils be paid off and dismissed. I also demanded that the remaining ones be screened for leprosy, syphilis, gonorrhea, measles, whooping cough and mumps. While it was being done I obtained a large bottle of Lysol, hied myself to the hotel and damned near burned my hide off in an effort to make myself antiseptic.

The only fond memory I have of that location was my departure, after eight long weeks of frustrated effort. Accompanying me on the train were two large commercial sample-trunks packed tightly with fine liquors and decorated with the official seals that proclaimed diplomatic immunity. It tickled me that with the connivance of a high government official, I was thus able to strike a blow for freedom.

Back in Hollywood there was a two-week interim while the studio big-wigs looked over the stuff we had shot in Mexico and debated on what to do with it. They ignored my suggestion that the film be cut up and sold as mandolin picks and, after much deliberation, decided to throw more of the stockholders' good money after bad.

The director was fired—there always had to be a scapegoat—new sets were built, and we started over again, with Lionel Barrymore directing.

Lionel may have had talent as a director. I don't know whether he did or not. But if he had he damned well kept it a secret during that assignment. Most of his time on the set was spent in sleeping. I excused it on the assumption that he was ill.

The inept script was still in evidence, no attempt having been made to improve it. And the situation appeared more hopeless than ever. To render my frustration more complete, Irving Thalberg was absent from the studio for an indefinite period. As instinct warned me to keep my distance from Mayer, there was no one for me to scream at.

On the first day of actual shooting, the cast was notified to make no evening engagements for the duration as it would be subject to after-dinner calls until the picture was finished.

Via the assistant director who functions as liaison officer for the production department, I served notice that I would be unavailable for after-dinner calls. I explained that to work such long hours would tend to jeopardize my health and therefore lower the standard of my work as an actor.

At six o'clock that evening the company was released one hour for dinner to be back on the set at seven.

After reassembling at seven, the cast, the director and the crew sat for hours doing nothing; overtime costs piled up the while. This stupid procedure was followed for several days. Word was spread that the costs were being charged to me.

Came the day of the big wind; a veritable hurricane it was. I had received an urgent message requesting my presence in Louis B. Mayer's office, immediately.

Knowing his reputation for ruthless and bullying tactics in his dealings with talent, I paused before entering his office and while marshalling my defenses, indulged in a deep-breathing exercise, hoping thereby to envelop my own explosive temper in a protective covering of tranquility.

I was met in the outer office by his secretary for personal affairs. Her manner was frigidly polite. "Mr. Mayer is waiting for you," she said. "And a word of advice, young man. Don't cross him. He's not feeling too kindly toward you this morning." With these words of warning, or threat, she ushered me into the presence chamber.

To my great surprise, Mayer, instead of launching the expected tirade, came forward smiling broadly and with his hand extended in greeting. "Good morning, Charlie. I'm glad to see you. Sit down."

Taking his cue, I responded in kind. "Thank you, Mr. Mayer," I said. "It's good to see *you* again."

After seating himself behind his desk, he eyed me quizzically for a moment, then, nodding his head, voiced his conclusion. "You're looking great, Charlie. Just great. Mexico evidently agreed with you."

"Thank you."

"You've put on too much weight, though. Get rid of it. It's unbecoming."

"Yes, I know. I'm working on it."

"Good."

With the niceties disposed of, he got down to cases. The joviality was replaced by a manner of grim concern. "I don't have to tell you, Charlie, that your picture has gone way over the budget."

"I presumed it had. Yes."

"It's going to cost more than a quarter of a million more than it should. So it's up to everybody concerned to put their shoulders to the wheel and take up as much of the slack as possible. Agreed?"

"Certainly."

"Then why is it that everybody is cooperating but you?"

"That's kind of a loaded question, Mr. Mayer. It's like

asking a man why he doesn't stop kissing a pig. I don't know what you mean by it."

"Don't quibble with me, Bickford. Do you call it cooperation to keep an entire company and crew sitting night after night while you fail to show up?"

"I won't accept that responsibility, Mr. Mayer. Your flunkies down there knew I wasn't going to show for those night-calls. I told them I wouldn't, and why."

The rise in his blood pressure was almost visible. The thin veneer of urbanity cracked. "*You* told them," he yelled. "What the hell right have you got to tell us what you'll do or what you won't do? You're under contract here. Don't forget that."

I tried logic. "Mr. Mayer," I said. "When I started work on 'Anna Christie,' the picture I was doing at Universal was still unfinished. You refused to allow me to go over there and work four hours a night on the premise that it would wear me out and jeopardize my work on 'Anna Christie.' How about that? Why the concern about me then and not now?"

I shouldn't have brought it up.

"What are you trying to hand me?" he yelled. "You did go over there and finish it."

"But that was an emergency."

"So is this an emergency."

"I don't consider it so."

That blew the lid. His temper boiled over.

"God-damn you, Bickford, you've been getting away with murder around here. But it's ended. From now on you're going to toe the mark. You're going to stop shooting off your mouth to the press, panning every picture you're in, giving out outrageous lies to interviewers. And you're going to quit fighting with everybody. I've had enough of your lousy temperament."

"I'm afraid you've got me wrong, Mr. Mayer. I'm no temperamental actor stirring up trouble just for the hell of it. It's a matter of principle with me."

He snorted in derision. "Principle? Nuts. You're a God-damned Bolshevic. But from now on you'll do as you're told, or you're through."

"You mean you're firing me?"

"I mean you're through in the picture business."

"Well, I guess that does it," and I spoke with icy calm. "O.K., Mr. Mayer, I'm through in the picture business, as of now." I started for the door.

"Wait a minute," he yelled. "I'll tell you when to go. I can fire you any time I like but you can't quit until I say so. Remember that. Right now, you'll go back on that set and go to work. And you'll work tonight—and every night until the picture is finished. Now get out of here."

The man thought he held all the aces. We had reached the line of demarcation. This was the moment when I was expected to put my tail between my legs in submission. And, to my shame, I thought of doing just that. All I had to do to get this monster off my back was to apologize abjectly and promise Daddy that henceforth I would be a good boy. Then, all would be forgiven and, who could tell, perhaps I would be the white-haired boy on the lot.

But I had no talent for fakery or finagling and I could not have uttered the words without vomiting.

I made one more effort to resolve the issue. "All right, Mr. Mayer, I'll make you a proposition. I'll finish 'The Sea Bat' and work any hours you care to impose—if you will agree to release me from my contract immediately the picture is finished."

He smiled nastily. "You'll finish 'The Sea Bat,' all right, and I'll agree to nothing."

"Why not? It seems to be the obvious solution to both of our problems. Look, I'll pay a hundred thousand dollars for my release."

"Ah!" he exclaimed. "So that's it. I should have known. Which studio is putting you up to this?"

"No studio. It's my own money."

"You're a God-damned liar. You haven't got a pot to piss in. You can tell them it's no deal. We're holding you strictly to the terms of your contract. Get out."

"O.K., Mayer. But paste this in your memory book: I'm not working tonight, nor any other night. And if you think I've given you trouble, you ain't seen nothing yet."

As I reached the door, he screamed after me, "You're nothing but a lousy, red-headed mick son-of-a-bitch."

In retrospect, I can say in all modesty that up to this moment I had done an admirable job of controlling my temper. I remember standing there, speechless for the moment, then as I turned and looked at his ugly puss, I thought, "Of all the sons-of-bitches I have ever met, this son-of-a-bitch is the most despicable son-of-a-bitch of them all. I've got to cut him down."

And I did. I threw the gauntlet, not at his feet but in his teeth. I deliberately locked horns with this man, bloated with arbitrary power and authority, a man recognized as the most powerful Mogul in the industry and whose vindictive nature was known and feared throughout the film world.

Such was my arrogance, anger, strength of character, or sheer stupidity that I was not even slightly awed by his threatening attitude, his money, his power, or his position.

For the first time during this fantastic interview, I cast aside all effort to be tactful, diplomatic, or even civilized.

I didn't even choose my words. They just tumbled out of me.

"I'm red-headed all right, and I may be a son-of-a-bitch. But I'm not lousy, nor am I a mick. And if I were a mick, it wouldn't hurt my feelings a bit to be called one. I rather like the micks. But I am outraged to be called one by a venomous little junk peddler like you. To hell with you—you posturing little ignoramus."

I had really touched him on the raw. Livid, and shaking with anger, he said quietly, "One day you'll come crawling on your knees to apologize for that."

"Fuck you, Mayer," I said, and as I closed the door after me I knew I was ear-marked for the slaughter house.

In the commissary that noon the long table at which I usually ate with five or six companions was strangely empty. Acquaintances with whom I had fraternized in a spirit of camaraderie either avoided me or greeted me with surreptitious nods from across the room. The only friendly faces I saw were those of the waitresses.

News does indeed travel fast in the studios. I had tangled with Mayer; therefore it was not politic to appear friendly toward me. Outstanding were the publicity people who seemed suddenly to be stricken blind when I came into view. Not that it bothered me too much.

There were a few others, a handful of actors and writers, whose attitude did surprise and hurt. None of them cared to jeopardize his rich field of clover by making a decent gesture toward a lone maverick.

Significantly, there were no more night-calls issued to "The Sea Bat" company and work on the production proceeded as well as could be expected under the circumstances.

For the sequences involving the fight with the Sea Bat, the studio had constructed, at great cost, an enormous mechanical fish built of steel and leather and equipped with electrical motors which propelled it through the water and operated its great winglike fins, tail and mouth.

It was an ingenious contraption and certainly looked devilish enough in operation. The sequence, which was shot in a tank at the studio, might have been exciting had it not been for the fact that every time I hit the metal body of the thing with my three-pronged spear, the recoil would bounce the spear back, nearly upsetting me. The only times it didn't bounce were when the prongs bent. In either case, the effect was ludicrous and, as the sequence was the climactic one of the picture, disastrous.

After the preview of the picture, at which the audience had hilariously kidded the battle with the armor-plated fish, Mayer was heard to say, "The thing is a disaster and it's all Bickford's fault. He laid down on the job. But I'll fix him. This picture will never play a major theater in the country."

One of Irving Thalberg's first acts on returning to the studio was to send for me. His attitude towards me was unchanged and after a cordial greeting, he insisted upon a verbatim account of the blow-up with Mayer.

He listened with concerned interest, interrupting only once to ask if the hundred-thousand-dollar offer for a release was really my own idea. My final blast at Mayer intrigued him and he laughed heartily at the mental image of Mayer being called "junk peddler" and "ignoramus."

Then he became very serious. "It's a bad situation, Charlie. Why in hell didn't you stay away from him?"

"How could I? He's the head of the studio and he sent for me. I could hardly refuse to talk to him."

"No. I suppose not. But you didn't have to run off at the mouth."

"I couldn't help it. Believe me, I did my best to be reasonable. What was I supposed to do? Just lie down and let him walk all over me?"

"When are you going to smarten up? You can't tangle with men like Mayer and Hearst, and get away with it. A man of your intelligence should know that, for Christ's sake. But of course, that's part of the trouble. You've got the stink of intelligence about you. They know you're onto them and it grates on them."

"My heart's bleeding. It's just too God-damned bad about them."

"Yes, it is. And you'll have to do something about it."

"For instance."

"You'll have to square things with Mayer."

"Just like that, huh? Just like he said. I'm to crawl to him on my knees and kiss his ass. Not by a damn sight. Wild horses couldn't drag me. So where do we go from there?"

"I don't know. You're making it awfully tough, Charlie. I don't know what to do about you. You're a hard man to deal with."

"Not really, Irving. Only when I'm pushed around. There's nothing complex about me. I have no pretensions. And believe it or not, I have much humility. Stubborn, yes, but honest. And I expect honesty in return. This, I'm not getting. All I'm asking is for the company to live up to its promises to me."

"You'll never get option over your material, Charlie, so that's one idea you may as well forget."

"Then the studio may as well forget any idea of co-operation from me."

Thalberg's patience had run out. "Now you're talking like a loud-mouthed jerk. Mayer may be all and more than you say he is. But he holds the power, my friend. He can make or break you. You can't fight City Hall. You don't throw punches at a man like Mayer, not if you expect to get anywhere. So get onto yourself. Play the game like everybody else. Butter the guy up a little and he'll eat out of your hand. Apologize to him. What in hell have you got to lose?"

"My self respect, Irving, and that's worth more to me than a few lousy bucks. Listen, it seems that I'm getting to be a problem to *everybody* in this joint, including you.

"I wouldn't lie to you."

"So we're even. Everybody in the joint is getting to be a pain in the ass to me. But there's a simple solution. Get me out of your hair. Release me."

"Not a chance. This company has no intention of allowing another studio to cash in on what we've built up. So that's another idea you can get out of your mind."

"There's no other studio involved."

"I don't believe it."

"I'll agree not to work for another studio for two years. That should prove something."

It did. I'd really gotten through to him. I think up to that moment it was incredible to him that I was willing to sacrifice a potential fortune.

"My God," he said, wonderingly. "You really do hate us, don't you?"

"I hate the screwing I've been getting."

He rose and stood for a moment, gazing out of the

window. Still with his back to me, he said, "I have to admit you've had a lousy break on scripts. But there's one in the works now that should be right up your alley."

"Oh?"

He turned. "Yes. It's a prison story with a great, gutsy role for you. Frances Marion is writing it. This will be a big one, Charlie."

"Great. When do I get a look at it?"

"We should have a first draft in three or four weeks. I'm going to have to straighten out this thing between you and Mayer, though. In the meantime, steer clear of him. If he should call you, get in touch with me."

"Right. Thanks, Irving."

The interview raised my spirits considerably. With a major picture in preparation, it appeared that my fight for good roles in literate vehicles was about to pay off. The fact that they were adamant against releasing me was proof that they considered me a pretty hot property.

I meticulously followed Thalberg's injunction to stay away from Mayer. Not only that, I gave the studio a wide berth and for several weeks curbed my impatience while waiting to get my hands on the promised script.

Late one evening a studio messenger delivered it to me at my home. The script did not have Frances Marion's name on it, nor was it a prison story. Instead it was another prime example of glamorized garbage.

My reaction was mostly bewilderment. I guess I had been kicked below the belt so many times that I was too sluggy for anger. But I was puzzled as to who was doing the kicking, and why.

Certainly Mayer had left no doubt as to his attitude. But what about Thalberg? Was he really championing my cause against great odds, or was he a blue-faced little

Machiavelli lulling me with soft words so he could destroy me piecemeal?

Of one thing I was sure. No longer would I fall for the soft-sell. No one would con me into playing this latest insult to my ability as an actor. For me, Thalberg's charm had lost its potency. Come morning I would have it out with him.

If my resolution had needed bolstering, which it didn't, an item in next morning's newspaper would have more than sufficed. MGM's most favored columnist proclaimed in her lead that Wallace Beery was to star in "The Big House," a prison story especially tailored for him by Frances Marion. "The Big House" was scheduled for immediate production at MGM.

Even after reading this shocker, I was more resigned than angry. It must have been that I more than half-suspected some such double cross and it left me cold. Suddenly it didn't matter a damn who was responsible. All I wanted was to get clear of Metro-Goldwyn-Mayer.

When Thalberg arrived at his office that morning I was there to meet him. And an icy meeting it was. There was no hint of friendliness or interest in his manner, nor in mine.

"I'm tied up this morning, Bickford," he said, brusquely. "Call me this afternoon."

"It won't wait, Thalberg."

"Sorry," and he proceeded into his private office.

I followed close on his heels, closing the door behind me.

Accepting the inevitable, he said grudgingly, "Well, all right. As long as you're here, let's have it. But make it brief."

"I'll do that. I came in to tell you that my career as a

prostitute has ended. I'll play no more of your garbage. That's it. That's all I have to say. Brief enough?"

"Quite. Do you still want a release from your contract?"

"More than anything I can think of."

"You've got it. Come back late this afternoon. The papers will be ready then."

That was it. No apologies, no regrets, no farewells.

I walked out of his office and that was the last time I saw Irving Thalberg face to face.

Jubilantly I went to my dressing room, gathered my belongings together and left the lot.

Late that afternoon when I returned, I was directed to the legal department where sure enough the papers were waiting my signature. I signed, took my copy in my big, hot fist, said "Goodbye" to no one and made my exit from the Metro-Goldwyn-Mayer studio.

I immediately called my agent and instructed him to get on the phone and acquaint every major studio with the good news.

The following morning he called to tell me that I was as hot as a pistol. I told him to give Darryl Zanuck the first crack at me, outlining the deal I wanted.

Zanuck went for it in general and within another twenty-four hours we had come to terms. The details were relayed to the Warner Brothers attorneys, who were to have the contract ready for signature within a week.

It was an extremely advantageous contract for me and I couldn't have been happier with the course of events.

One week passed. No word about the contract. Then another, at the end of which I again awakened my agent and suggested he find out "how come?".

He reported that something strange was going on; that

Warner Brothers were stalling, and in his opinion, had no intention of going through with the deal. "I'm afraid," he said, "that MGM has put the Indian-sign on you."

"What in hell does that mean?"

"It means that they've got you blacklisted. And if they have, no other studio will touch you."

"Well, you'd damn well better find out. Feel out the other studios."

He reported back that no studio in Hollywood was interested in a deal with Charles Bickford.

I had heard of black lists, but for the first time, it appeared, I was featured on one and I didn't appreciate it. It amazed me that any one studio, or one man, was powerful enough to frighten an entire industry into boycotting one defenseless actor. This was restraint of trade with a vengeance.

I told my agent I intended to fight MGM and asked if he could, or would, help me to get the goods on them. His answer was "No." So being of no further use to each other, we severed relations.

I then engaged the services of one of the top investigative agencies in America and for several months one of their crack operatives was planted in the MGM studio, searching for evidence substantial enough to build a case against them.

Unfortunately—for it would have delighted me to take over the MGM factory—the investigation was unsuccessful. The black list was intangible. Not one scrap of concrete evidence did the investigation turn up.

Meanwhile, the publicity hatchet-men had been put to work. More contemptible even than their bosses, they did a magnificent job; a much more efficient job of tearing me down than they had in building me up. It was a galling, but at the same time fascinating, experience to stand by helplessly and watch myself being crucified. The whispering campaign was the most effective. The saboteurs spread the word. Overnight I was miraculously transformed into box-office poison. No longer was I a great actor; I had suddenly become a mediocre ham. I was a troublemaker. I was impossible to handle. I had no sex appeal. I dyed my hair. I was a Bolshevic. I was having sexual relations with my mother.

Although seething inwardly, I assumed an indifferent attitude toward this hiatus in my film career. I could of course have returned to New York where the Broadway producers still held me in great demand. But this would have been synonymous with surrender, a word not contained in my lexicon. Having chosen the motion-picture industry as my field of activity, I was determined not to be driven out by any group of gangsters.

So, I attended to my nonprofessional business interests and, like Mr. Micawber, waited for something to turn up; the something being the ammunition which I hoped the detectives would eventually place in my hands, evidence which would enable me to fight the enemy on even ground.

Months went by. Then I received a telephone call from a man who claimed to have vital information concerning me, information which he could not reveal over the phone. He requested a personal interview. I granted it.

This man, whose first name is Harry—I can't recall his surname—said that for many years he had functioned as personal representative and business manager for various silent-picture stars. In that capacity he had been instrumental in settling many disputes between his stars and the studios.

On the preceding Sunday he had been a guest at a brunch party at Louis B. Mayer's beach house. There, he said, a conversation had taken place, directed *at* him and which, in effect, commissioned him to feel me out in respect to a new contract at MGM.

The word flabbergasted best describes my feelings at that moment. I just could not credit what the man was saying. But he went on to specify the terms of a proposed contract containing concessions which made it interesting to me. In return, certain concessions were demanded of me. A sort of give-and-take proposition which, under the circumstances, I would have been idiotic to refuse.

"If," I said, "you can come up with a firm deal on those terms, the answer is an unequivocal 'yes.' "

"You'll hear from me within the week," he said, and departed.

Two days passed. Then he called again. A fast worker, that Harry. He was no waster of time nor words. "Be in Louis Mayer's office at ten tomorrow," he said.

"Yup," was my even terser reply.

Remembering my last meeting with Mayer, I was slightly embarrassed and more than a little unsure as to the proper attitude with which I should approach the coming interview. Crow had never been my dish.

I was bewildered by MGM's seeming change of face, suspicious that there was a skunk in the bushes, and at the same time hopeful that the proposed deal was really on the up-and-up. I decided to play it by ear and let Mayer carry the ball.

It was a wise decision

No errant son just returned home after long years of wandering could have received a more effusive welcome. The man actually had tears in his eyes as he came for-

ward with out-stretched arms and enfolded me in a fa-
therly embrace. For one desperate moment I was afraid
he was going to kiss me.

"My God," I thought. "Anything but that," and prepared to duck.

The tension was relieved by a short chubby individual
who emerged from a corner of the office. He had evidently been hiding. Smiling broadly, he held out his hand
in greeting. "Hello, Charlie," he said. "I'm Jerry Mayer."

I was so relieved by the timely interruption, I didn't
even case him for a weapon. Nor did I question the reason for his presence. I returned his greeting with all the
warmth I could muster.

Well pleased, he retired to the shadows while L.B. sat
me down and went into his act. With variations and a
few additions he delivered the same speech he had made
in De Mille's office at our first meeting. In contradiction
of the whispering campaign being waged by his hatchet
men, he again told me that I was one of the great actors
of the age; I was loaded with sex appeal; I was a combination of Tommy Meighan, Wallace Beery and Rudolph
Valentino; and, apparently, I was no longer co-habit-
ing with my mother.

Soon he motioned the other little man to come forth,
and two documents were placed before me. One was in
the form of a letter containing the salient points of the
new contract. The other was an agency contract.

Thus did I become aware that the new deal was being
negotiated by a theatrical agency, of which Jerry, brother
of Louis, was the head. And, it turned out, the mysterious Harry was in the employ of Jerry. And so Jerry was
to collect ten percent of every dollar paid me by Louis.

How nice, I thought. What a touching example of

brotherly love. Swallowing my nausea, I signed both
documents, wondering what part of the commission
Jerry would kick back to Louis.

Ironically, at the very moment I was signing the contract, a detective in my employ was somewhere in the
studio digging for proof that MGM was conspiring to
prevent my earning a livelihood in motion pictures.

That very day, of course, I cancelled the investigation.

My erstwhile agent eventually got wind of the new
deal and tried to horn in. He threatened suit, contending
that the contract was simply a continuation of the original contract. His squeals were soon silenced, however;
probably by threat of boycott.

With the new deal consummated, it was natural that I
should assume my troubles to be over. I could expect,
reasonably enough, that something worthwhile would
result.

I waited patiently.

Weeks passed. The promised fat roles in important
vehicles did not materialize.

On each payday, a check was deposited to my account
in the bank. And although I was probably the highest
paid unemployed actor in America, it was becoming
more and more apparent that a whole family of skunks
was hiding in the bushes. The aroma was unmistakable.

Perplexed and disturbed, I did not allow the frustrating situation to weigh me down. Fortunately my outside
business interests occupied most of my time and diverted
my attention from the snake-pit in Culver City. One of
my prime interests at that time was in a new invention, a
dry concentrator, which in laboratory tests was successful

in recovering ninety-nine percent of the fine gold and platinum contained in mine tailings.

Having acquired a controlling interest in the invention, I set up a mill for experimental purposes and employed engineers to prospect certain gravel deposits and old tailings dumps. As prospecting was a perfect complement to my love of the open, I devoted as much time to it as possible.

At about six o'clock one evening, having driven north on my way to examine a placer-mine in Oregon, I pulled into the town of San Luis Obispo.

An actor acquaintance of mine was a member of a cast rehearsing at San Simeon, preparatory to shooting a Marion Davies picture. As the Hearst ranch was close to the town, it occurred to me to phone and invite him to come down from the mountain and shoot the breeze over a delicious Greco-American Blue Plate Special.

Fortuitously, the operator put my call through over Marion Davies' private line. Marion, assuming that I had called *her,* hospitably suggested that I dine and spend the night at San Simeon. I found it difficult to explain the operator's mistake, so declining the invitation with thanks, I said that I had called simply to say "Hello" and that I wouldn't consider imposing upon her hospitality.

She was insistent, saying that once having been a guest at San Simeon, I was welcome evermore, and that she would feel affronted if I didn't come.

I compromised, insisting upon dining in town, but promised to drive up afterwards and have a drink before continuing my way north.

After a leisurely and boring dinner at the local greasy spoon, I drove the forty miles to *La Cuesta Encentada,* timing it to arrive before the portals of *La Casa Grande* at about nine o'clock.

The major-domo was waiting on the big porch. After her formalized greeting, she insisted upon having my bags taken from the car. Ignoring my protestations, she affirmed that it was Miss Davies' explicit instruction that my things were to be taken to the same suite I had previously occupied.

How does one argue against such determined hospitality? I acceded.

My timing had been perfect. Dinner was just over and as I entered the great hall, the guests came streaming from the refectory. Most of them were acquaintances—Hedda Hopper and Sidney Blackmer among them—and as they gathered around me their surprised greetings made me feel quite the most popular man at the party.

Then Marion came into view, followed closely by Hearst. I was about to step forward and pay my respects when Hearst saw me. Stopping in his tracks, he glared for a moment in astonished dismay. Then, his expression changing to one of malevolent fury, he grasped Marion's arm and strode quickly from the room.

Fortunately, most of those present were unaware of the incident, a fact which helped enormously as I struggled to hold my temper below boiling point.

Someone thrust a drink into my hand and I continued to chat with the group around me, intending after a minute or two to make as swift and unobtrusive an exit as possible.

But even as my mind was formulating this plan of voluntary retreat, the enemy struck again.

The major-domo entered the room. Tactfully drawing me aside, she gave me my congé. "I'm sorry, Mr. Bickford," she said sympathetically, "but something has come up and we are going to need your rooms. Your bags have been repacked and are in your car. You are to leave immediately."

It was with difficulty that I curbed a compulsive urge to seek out Hearst and flatten him.

Luckily for us both, I kept control and after mumbling a hastily contrived excuse for my quick departure, I left the house, accompanied by the major-domo.

My car, with the motor running, was just outside the door. Parked behind it was a Ford pick-up truck. Standing beside the truck were two rough-looking men.

The major-domo volunteered an answer to my unspoken inquiry. "These men will see you safely off the property, Mr. Bickford."

"That's nice," I said. "You're certainly doing your best to speed this departing guest."

"I do what I'm told, Mr. Bickford."

"Yes. Of course you do. Tell me, Mrs. Scully," (I seem to recall that as her name), "do you know the alleged whys and wherefores of this affair?"

"I know nothing about it."

"Well. Will you convey a message to that perambulating oyster that pays your salary?"

"I prefer not to be involved."

"That's understandable. But it's just possible that he will be interested in my reaction to his gratuitous insult. If he should ask, will you please tell him that he is in my opinion the littlest big man extant? And that I hope the world will soon be rid of him? It would afford me enormous pleasure to dance on his grave."

The woman probably never delivered the message. But if she did, I'll gamble that he chewed the carpet for days afterward. He had a horror of the very mention of death.

And so, literally at gun point, I left *La Casa Grande* and as I drove down *La Cuesta Encentada,* the sinister truck close on my tail, my sense of humor asserted itself and I chuckled at the thought that I was probably the only actor in the world who had been given the bum's rush from the Hearst domain. And, with the added distinction of being escorted to the border by two *pistoleros* . . .

The megalomaniacs of this world always have reasons, real or fancied, for their petty or significant acts of evil. I assume this picayune insult was tendered me because of my refusal to do a picture with Marion. Perhaps, but I found it hard to credit.

It could be that Marion *was* the cause. I had heard of Hearst's insane jealousy. It was common knowledge that he had relentlessly persecuted young virile actors whom he suspected of seeking Marion's favors. Was it possible he had the mistaken idea that I had a yen for Marion? I discounted the thought. I had never stepped beyond the limits of the amenities with her.

Or was the incident tied in with the strange things that were happening to me at MGM? Why not? Hearst and Mayer were closely associated. It was reasonable to suppose Hearst was aware of my status at the studio. Consequently, if he felt free to knife me with impunity, it followed that I was already earmarked for execution.

Upon my return to Hollywood a couple of weeks later, my first order of business was to confer with Jerry Mayer.

Jerry pooh-poohed my suspicions of dirty work at the

cross roads, insisting that his brother Louis held me in
high regard, both as a person and as an artist and that big
things were in store for me. He cited a production that
was in preparation, a story in glorification of Pancho
Villa, the Mexican bandit. As Jerry put it, "They're tai-
loring the role for you and if it turns out to be good
enough, Louis intends to star you in it."

I swallowed it. After all, Jerry was my agent. He col-
lected ten percent of my salary, therefore my interests
were his interests. What possible reason could he have
for lying to me?"

Again I marked time. The idea of portraying Villa
appealed to me. I read everything I could lay hands on
that had to do with the colorful cutthroat. At last I was to
be cast in a role in which I could sink my teeth.

But time marched on. Several more weeks passed with
no word of activity. I again pressed Jerry Mayer. Rejecting his soft soap, I insisted that the situation stank to high
Heaven, and demanded that as my agent he find out the
score.

He reported back that the studio was high on me; that
the delay was because Mayer was waiting to find just the
right story for me.

"Nonsense," I said. "That doesn't make sense. What
about the Pancho Villa story? That's a *great* vehicle for
me. I'd settle for it sight unseen."

"We were wrong about that one, Charlie. You
wouldn't play it. The part didn't work out so good.
They're going to throw Beery into it."

He really hit the fan with that batch. I no longer had
occasion to wonder about MGM's bad faith. I was mad. I
laid it on the line. "Don't hand me that crap, Jerry.
Those bastards over there are still handing me a screw-

ing, and you know it. Why don't you level with me? Why did they re-sign me? They had me completely hog-tied with their God-damned black list. They are still keeping me out of circulation. The only difference is that they're paying me. Why?"

My guess, which I did not reveal to Jerry, was that they had learned of my investigative operation. By re-signing me they forestalled the possibility of legal action on my part and at the same time insured the success of their plan to keep me off the screen until I was professionally dead.

Jerry insisted there was no plot. "Believe me, Charlie, my part in it was on the up and up. And I know that Louie signed the contract in good faith. If anybody is putting the boots to you over there, it's the Thalberg bunch. They're trying to get control from Louie. But they'll never make it. He's too strong for them. Just be patient a while longer. Everything will work out all right, believe me."

But I'd had it. "Patience be damned," I said. "I want out. I don't care how you do it. Coax him, kis his ass, or blackmail him—you must have plenty on him—but get to Louie and wangle me a release. Otherwise, I'll air the whole stinking mess in court. It'll be interesting to hear what those guys have to say about all this, under cross-examination."

I don't know which of the suggested methods Jerry adopted; probably a bit of each. But a month later he came up with the welcome news that the fantastic war was over; Mayer had agreed to a release.

I was jubilant. Now I'd be able to think and act without compulsion or arbitrary restriction. As a free lance actor, I could sell my services to the highest bidder. I was free.

My naïveté was extraordinary. I really did believe I had been emancipated. So in celebration of my fancied liberty I decided to satisfy an old yen . . .

Since early childhood the name Damascus had held a strange fascination for me. It was one of the far places my grandfather had talked about—the city that was old when ancient Rome was young; a city that has survived countless invasions, that was captured by David, Alexander and Pompey, that was sacked and burned, and still lives on.

Above everything else, I think my imagination was fired by the belief that here was the Garden of Eden. I wanted to see this place where Eve handed Adam the apple and thereby exploded a bomb of such explosive force that its chain reaction has made of the world a teeming jungle . . .

I doubt that any city in the world excels Damascus in the dreariness of its surrounding terrain, a bleak and barren wasteland that extends for miles in all directions.

In startling contrast, Damascus itself, blessed by two rivers—the Barada and the Pharpar—appears as a shining jewel, set in a wide belt of lush greenery. These fertile gardens, producing barley, wheat, various vegetables, fruits and nuts, constitute the life-blood of the city and offer a vivid explanation of its ability to endure through the centuries.

In a little inn at the edge of the Barada river, I was furnished clean comfortable quarters and, delightful surprise, excellent meals. This was my headquarters during my two-week stay and it was from here I set out every morning to explore the city, guided by a fourteen-year-old Bedouin named Abrahim. He was very pleased to have me address him as Abie.

Together we haunted the bazaars in the narrow crooked alleys, roofed with palm thatch and lined with little shops and stalls. I spent countless hours watching the various artisans work at their crafts—goldsmiths, silversmiths, coppersmiths, leather workers, wood workers, shoemakers, gunsmiths, and numbers more. With Abie officiating as my purchasing agent I bought a crateful of articles for which I had no earthly use. The smells, noises, colorful costumes, babel of voices and the motley crowds held my unflagging interest.

Abie himself would have interested a student of criminal psychology. He spoke a kind of pidgin English which he had picked up during his five-year experience as a tourist guide. Utterly amoral, he was one of those unfortunate waifs whose eyes have looked upon every known evil.

One example. He did his best to pressure me into visiting a specific whorehouse. When I demanded to know why, he confessed that two of the girls there worked for him.

He tried to sell me dope, hashish and filthy pictures. I'm sure he would have stopped at nothing in order to make a buck.

Nevertheless, he was a competent guide and led me to many places of interest. He failed me completely, however, when I demanded to be shown the exact spot where Eve gave Adam the business. He knew of several Gardens of Eden but had never heard of Adam and Eve. After hearing the story he laughed scornfully. "What kind of guy would be satisfy with a apple?" he demanded to know.

I think a great part of my pleasure in visiting this city was due to my complete anonymity. The fawning adulation of picture personalities by the mob has always disturbed me and the absence of it here was marked. It was my impression that few of these people were aware of the existence of such creatures as film stars, possibly excepting Charlie Chaplin and Bill Hart. My presence was all but ignored.

A few days before the end of my stay I experienced a delicious example of Bedouin hospitality. Abie's uncle Josef, a breeder of camels, invited me via Abie to dine and spend a night at his farm, situated in the desert about twenty-five miles east of the city. In extending me the bid, Abie assured me that as his uncle was a wealthy man everything would be hunky dory and that I would have the time of my life.

I was intrigued.

I chartered a small car for the excursion and on the appointed evening we set out. Although Abie was not included in the bid, he was to accompany me as guide and interpreter; Josef spoke no English.

I felt the first qualms when, following Abie's direction, I turned from the highway onto the desert floor. There was no road. About a mile distant there was an oasis, indicated by three anaemic-looking date palms. Pitched in a semi-circle around these was a cluster of black tents.

"What the hell am I getting into?" I asked myself. "This is no farm."

Then I smelled them. The camels. About thirty-five of them, tethered in a long picket line.

A man emerged from one of the tents and from the enthusiastic screeches of greeting emitted by Abie I knew that this must be the place and that the man could be none other than mine host, Josef.

Tall, rangy and sun-blackened, he was dressed in baggy cotton trousers tucked into soft leather boots. Over this was a long robe with a sash, the whole topped off by a tarboosh worn rakishly tipped to one side. White teeth flashed at me from beneath a very black mustache. I got the distinct impression that he considered himself the very devil of a fellow.

Holding my proffered hand between both of his, he bade me welcome, via Abie, and proclaimed that his poor establishment was mine to do with as I wished.

Hovering about a camel-dung fire as they prepared food were five females. One, about Josef's age, I presumed to be his wife. I was not introduced. The others ranged in age from fourteen to sixteen. I took it for granted they were his daughters. All wore shapeless, groundsweeping skirts, rusty black in color and of rough material. They kept their eyes discreetly averted from me except at times when they felt I wasn't looking.

Josef was a man of direct action. I had been asked there to dine. So, I must dine. Immediately.

Torches were lit, a rug was spread, a cushion was placed and Josef, after indicating that I was to use the cushion, sat crosslegged on the ground. A huge platter of what appeared to be lamb stew with rice was placed on the rug between us, together with a stack of thin, round cakes similar in appearance to Mexican tortillas.

That was it. There were no superfluities such as knives, forks and spoons.

Abie placed himself on the ground a short distance from me and Josef motioned me to begin. Politely, though shuddering slightly, I dug in.

Josef ate monstrously. I, daintily, I fear. I was in constant fear of nausea.

No conversation was attempted. The only sounds were the squeals of the camels, the belches of Josef, the muted chatter of the women and the rumble of my stomach.

The scene, though decidedly picturesque, had overtones of portentous evil and I began vaguely to wonder if my affairs were in decent order. The meal seemed interminable but finally Josef arrived at repletion and signaled the women to take away the remnants which I presumed were to be divided among them and Abie.

I took this opportunity to excuse myself, through Abie of course, pleading fatigue and expressed my appreciation for the delicious meal. Josef was pleased. "I am one of God's favored sons," he replied. And picking up a torch, he led the way to my tent, handed me the torch, bowed and said, via Abie, "If God wills, we shall meet when the sun rises."

Bemused, befuddled and half expecting that at any moment my throat would be cut, I sat on a pile of rugs, the tent's only furnishings, and deliberated. It would have resolved the question very simply had I stepped into my car and left. On the other hand I certainly did not wish to insult the man. Also, in spite of my queasiness, in stomach and in mind, my adventurous spirit exalted in the strange situation and I didn't wish to miss any part of it.

Suddenly, and to my utter astonishment, two of the girls slipped shyly into the tent. They were the youngest of the four. I doubt that either of them was over fifteen.

The meaning of the invasion escaped me completely. They just stood there silently, their eyes downcast. "They're like frightened little gazelles," I thought, and wondered what they wanted of me.

As I was about to call the indispensable Abie to interpret, I remembered Josef's greeting, "My poor establishment is yours to do with as you wish."

"Good God," I thought, "the man is sacrificing his daughters to me."

Appalling but illuminating. My skepticism vanished.

Suddenly the situation had taken on the aura of rare adventure. This was primitive hospitality in the raw. I was strangely touched. At the same time my sense of humor took over. I laughed. To the girls, my laughter spelled acceptance. They laughed with me.

But even though solved, one problem usually begets another. Where was I to take it from there?

Even a child molester could have withstood the charms of these pitiable youngsters. One of them was so lousy I could see her hair move as the critters played hide-and-seek in it. Both smelled exactly like the camels. My only problem was how to get rid of them without offending.

I tried charades. In pantomime I told them of my terrible stomach ache, my overwhelming fatigue and my necessity for immediate rest. My acting was a flop. They just giggled.

Finally I divided the rugs, spread the second pile at the opposite side of the tent, gently pushed them towards it, parked myself on the remaining pile and pretended to sleep.

For a long time I heard them whispering and giggling. Then I really slept.

When I woke it was daylight and they were gone.

Josef had already departed for the camel market but sent greetings, through Abie, assuring me that as long as God willed it, I would walk in the light of his eyes.

But for some strange reason I had lost face with Abie.

The girls, I discovered later, were not Josef's daughters. They were concubines . . .

I'd been away from Hollywood for four, carefree,

stimulating weeks. I returned to bitter disappointment. Not that there was any question of my liberation. I was free all right. Free as a bird. A dodo bird. There were no bidders.

Months passed. Around the major studios my name was synonymous with unadulterated poison. In Hollywood jargon, I was washed up, finished, dead.

Refusing to allow my battered frame to be properly interred, I raucously proclaimed the rumors of my death to be grossly exaggerated. I had but one foot in the grave. The other was set firmly on solid ground. Furthermore, my ears were flattened against my upright hackles, my back was itching, my tail was straight-out against the wind and I was determined not to be driven into limbo by the barbered apes who held sway over the motion-picture industry.

Independent production was virgin territory to me. Provided I was willing to put aside my artistic pretensions and work for mere money, I should be able to remain on the field, garnering plenty of shekels while I thumbed my nose at the enemy.

I instructed my agent to explore the possibilities. The result was flattering. Almost immediately I was up to my hips in submitted scripts. I committed myself to four of them, to be shot during that current year.

Meanwhile, so old acquaintance be not forgot and as a constant reminder that I was still around, I installed a huge sign over a garage which I operated as one of my extra-curricular activities and which was situated directly across the boulevard from the MGM executive offices. In block letters two feet high, the sign extended seventy-five feet across the front of the building, spelling out the name C H A R L E S   B I C K F O R D.

No one looking out from L.B. Mayer's office windows could have missed seeing it.

Perhaps it was coincidental but shortly thereafter MGM announced plans to construct a new administration building. The site? On the opposite side of the studio . . .

For the next ten years I averaged about four pictures annually. A few of these productions were passably good; most of them were just plain lousy. All of them were undistinguished.

But to give credit where it is due, those films were made the hard way. The independent product of that time was excluded from the cartel-controlled theater chains thus limiting the market to the comparatively puny independent exhibitors. The pictures were made on tight schedules with painfully limited budgets and with no major star names. The independents could not afford tremendous publicity organizations and so the glamor process was sadly lacking. Distribution facilities left much to be desired. The pictures and stars had to stand or fall on merit alone.

On the other hand, the major producers, with millions of dollars to work with, the world's greatest acting, writing and directing talent at their beck and call, plus the finest equipment and facilities, giant publicity organizations and world-wide distribution could only on extremely rare occasions come up with a film of genuine merit.

Those struggling little independents had more on the ball than their more fortunate brethren. In retrospect, I salute them.

Considering my theatrical background, my ambition

and my ego, those years spent in the quickie factories should have been horrendous to me. They were not. The work was uninspiring. Scripts were constructed to formula, each story much like another. The difference was in the locales and the names of characters. But even though at times I likened myself to a former derby winner running for hay money at county fairs, I was not unhappy. Under wraps perhaps but still a prospective winner. The years sped by.

One day while I was on the Universal lot playing in "East of Java," a real little melodramatic doozy, my agent appeared on the set bearing welcome news.

An old acquaintance, Darryl Zanuck, now production chief at the Twentieth Century Fox, was about to start production on "The Littlest Rebel," starring Shirley Temple. He was making me a firm offer to play the male lead, the engagement to be the start of a long term contract.

I did not like the necessity of restricting myself to the provisions of a long term deal but curbed my inclination to balk and grabbed the deal.

I was elated. Shirley was the hottest young star since the heyday of the fabulous Jackie Cooper. The picture would be an important one. I was about to make a triumphant re-entry into major production. Or so it appeared.

But fate, or something, took a hand . . .

Years ago when I was a brash kid, I used to believe man held his destiny in his own hands. I have long since rejected that idea. I believe now that we are all victims of accident, lucky or otherwise. Who really knows what lies in wait around the corner?

And what lay ahead for me next is a fair example . . .

Unimportant as it was, the picture, "East of Java," played a vital role in my life. It was a wild-and-wooly action picture in which I was a sea captain. My schooner was carrying a cargo of wild animals—lions, tigers, leopards, big apes and snakes. Also aboard were four passengers—the inevitable boy and girl, a villainous white hunter and a scheming Chinese opium smuggler.

Briefly, the plot was this: During a violent storm, the vessel is wrecked. The passengers, I and most of the animals survive to find themselves cast away on a small uninhabited island.

The girl, a desirable bit, is persecuted by the unholy attentions of both the brutal hunter and the villainous Chinese.

I too have a yen for the lass, but perceiving that true love exists between the young ones, I suppress my own desires and dedicate my efforts to save them from the evil machinations of the bad men, both of whom I am subsequently forced to kill.

Finally, and in proof that my heart was made of twenty-two-carat gold, I sacrifice my life in order that the young lovers escape.

Contrived, melodramatic and utterly unbelievable as this story may sound, it was real enough in the making to come within a cat's whisker of resulting in tragedy for me.

The escape sequence was shot in a back-lot jungle set at Universal studio. The scene represented a desolate spot where the jungle met the sea. In the foreground was a strip of beach, then a tangle of brush extending back to a rocky cliff rising almost perpendicularly sixty feet into the air.

As the action opened, the boy and girl, panting in

exhaustion and running for their lives, appear at the top of the cliff, closely followed by me. With only a burning brand as a weapon, I hold back two ravening lions while the boy and girl make their precarious way down the face of the cliff and to safety.

I make my move but as I am half way down the cliff one of the lions leaps from the top and knocks me to the ground. Other lions close in and after a hopeless fight, I am torn to pieces.

The set was enclosed by a steel fence high enough to ensure perfect safety for the director and crew who shot the action from the outside.

Everything went well enough as the long shots were photographed. The actors, of course, were doubled by stunt-men.

In the closer shots, and particularly the scene involving my fight with the lion on the ground, the use of a double was quite apparent; as the scene was the big dramatic climax of the picture, I, motivated solely by my wish to help the production, volunteered to get in there and play the scene in close-up.

The assistant director objected vehemently, insisting that the risk was too great. Always more fool than angel, I laughed away his concern. The director also pooh-poohed his qualms. "What the hell," he scoffed. "They're trained cats, aren't they? Charlie is right. We've got a chance here to get a spectacular scene. Let's go."

And so the scene was set up. Four cameras were used, two of them to shoot in close-up from two different angles. A rifleman stood ready to shoot in case the cat went savage and when the cameras were ready to roll, I went into the enclosure.

Although this incident occurred nearly thirty years

ago, it's one for which I have total recall. The scene
could not be clearer in my memory had it happened yesterday.

The animal was a magnificent specimen. In the prime
of life, it weighed some four hundred pounds and was
possessed of a beautiful tawny coat and armed with truly
awe-inspiring fangs and claws.

As the gate closed behind me, he came bounding toward me, fangs bared in what was evidently meant to be
a ferocious snarl, a tactic very similar to the mock attacks often staged by my dog, Rocky, in a design to scare
me.

To the beast's astonishment, I reacted exactly as I
would have had he been Rocky. I cooed baby talk to him
and as he stopped an arm's length away, I held out my
hand for him to sniff. For a moment he stood foursquare, his eyes showing nothing but feral glare and his
tail lashing.

Then, I swear, that snarl became a grin. A bit sardonic
perhaps, but nevertheless a grin.

I scratched him gently behind the ears and after a
moment he came close, rubbing himself against my legs.
He capitulated completely and began to purr, exactly like
a great house cat.

I played with that regal creature as one would play
with a dog. Sitting on the ground, I petted him, pulled his
ears, roughed him up and pushed him around, all the
while maneuvering him into proper position for the cameras. When I was flat on my back with the big cat standing over me, I passed the word and the cameras began to
roll.

The only justifiable criticism of that lion's acting was
that he was cast to type. He reacted perfectly to my simu-
lated efforts to fight him away from me, snarling, baring

his fangs and striking at my face with his enormous paws. The scene ended only when the cameras ran out of film. So realistic had been his performance that I was near exhaustion.

Using a hunk of beef, they enticed him to the far side of the enclosure while I made my escape through the gate.

The director was delighted with the scene. I was pleased, and the crew was sufficiently impressed to give me a big hand.

Then the director, poor stupid man that he was, who should never have allowed me to do it in the first place, compounded his stupidity by asking for another take, this one for protection just in case something unforeseen should happen to the film.

I, more culpable even than the director, for it was my life that was at stake, agreed, and we set up for another take.

The action was about the same as before, except that this time as I maneuvered the cat into position, I became aware of a breath-holding tension among the men outside the fence. Realizing that these men were desperately afraid for me, my own imagination began to work and by the time the scene was under way, the aura of fear that pervaded the place had infected me. For the first time since I had involved myself in the foolhardy stunt, I was afraid for my life.

Men whose vocation it is to work with wild animals hold that the beasts are acutely sensitive to fear, that they can actually smell it. I can well believe it. The lion, which up to this instant had been instinctively afraid of me, suddenly regarded me merely as a hundred and eighty-seven pounds of live meat.

His eyes flashed green and with no further ado, he

sank his fangs into my throat and picked me up like a sack of peanuts.

I should like to be able to record that I put up a brave fight and vanquished the critter. I did try. With both fists I punched away at his nose but there was no force in the blows and I was as helpless as a baby as he dragged me toward the thick brush.

The cameras continued to roll as the men stood immobilized and horror-stricken.

First to break the *tableau vivant* was the sharpshooter who, as he maneuvered to get a shot at the lion without endangering me, repeatedly shouted, "Quiet, everybody. And don't move." He could have saved his breath. They were all frozen stiff.

Then, for whatever the reason, the cat dropped me, leaped across my prone body and disappeared into the brush.

Clamping my hand to my mangled neck, from which the blood was spurting in jets, I tried to get to my feet but only made it to my knees. Because of severed nerves, my limbs were twitching and I had no coordination.

All of this happened in less time than it takes to tell it but because of my racing pulse I was seeing everything in slow motion. As I knelt there dying, conscious that the lurking lion might pounce again at any second, my indignation knew no bounds as I waited, seemingly for minutes, for someone to come to my assistance.

No one moved. I began to yell. And despite my condition, my yells were hearty, profane and abusive as I demanded to know when some of the stupid sons-of-bitches were going to open the gate and get me the hell out of there.

A ludicrous note was provided by the director who

unconsciously was repeating, at the top of his voice, every word I uttered.

The men understandingly discounted the abuse and in jig time, three of them, covered by the sharpshooter, entered the enclosure and carried me to a waiting car.

I was speeded to the emergency hospital on the lot and from there to the Hollywood hospital where, forty-five minutes after the accident, I was on an operating table.

The prognosis was bad, but skillful surgery plus my iron constitution pulled me through the operation. During the weeks that followed there were times when the odds against my recovery were ten to one. But I eventually began to mend and went on record as the only actor to place his neck in an angry lion's mouth and live to tell it.

I must say that the Universal studio executives made no insincere gestures, not even to the extent of sending a bunch of lilies. Not that they were unconcerned. They cared very much indeed and inquired repeatedly as to if, and when, I would be able to finish the picture.

And so when the time came for Twentieth Century Fox to start production on "The Littlest Rebel," I was still in the hospital, delayed there by a persistent infection that kept my temperature hovering between a hundred-and-one and a hundred-and-three. Zanuck agreed to shoot around me for a week. When I was unable to deliver myself, he extended the time for a second week. When I was still unable to report, he gave me a third week, this time however with a deadline. If at the end of this third week I was still unfit, he would be forced to recast the role. He was given every assurance that I would be ready.

On the eve of the deadline, I found myself engaged in

a hassle with my doctor who refused to sanction my release because I was running a temperature of a hundred-and-one plus.

When I ridiculed him as an alarmist, he pointed to my still-swollen and unsightly neck and asked, "How in hell do you propose to hide that from the camera? You look like a refugee from a slaughter house."

I snapped back. "Don't pull your bedside charm on me, Doc. It just won't work. And don't worry about your precious reputation as a surgeon. I'll cover for you. I'll camouflage your botched up butchery with an expert makeup job. I'm not jeopardizing that Zanuck contract because of overcaution on your part and whether you like it or not, I'm going to be in that studio at eight o'clock tomorrow morning."

The Doc and I knew each other pretty thoroughly. This wasn't the first time we had gone to the mat and now, seeing that my ears were laid back, he recognized the futility of further argument and reluctantly gave in, stating for the record that I was acting in defiance of his professional advice and stipulating that he, and a nurse, must accompany me.

At eight o'clock on the following morning, the doctor and a uniformed nurse sat in my studio dressing room watching in solemn disapproval as I, weak, feverish and irritable after a restless night, labored industriously to make up the misshapen thing my head rested on into a reasonable facsimile of a healthy neck.

After changing into my costume, I surveyed myself in the full length mirror and was highly pleased by the overall result.

Owing to the fact that my temperature had risen to a hundred-and-two, my vision must have been a wee bit faulty because when I opened the door to the assistant director, who came to call me to the set, the man, after an astonished double-take, turned tail and ran.

I realized he had been shocked by my appearance and that he was on his way to report to the front office. My camouflage was a flop. With mixed feelings of perplexity and angry frustration, I turned back into the room.

The doctor was of no help. "Why don't you give up, Charlie? You scared that guy out of his old-age pension. You really look like death warmed over, you know."

"Whose side are you on?" I snapped. "If you can't say anything constructive, keep your trap shut. It's you who frightened him, you and your assistant cut-up there. You look like a couple of ghouls about to snatch a corpse. You're enough to terrify anybody, for Christ's sake. . ."

He refused to be insulted. Grinning cheerfully, he turned to the nurse. "Check his temperature, Mrs. Carew."

Mrs. Carew, a mustached grenadier of a woman, thrust me into a chair and as she stuck a thermometer into my mouth, the doctor moved up on the other side and proceeded to count my pulse.

This was the charming little scene of unhealth and imminent collapse that met the eyes of Darryl Zanuck as, a moment later, he hurried into the room.

I had already tabbed Zanuck as a man of quick decisions. This one probably established a record, even for him. He threw one horrified glance at me and without breaking his stride turned on his heel and rushed out again, muttering something that sounded like "For God's sake take him back to the morgue."

I didn't get to play the part.

Three weeks later, my vitality almost nil, one side of

my body semi-paralyzed because of severed nerves, a three-inch scar standing out above my collar line like a brand of the Mafia and the prognosis of probable loss of sight in one eye, I departed the hospital.

Destination? Ostensibly, the scrap heap . . .

Thanks to my superb physical condition in general and my stubborn determination to beat the rap, I mended rapidly. Six weeks later, a reasonable facsimile of my former cocksure self, I appeared in person before the equally cocksure Mr. Zanuck and reported myself to be fully recovered, full of vim and vigor and eager to start on my first assignment under the contract.

Mr. Zanuck was also in fine fettle. Evidently he had been playing polo that morning. Still in costume, he looked quite the Pukka Sahib as he strode up and down his impressively enormous office, talking as he walked and emphasizing his points with dramatic swishes of a slender malacca cane. He seemed genuinely pleased to see me in good health, complimented me for bravery over and beyond the call of duty, congratulated me on my quick recovery and castigated me for criminal negligence in doubling for the double. He went all out to show me he really cared.

While I was silently vowing my undying fealty and devotion to his service, he squinted at my indubitably ugly scar and said, his voice quivering with sensitivity, "Of course you're all washed up, you know that."

Quite taken aback, I said, "Huh?"

"That mangled neck. You're through as a leading man."

Narcotized by what I had interpreted as his overwhelming concern for me, I failed to catch. Face to face with my congé I didn't recognize it. Too, it had not occurred to me that my contract may have been cancelled.

"So what?" I countered blithely. "I'd much prefer to play character roles, anyway."

"Fine, Charlie, fine. I'm glad you agree. The contract is right here in my desk. We'll change the date and reactivate it just as soon as I can find the right role to start you off. Meanwhile you're free to accept any outside engagements that may come along. Okay?"

A great light burst over me.

Thanking him for his courteous manner in giving me the finger, I left. And as I strode down the long corridor towards the nearest exit, I muttered to myself, "Up yours too, Mister Zanuck."

Not that I felt any real bitterness toward him. The guy was merely doing his job. Obviously his interest in me had been primarily for the role in "The Littlest Rebel." Because of its hit potential it had seemed a good idea at the time to secure an exclusive on my services. When I failed to deliver the body, his interest had lapsed. Simple.

So I wasn't really mad at anyone. Not even the lion. Undoubtedly he was British and had sensed the Irish blood in me.

Nevertheless it was a bitter pill. And as I swallowed it, I felt kinship with that mythical character, Sisyphus, who was condemned to spend an eternity rolling a heavy rock up a hill, only to have it roll down again each time he neared the top.

Back to the sticks I went. And there, among the never-wases and has-beens, I again put my shoulder to the rock and pushed. And the rock seemed heavier and heavier during the next decade as my career, though active, remained in comparative eclipse. . .

Contrary to Zanuck's ukase I continued to play romantic leads, always, I hasten to add, in unimportant "B" pictures. There was an occasional bid from major studios but never anything of real importance.

And then, suddenly as always, came another red-letter day. A major studio production chief, who for obvious reasons shall be nameless, invited me to lunch with him at his studio. It transpired that he was interested in having me play the male lead in a forthcoming production, the femme star of which was his current light-o'-love.

The lady, a prominent star, joined us at the luncheon table and not being too heavy in the brain department soon made it evident that I was on display for her benefit. The situation did not please me one little bit but knowing that this engagement could be my means of getting that damned rock up and over the crest, I showed her ladyship my best leg while her protector outlined the story to me.

I liked it and expressed my approval.

Gratified, he assured me he would be in touch with my agent forthwith. I was in.

I was so delighted I could have kissed the producer. And that is really saying something. You see, he was one of those Hollywood golf athletes with a face bearing a remarkable resemblance to the sunburned underside of an unripe summer squash.

A couple of days elapsed. My agent, hearing no word from the producer, called upon him at his office only to discover that the deal had collapsed.

Reason?

The lady had balked, declaring that I was much too old to carry her romantic interest.

My immediate reaction to this unkindest cut of all was

violent. I could have found sheer delight in strangling her. Due reflection, however, brought the realization that I must have shaved every morning for the past fifteen or twenty years without looking at anything but the whiskers. My vitality had blinded me to the fact that I was nearing my fiftieth birthday, that it was high time I quit chasing chicks (on the screen, at least) and leave the romance to the pretty boys. My anger cooled. The little glamor-puss was right.

Nevertheless, the revelation knocked me flat on my butt. A new look was indicated. A long, close, agonizing reappraisal.

My Gethsemane was the Grand Canyon which had long been a must item in my mental catalogue of places I must see. There, feasting my eyes upon the glories of that wonderful place, I pondered my professional future for three soul-searching weeks before coming to the wisest decision of my on-again, off-again, Finnegan career.

I resolved that I would play no more romantic leads. Further, I would play in no more independent quickies. I would become a character star. I would accomplish this by playing important character roles in major productions. And if the important roles did not materialize for me, so be it. I would acknowledge my defeat and hang up my sock and buskin. Under no circumstances would I become a dime-a-dozen character bit-actor.

I said a silent prayer for my old friend, Dave Weston, and returned to Hollywood.

Came the drought.

The major producers were unaware that a great character star had arrived in their midst. For an entire year I threw my agent's nose out of joint by refusing even to read scripts proffered by the small studios. His commissions were nil and my bank balance was lean. My only satisfaction was that the income-tax boys could find nothing to grab.

But my patience paid off.

I was in my agent's office on the day it happened. He was talking on the telephone when suddenly I heard the click as his nose snapped back into alignment.

Twentieth Century Fox studio had cast me as Peyremale, Dean of Lourdes, in "The Song of Bernadette."

Thanks to the perspicacity of George Seaton, the writer who recommended me for the role, the understanding and directorial skill of Henry King and the beautifully written, well-rounded character of Peyremale, I was able to push that God-damned rock up to and, this time, over the crest. After the premiere, I was newly discovered and literally overnight leaped into great demand as a character star. The success of this unforgettable production had opened up an entirely new vista for me.

To the little sex pot who had forced my decision, I sent a telegram, "Yours not to reason why, but thank you, my dear."

Since then I've been in many pictures, some of them memorable—"Not As A Stranger," "The Farmer's Daughter," "Johnny Belinda," "A Star Is Born" and "Days Of Wine And Roses."

A few occupy a niche in my memory labelled Superabundant Pseudo Epics That Bombed.

In this category was one to which I committed myself, not because I was in love with the trite story but because it was to have a lavish production, a star-studded cast and a director who was rated nonpareil in the industry—

ingredients which ordinarily should furnish reasonable insurance of box-office success.

My enthusiasm was dampened by one reservation. Thoroughly aware of Hollywood's proneness to worship false Gods, I was not impressed by the reputation of the nonpareil. The director, that is.

Ah, yes! The director . . .

Nearly thirty years had passed since I had last seen him. During that span he had acquired fame, wealth and influence. It couldn't have happened to an unworthier guy.

I did not exclude the possibility that his success was merited, in part at least. Surely, I thought, in order to achieve his position he must have developed some degree of talent. The years must have abraded the rough edges and sharpened his mental faculties. Perhaps, I considered, just perhaps I had misjudged the guy.

And so, with open mind and hopeful heart, I approached the first day of shooting. It was on location in one of California's inland valleys. At seven a.m. the company, made up and ready for action, was assembled on the set which represented a Western town. Built at enormous expense by the production department, it lay in the center of a vast plain, surrounded by low mountains. Designed and constructed by experts, it was perfect in every detail.

The number of people, animals and equipment involved in a top-flight operation such as this makes for costs that would tax the imagination of a CPA. The salaries of the stars alone reached astronomical figures, to which must be added the supporting cast, an army of extras, stunt men, cowboys, horse wranglers, grips, property men, electricians, sound technicians, camera men, makeup men, hairdressers, green men, truck drivers, bus drivers, chauffeurs, production men and assistant directors.

Include the costs of a dozen buses, a fleet of limousines, twenty trucks, fifty horses, a herd of a thousand cattle, the rental of the ranch we were working on, plus the catering service which was there to provide daily hot lunches for two hundred people and it can readily be seen how extremely important it was to take full advantage of every minute in the working day.

At times it can be uncomfortably hot in our inland valleys and on this particular morning the temperature kept pace as the sun rose higher. At nine o'clock it had reached the high seventies and by ten was nearing ninety.

Meanwhile, the cast had been impatiently waiting to be called into action. Enthusiasm was waning. They bombarded the assistant directors with questions. "Why the delay? Why don't we get started? Why were we called here at seven o'clock?"

I had no need to ask. The situation was distressingly familiar.

Out there on the plain, about a half mile distant from the set, a stubby little figure was pacing. Back and forth he went, pausing occasionally to scratch his pointed head as he tried desperately to think.

I knew why he was there. I'd seen the performance before.

He was groping for the answer to a most difficult question: "Where should he set up the camera for the opening shot?"

I found a comparatively cool spot in the shade of a property truck and settled down for a long wait.

Two more hours passed. The heat pressed down over

the valley like a low-lying blanket. The people, two hundred head of them, were by now aware of the farcical situation. A few were amused, many ribaldly contemptuous; the majority were peevish and hungry. It had passed lunch time.

Suddenly there was a stir. The first-assistant-director mounted a horse and rode at a furious gallop toward his master.

With bated breath, the wilted horde watched from the town as the assistant director, yanking his horse to a sliding stop, dismounted and handed the great man a corned-beef sandwich.

A shriek of anguish rent the sky. The hungry multitude, shocked and angered by this cynical display of inconsideration, turned their eyes away. Ignoring the frantic pleas of the assistant directors, they stampeded for the commissary tent.

During luncheon word came that the company was dismissed. There would be no shooting on the Western town set that day. Nor for many a day.

Not that the stubby little fella hadn't reached a decision. He had. Therein lay the difficulty. You see, after choosing a specific spot to set up the camera for the opening shot—about thirty seconds on the screen—he had discovered a certain mountain in the background which disturbed his sense of composition.

Ergo, either the mountain must be eliminated or the town must be uprooted and transplanted a hundred feet to the east.

My judgment was vindicated . . .

The Golem was still—the Golem.

On the following morning we were called to work on a different set. From the beginning it was apparent that

nothing I could do was going to please him. Maybe it was
my own fault. It could have been that my disdain was
showing. Or possibly he had never forgiven me for having forced him onto the road to fame and fortune.

First, it was my costume, which to me was comfortable
and right. For two hours the company waited while he
rummaged in the wardrobe truck, searching for a shirt
and a pair of pants which in his judgment better fitted the
character I was to play.

Next, my makeup. He was insistent that I wear a huge
handlebar mustache. I considered it unsuitable for the
character and refused to wear it. We argued the point.
Hours passed. Finally lunch was called. The entire morning had been wasted.

After lunch he conceded that I was right on both
points, costume and makeup. We rehearsed. All afternoon we rehearsed. It was a two-page scene.

The Golem was running true to form. At the end of
the second day we were two days behind schedule.

The cameras turned on the following morning. We
shot the scene. Again and again and again we shot. The
cast was bewildered; I was infuriated. After the twentieth
take I inquired, "How many more times do you intend to
shoot this scene?"

"Until its right."

"It would help a lot if you told us what is wrong with
it."

"You. You're what's wrong"

"Oh! Well now, that's very interesting. Would you
mind telling me why?"

"You're not playing it right."

"I see. Well, that's clear enough. But if you don't mind
telling me, I would appreciate knowing just what I'm
doing wrong."

"You're not giving me what I want."

Knowing that this scintillating dialogue could continue ad infinitum I decided to end it.

"All right," I suggested pleasantly. "Supposing you step right in here and play the part yourself."

"Don't be ridiculous," he sneered.

"I'm not. Furthermore, I don't intend to be. Now you hear this. I'll play this scene just one more time. That's it."

I'd gotten to him. His face reddened, the color quickly spreading across his forehead and over his bald pate. The obsidian-colored eyes glinted dully as, drawing himself to his full height, he glared up at me.

"I never heard of such a thing," he said.

This unexpected killer-diller of his nearly floored me and for a moment I floundered as I groped for an equally brilliant retort. My quick wit responded and I let him have it.

"Well, you've heard it now," I snapped and turned away. I felt like a guy who had gone hunting for bear and came back with a chipmunk.

As we shot no more takes of the scene, I appeared to be the winner. Not much of a victory, to be sure, but assuming the Golem must have been convinced I was not to be crowded with impunity, I dismissed the incident as water under the bridge. From there on, I decided, I would do my damndest to avoid friction.

My damndest wasn't enough. The stupid oaf was obsessed. For the next ten weeks, the duration of the engagement, he missed no opportunity in his attempts to belittle me.

I retaliated. Naturally.

Refined cruelty I suppose one could term it. Never voicing my disapproval, I managed by looks and gestures to express my supreme contempt of his fumbling efforts to direct.

These tactics proved most effective. There were times when he visibly shook with rage and within a week one of his intimates informed me that I'd driven him into a state of chronic constipation.

Needless to say, this was one engagement I shall always remember with distaste.

But, I must also candidly admit that the finished picture was a good one. And I was genuinely pleased by my contribution to it. No thanks to the Golem.

The film was not good enough, however, to survive the excess cost of making it—a couple of million dollars; all thanks to the Golem.

A few final words anent this exalted jerk. Undeniably he was shrewd. His *modus operandi* consisted of packaging salable merchandise—tested material, successful plays or books, top writers to adapt the stories and box office star names to impress the bankers.

Such wares seldom fail to elicit unlimited financial backing. One cannot fault him for this procedure. Most successful pictures are promoted in the same manner.

Once underway with a production, however, this man, utterly unsure of himself, proceeds to shoot take after take, sometimes up to sixty, of every scene. It needs no stretch of imagination to picture the effect of this fiendish torture upon actors, not to speak of the anguish visited upon the bankers.

Finally, when the production is finished, the miles of celluloid are placed in the hands of an expert cutter who strives to put together a picture.

Trial and error. And sometimes it works. But it is my contention that a normally intelligent child, given the same indulgence, would achieve the same degree of success. Imagine General Motors or United States Steel being operated in that fashion. Lo, the poor stockholders . . .

In direct contrast to that Golem-haunted clambake are my recollections of an engagement which followed on its heels. This one, also boasting a star-studded cast, was directed by a man possessed of a *bona fide* touch of genius, John Huston—eccentric, unpredictable, nonconformist and flouter of the conventions. No criticism intended.

He is also extremely intelligent, loaded with talent and blessed with a personality capable of charming anybody but an income-tax collector.

For reasons known only to God, to the producers and Huston the picture was shot in Durango, deep in the heart of Mexico. Off the main line, the place was not easily accessible either by air or railroad and the company was flown to Mexico City. There they boarded a chartered ship and were flown to a town, the name of which escapes me. From there they were treated to a two-hour automobile ride, finally arriving in Durango more dead than alive.

I escaped this delightful excursion. Flying doesn't agree with me and as I wasn't scheduled to begin work until a week later, I elected to get there the really hard way, by railroad. As this was to be my first visit to that area, I looked forward to seeing the country.

The journey, an inordinately long one, consumed two days and two nights and although it was uncomfortably hot, dusty, monotonous, stinky and at times dangerous, I found it not only interesting but exhilarating. And though not pressing for an encore, I wouldn't have missed it.

It began in the Union Station, Los Angeles, where I boarded the crack Southern Pacific Streamliner which was to take me as far as El Paso, Texas.

I had grown a beard, a real hirsute masterpiece— white, sprinkled with red and bushy. My clothes were homespun, badly fitting and styled *à la* the West of a century ago. The combination constituted my makeup and costume for the picture and I was wearing the clothes which had been custom built for my use in order to rough up the newness and mold them to my contours.

I became aware that my appearance was a bit startling when the Pullman porter, an old acquaintance—we had travelled together before—chuckled slyly as he greeted me. As he ushered me to my room, I said, "Tom, your ivory is showing. What's so funny?"

He laughed heartily. "Mr. Charlie," he said. "If I didn't know you, I'd swear you were old Silk Hat Harry himself." Silk Hat Harry being a comic cartoon character of a former era.

All that can be said of this first leg of the trip is that I wallowed in luxury. The spacious, air-conditioned drawing room, excellent food and flawless service left nothing to be desired. But it was only the prelude.

I left the train at El Paso, carrying my one piece of baggage, a small overnight case. Stepping into a taxi, I directed the driver to take me to a hardware store where I had him wait while I purchased a large wicker laundry basket, two large thermos bottles, a couple of aluminum cups, saucers and plates, a pair of salt and pepper shakers and two each of stainless steel knives, forks and spoons.

The driver was Mexican, about fifty years old and spoke with a marked accent. His pop-eyes and bristling mustache would have qualified him as a perfect stand-in for Jerry Colonna.

He eyed me suspiciously when I emerged bearing my out-sized basket but offered no comment nor assistance, as with some difficulty I maneuvered the basket into the seat beside me.

The next stop was at a super-market where again he waited while I bought milk, crackers, cheese, apples, oranges and a bunch of bananas.

This time my emergence was ignored. Grim and silent, he stared straight ahead. I vaguely wondered what the hell was eating him.

"Now take me to the best hotel," I said, straightaway discovering the answer.

"You're running up a big fare, Mister."

"I know, Jerry, I know. But don't worry about your money. I'm going to stick up the joint."

His eyes rolled.

But he was an excellent driver. During the eight-block drive to the hotel, one eye studied me in the rear view mirror while the other scanned the roadside for a cop. Contrary to my expectations there was no smash-up.

Arrived at the hotel, I instructed him to wait, saying that I'd need him to drive me across the border. His reaction was explosive.

"No! No, Señor, I can't do that. I have to report in. You pay me now."

"All right," I answered, and hauled my unwieldy baggage from the cab. "How much do I owe you?"

"Three dollars and seventy cents."

Stripping a ten dollar bill from a sizable roll I handed

it to him and headed for the hotel coffee shop, saying as I went, "Okay, Jerry. Keep the change but keep your lip buttoned."

At the door I glanced back. He was motionless, his eyes like saucers as he stared after me, the bill still clutched in his hand.

The coffee shop people recognized me at once. Although an eyebrow or two was raised, my incongruous appearance was taken for granted. No questions were asked. No explanation was offered.

I ordered the thermos bottles filled, one with hot coffee, the other with ice water; a variety of sandwiches, an apple pie, a dozen doughnuts and a pound cake. All of this was neatly stowed in my trusty basket, together with my overnight case.

At the restaurant door, grinning from ear to ear as he relieved me of my now hefty burden, was Jerry. It was painfully evident I had bought myself a Man Friday. "How sad," I thought. "He hated and feared me. Now ten bucks makes all the difference."

After crossing the bridge into Mexico, he proved invaluable, first at the bank where I exchanged American currency for Mexican, then at the railroad terminal where my train tickets, passport and visa were not only checked, but questioned. After interminable discussion, Jerry informed me that the department of immigration had entered into the argument, withholding permission for me to proceed until it was decided whether or not I was entering the country as a tourist or as a worker. In the latter case, the department was not about to allow me to steal the bread from the mouths of honest Mexican nationals.

In view of the fact that a permit granting me the right

to work in Mexico for a period of six months had been issued and forwarded to the said department by the Mexican Consulate in Los Angeles, I considered the attitude a bit far-fetched. I was angry and disgusted. My hackles were as stiff as pig bristles.

But remembering where I was, I swallowed my disgust. Arming Jerry with the equivalent of fifty dollars, I instructed him to re-enter the fray and at his discretion use the money to convince the patriotic bureaucrats that I was but a harmless tourist.

Jerry was an excellent negotiator. In jig time we had passed immigration and entered customs.

This should be a breeze, I thought. I was wrong. My unconventional baggage, plus my personal appearance aroused the suspicion of the beggar-on-horseback to whom I was assigned. He insisted that I take every item from the basket for his examination. He declared my food supply as contraband. Pushing it aside on the filthy counter, he motioned me to take the rest of my belongings and scram.

Again Jerry went into action and there ensued a verbal battle which by all the rules should have ended in gunplay. Or so it appeared to me until I saw Jerry slip the bandit a fistful of pesos.

Open sesame. Money, I love it. The bandit helped me repack the food in my basket and waved a gay *adios* as I passed into the train shed.

Peons of every description milled about a train, which, overflowing with passengers, waited the highball to pull out. The scene was colorful, smelly and noisy. A thousand insane parrots would have had a rough time topping the bedlam as a thousand seemingly insane people shrieked their farewells.

It was the train that above everything else excited my interest. I had ridden railroads in many lands, but never in this wide, wide world had I seen its equal in squalid dilapidation.

The day coaches were battered, wooden relics of by-gone days, some of them with great holes gouged in their sides, patched here and there with strips of tin. Obviously years had passed since any of them had been painted or washed. The glass was missing from many of the windows, the openings of which were now glutted by masses of humanity; with each doing its damndest to outscream its counterpart on the platform.

I seemed to recognize the locomotive and tender as specimens I had seen at the Smithsonian Institute in Washington, D.C. In any event, they certainly had seen service on some American line during the Civil War.

The sleepers, three of them as I remember, were distinguishable from the coaches only because the windows were wider and, oh! yes, there was a diner, equally anti-quated, dirtier if that was possible, and the more depressing because of the flowers. On each table was a small vase containing a single rose, an aesthetic touch which only succeeded in accentuating the overall shabbiness.

"Ye Gods.!" I thought. "What an unholy collection of crud buckets." Wrapped in my mantle of smug superiority, I pitied the unfortunate wretches who found it necessary to travel in such degrading fashion.

Suddenly my ears were assaulted. Decrepit as that old iron horse may have been, its whistle, or horn, still had plenty of authority. Echoing from the rafters, the sound was mournfully urgent and poignantly reminiscent of the wail of a calf upon his painful discovery that he has become a steer.

Jerry was galvanized into action. Picking up the basket, he yelled, "Quickly, Señor. We must hurry." Then he ran. At that instant the awful truth smote me. What I had derided as a ridiculous collection of antiquated equipment fit only for the junk heap was, in reality, the luxury flyer on which I had booked expensive accommodations!

For one bad moment I thought of chickening out. But I'm really a brave man. "What the hell," I thought. "A guy has to die sometime." So I took off after Jerry.

A moment later, in the musty confines of my drawing room, Jerry and I bade each other farewell. He was genuinely emotional, affected no doubt by my more than generous tip.

The train had barely pulled out of the station before I was visited by the conductor. His manner was surly, so resentful, in fact, that I fully expected him to say, "Mexicans, *Si—Gringos, No.*" But he uttered no word and after processing my tickets, cast a last suspicious glance at my unconventional baggage and departed.

Close on his heels came the dining-car steward. This one was a charmer. Deferentially polite, he welcomed me aboard in the name of the National Railroads of Mexico, presented me with an elaborate menu and assured me it would be his pleasure to cater to my every desire during the coming day and night.

He too cast a curious eye at my basket as he left. I wondered what his attitude would have been had he suspected what the basket contained.

I have no intention of deprecating Mexican food. It is, in general, excellent. But past experience had taught me that the American gastronomical system, mine in particular, must be acclimated if one is to escape the distressing affliction called *Tourista*. Therefore my stock of provisions. The basket was a convenient throwaway, to be disposed of after use.

Alone at last, I bolted the door against casual invasion and lifted my appalled eyes to my surroundings. It seemed incredible that at one time this cramped space had epitomized the height of travelling luxury. "Barely room to breathe" would have been an apt expression but for the fact that breathing here was difficult, regardless of space.

The upholstery, originally green in color, was now faded, filthy and torn. Through one gaping hole protruded moldy stuffing, the odor from which suggested the proximity of a long-dead 'possum.

The pattern of the carpeting was indistinguishable under a longtime accumulation of chewing gum, sputum, mud, grease, probably blood and only Heaven knows what else.

As for the tiny cubicle one usually dignifies by the word, "toilet", I could only guess what might have been lurking there. I opened that door only once and that but a couple of inches before slamming it quickly shut. The stench emanating from the fearsome place nearly floored me.

It was oppressively hot, one condition I managed to alleviate somewhat by forcing open the windows. Choking clouds of dust and sooty smoke poured in immediately, but by tieing a handkerchief over my nose and mouth, I filtered the air to an endurable degree. Not that I was comfortable but it was a decidedly preferable atmosphere to that deadly miasma which had preceded it.

As it was now past lunch time my always lusty appetite clamored for sustenance. I lunched heartily on two huge steak sandwiches, prime sirloin and wheat bread, both Texan products and a bottle of milk, gazing the while at the seemingly never ending expanse of flat country through which the improbable caravan was pounding. I'll swear every alternate wheel was flat.

Interesting? Exhilarating? I guess only to an incurable romantic like me. I loved the strangeness, the alien landscape—in appearance much like an extension of the Texas plains yet with a subtle difference. It smelled different. Mexico has been called "a land of sudden and violent death." I think that's what I smelled, death. The very dust reeked of it.

Or it could have been that my imagination was working overtime, aggravated perhaps by the occasional sight of animal remains and the omnipresent buzzards.

Pleasant? No! Interesting? Yes!

Came the dusk. The immense plain had been traversed, and the ancient locomotive puffed hugely as, at snail's pace, it edged upgrade into a mountain range. The dust clouds were falling behind; a blessing, but balanced by the fact the smoke became thicker.

"What the Hell!" I thought. "You can't have everything."

Onwards and upwards we ranged, the surrounding country ever more rugged, entering into a great timberland, passing by numerous small streams and occasional picturesque hamlets, the colorful inhabitants of which turned out en masse together with their chickens, dogs and burros to watch us. The magnificant vistas were reminiscent of our own Colorado Rockies. All of this beauty exhilarated me to the extent that I resented the coming of darkness.

When there was nothing to see but black void, I dined
—royally. Combination ham-and-cheese sandwiches on
toast, apple pie, fruit and hot coffee. And, sans dust and
heat. Who could ask for more?

And so to bed. Or let me say that was my intention.

After having the bed made up, I discovered the linen
was soiled and the blankets exuded a peculiar odor,
reminiscent of stale sweat and unwashed feet. I promptly
called the porter back and had him restore the room to
its pristine state of degraded gentility.

Sitting up for the rest of the night entailed no particular hardship. I dozed most of the time, resting better than
if I had attempted to sleep in the filthy bed.

There were a couple of stops made during the night
and it was interesting to sit in darkness, watching and
listening to the activity on the platforms which in both
places were seething with colorful crowds of people.
Primitives mostly, and it was my impression that they
walked hand-in-hand with poverty.

A woman, dressed in rusty black, her skirts brushing
the ground, approached my windows. She was about
thirty, emaciated, cow-eyed, a mantilla covering her head
and shoulders. With her was a little girl about five years
old, chubby and healthy looking.

Addressing the open windows—it was impossible for
her to see me—she rattled off a sentence in Spanish. As I
caught the words, *muchacha, dinero* and *hombre,* I interpreted it as a request for money to buy food for her
hungry child.

I decided to give her of my still plentiful supply of
food and as I reached for the basket, she picked up the
child and held it up to a window, at the same time repeating the request.

I placed a steak sandwich in the child's reaching fist. And as I was about to supplement the donation, the woman, moving as swiftly as a striking rattlesnake, snatched the sandwich from the child's hand and hurled it back through the window, missing me by a whisker. Muttering maledictions, she moved along to try her luck elsewhere.

Retrieving the sandwich, I tossed it to one of the starveling canines with which the place abounded. He devoured it in two gulps, waxed-paper wrapping and all. I couldn't have been more satisfied. If I had a tail, I'd have wagged it in unison with his.

Shortly after sunrise I breakfasted on oranges, bacon-and-egg sandwiches and coffee, and though the eggs were a bit glutinous, the bacon somewhat on the limp side, the toast excessively soggy and the coffee luke warm, everything tasted great. I was happy. In but a few short hours I would write finish to the second leg of this strange journey.

But the few short hours stretched into many long hours. The train pulled into Torreon, my immediate destination, some three hours behind schedule.

And when, carrying my trusty basket, I stepped from the so-called Pullman, unkempt, unwashed, my face blackened from dust and soot, my clothes bearing signs of having been lived in for decades; I was an offense to my own nostrils.

My feeling of exhilaration had vanished. I was tired, bored and angry. My mood was foul.

The trip was far from over. Here at Torreon I must transfer to another troop carrier which, providing I was extraordinarily lucky, would land me in Durango some four or five hours hence. Added to my discomfiture was the discovery that the said carrier had been delayed and that a three-hour layover in Torreon was indicated.

It was when contemplating this delightful prospect that I became aware of one man of the many that thronged the area. He appeared to be circling me at a distance of about ten feet, eyeing me dubiously the while from beneath a ridiculous pork-pie hat.

About fifty years old, he was of sturdy build and looked as tough and brown as a hickory nut. His sharp eyes, clipped mustache and square-toed yellow shoes gave me the impression he might be a police official.

I decided to find out. Smiling at him, I hoped winningly, I nodded and beckoned.

There was no answering smile. Wooden-faced, he advanced to a position about six feet away where, to my astonishment, he removed his hat and bowed.

Unequivocally, this was no cop.

I spoke up.

"What can I do for you, Señor?"

This time he grinned, disclosing a set of glistening brown teeth.

"Señor Beekfort?" he asked, tentatively.

"Yes," I answered. "I'm Señor Beekfort, all right. Or what there is left of him."

My acknowledgment delighted him. The leathery face split again in what I now interpreted as a derisive smirk.

"Jesus!" he said.

Well now. Admittedly my appearance was bizarre. And no one could have been more aware than I that my aura was highly suggestive of recently de-hibernated bear. But to have it thrown in my face by this total stranger . . . I was ripe for violence.

Then he rattled off a long sentence of which I understood exactly nothing. At the same time he grabbed for my precious basket.

I'm happy to be able to relate that I didn't belt him. I simply pinned him with a half-nelson whereupon he loosed a staccato volley of Spanish, of which I distinguished two words, Señor and Huston. I immediately released him.

At the same time, a passing samaritan entered into a short dialogue with him, afterwards interpreting to me.

The suspicious character's name was Jesus Delgado and he had been sent by a Señor Huston to meet my train and to drive me to Durango by automobile. His feelings had been badly bruised. The rugged exterior masked a very gentle spirit, but he graciously accepted my contrite apology conveyed via the kindly interpreter. With an air which proclaimed the end of any further nonsense he picked up my basket, motioned me to follow and took off.

"This," I thought, "could be the beginning of a perfect relationship. He speaks no English. I speak no Spanish. No communication—no arguments. Complete rapport."

And so began the third and last leg of this ill-advised journey. The car was a small coupe of American make. The highway was unpaved and badly in need of repair. Jesus' driving was unspeakable. He seemed to be subjecting the car and me to some sort of endurance test. At speeds between eighty- and ninety-miles-an-hour we slewed, rattled, skidded, squeaked, shuddered and bumped, shrouded the while in a cloud of dust raised by our own passage.

With the car windows closed because of the dust, the

temperature was furnace hot. I couldn't have been more uncomfortable, and as the minutes passed the more certain I became that we were headed for disaster. I tried to get the idea across to Jesus, pantomiming frantically for him to slow up.

Then it happened.

Wham!

The right front tire blew. Slewing violently to the right, the car left the road, plunged down a slight declivity, smashed through a barbed-wire fence and plowed some thirty feet into a field, dragging a section of fence after it.

For a long moment we sat, the dust settling about us, recovering from the shock of finding ourselves alive. Then Jesus turned to me and summed up the situation brilliantly.

"Sheet!"

"You sure said a mouthful," I agreed and a moment later upon discovering that he carried no spare, I doubled him in spades. "I didn't know you had it in you," I said, admiringly.

He did have a repair kit, however, and rejecting my offer to help, lost no time in getting to work.

Bisecting the field at a distance of about a quarter of a mile was a line of shrubbery, possibly an indication of a stream.

"*Aqua?*" I asked, fluently.

"*Si, señor,*" was the delightful answer, "*El Rio.*"

Hesitating only to grab up my overnight case, I ran for it.

El Rio was narrow, shallow and murky. Its water probably harbored amoebic monsters of every description, but to me at that moment it was *Aqua Puro,* crystal clear and cool as the soothing hands of angels.

For half an hour I revelled in it, my morale strengthening by the minute. Fresh underthings and a clean shirt completed the restoration, and brimming with *joie de vivre* I emerged from the fringe of shrubbery.

Meanwhile, back at the car Jesus was receiving visitors.

There were three horsemen, picaresque in their enormous sombreros, and armed to the teeth. Two of them sat their horses while the third investigated the contents of the car. Resenting this unauthorized probe into my belongings, I yelled, demanding that they keep their sticky fingers off my property.

All three turned to look, first at me then at each other, and laughed. My hackles rose.

The man afoot, after handing something up to each of the others, mounted and the three started in my direction, walking their horses.

I marched to meet them and as the distance between us lessened, I saw that they were hard-eyed, vicious-looking and altogether as sinister a trio as I'd ever laid eyes on.

"Oh, oh!" I thought, "Goodbye, Charlie."

But without favoring me with as much as a glance they rode past me and on, each of them munching a banana.

My anger fading, I watched them out of sight then rejoined Jesus at the car. "*Los hombres.*" I asked. "*Quien es?*"

"*Banditos,*" was his unconcerned reply, his tone indicating that banditry was a way of life in that area.

Ludicrous as this episode was, I think it is safe to assume that the shabby little car, my strictly-from-poverty luggage and my personal resemblance to Silk Hat Harry had convinced the sinister trio that I was not worth the effort to rob or to kidnap. Otherwise I might still be languishing in the wilds of Durango, waiting for someone to ransom me.

Jesus had done a remarkable job on the gutted tire and while he was mounting it, I examined the other three. All of them were worn as smooth as a baby's butt, the fabric showing in places.

Suddenly the whole bit struck me as hilarious. The unbelievable train, Jesus and his speed-merchant driving, the blown tire, the banana-stealing bandits and now the prospect of driving another hundred miles of bad road on paper-thin tires. I laughed.

Jesus, uncomprehending but *simpatico,* laughed with me. He didn't know, of course, that he'd just been demoted as chauffeur.

Driving at a maximum speed of forty miles an hour, avoiding the deepest holes and the larger rocks, we arrived in the environs of Durango without further mishap and I turned the wheel back to Jesus.

No longer *simpatico* and disgusted at what must have seemed to him old-womanish driving, he took off through the teeming city like a turpentined mule.

The mad dash was brought to a dead stop at an intersection where we were about to turn into the boulevard which led to our destination. A parade was passing, a funeral parade.

A revered churchman—an archbishop, I believe—was being borne to his final resting place and crowds of people lined the streets to watch.

In the vanguard trudged a group of about fifty little girls, all dressed in white. Then came the body of the deceased, lying in state on a catafalque which in turn was borne on a stake truck, evidently by courtesy of the Excelente Cement Company.

Next in line was a group of nuns, followed by a panel truck from which a voice loudly chanted in Latin over a public address system.

Bringing up the rear was a line of fourteen assorted trucks and cars, all late models, all scrupulously clean and all bearing the proud evidence that they were the property of Coca Cola.

Very sad.

Ten minutes later I said *adios* to Jesus before my two-bungalow reservation at the Campo Mexico motor court. Clean, modern and comfortable, the two little buildings would function as my castle for the next ten weeks.

Here also, extending a quarter-mile into a ten-acre meadow, was a semi-circular line of thirty bungalows, identical to mine and all occupied by members of our company.

And what a congenial lot they were. A nice bunch; so nice in fact that I find it difficult to write about them. It's much more fun to write about nasty people. Not that they didn't have their individual peccadillos, or eccentricities. Don't we all?

One of our character stars, Lillian Gish, was talented, possessed of a brilliant mind and blessed with a delightful sense of humor; she is the only character woman I have ever met who was never boresome. To the contrary, she was treasure trove.

Then there was the dedicated little virgin. Attractive, voluptuous and gay, she dearly loved to smooch. But when pressed too hard she would involuntarily enter into a series of violent belches. It had to be a persistent suitor indeed who came back for a second try.

There was another one—young, attractive and virginal. She also liked to play with fire. Around her neck she wore a thin gold chain with a pendant crucifix. Whenever the going got rough, she would thrust the crucifix before the astonished suitor's eyes and plead dramatically, "Please! I beg of you, in His name. No."

I understand that it worked. Either the guy laughed himself out of the mood or he got religion. I know that John Huston took her dancing one night, then went to early mass every morning for the following week.

Then there was the young war hero. He always carried a rifle and while driving back and forth to locations amused himself by shooting little birds from the speeding car.

This hero was involved in one quite dramatic incident. A boat he was in capsized in deep water and it turned out that he couldn't swim, being from Texas. So a lady photographer who happened to be in the vicinity plunged in and had him latch onto her brassiere while she towed him ashore.

And to our talented and gracious little top star, Audrey Hepburn, I quite lost my heart. If I attempted to express my true feelings, I fear she would emerge as something not quite mortal. So I'll settle by stating simply that she was a lovely lady—one of the few in the profession who really is blessed by that intangible quality a great star must have. Magic, I call it.

To balance the scales for that little lady's lack of peccadilloes, I offer myself. In the beginning I was considered the number one, dyed-in-the-wool, hundred percent eccentric. My two bungalows, for instance, one for general living, and the other for cooking and eating. I had a huge American refrigerator installed in the latter. It also had various cooking utensils, including four electric burners. Once a week I had prime meats, fresh eggs, milk, cream, butter, bread, fresh vegetables, fruit and bottled water flown in from El Paso, Texas.

I did my own cooking. During the entire time I was there not one morsel of Mexican food nor one drop of Mexican water crossed my lips. It was not at all surprising, therefore, to find myself the object of much good-natured ridicule.

But as the days went by, most of the scoffers, one by one, fell victim to the bug I was so successfully avoiding. Then it came to pass that I was looked upon, not as an eccentric but as a great and wise man. Unashamedly, casual callers began to drop by at meal times. The local merchants began to do a land-office business in kitchen utensils and electric appliances. The motel maintenance man began to spend most of his waking moments replenishing blown fuses and my name became a dirty word to the motel proprietor.

And now before I leave Durango, forever I hope, a few final words about the flamboyant, vital, cultivated, sensitive and lonely John Huston. Genius, or intellectual gangster, he may be. He has been called both. I found him the kind of guy I would like to have as a friend. I can pay him no greater compliment.

I have only one beef about him, and it is this: he has discovered that he is an excellent character actor, with the result that now, whenever a juicy character role turns up in a picture he is about to direct, the lousy rat fink casts himself in it . . .

There are many other pictures that come to my mind and a vast number of actors. Star, featured player, journeyman actor; you name him—I've probably played with him. Some of them have passed on, others have retired, many are still going strong. A few occupy a notch in my memory labelled sons-of-bitches, others hold my respect and admiration for their artistry. A handful, I liked.

And although I cannot claim to have been loved by any of them, some regarded me with liking, a few with affection; some detested me. Most of them, I think, respected me as a player and person of integrity.

I also have recollections, fond and otherwise, of many producers and directors of whom I omit mention because they had no important bearing upon my career. My intention has been neither to attack nor to defend Hollywood itself. It owes me no more than I owe it.

Nor am I mad at anyone. Not even the Golem. Nor the giant corporation which backs most of his pictures and which, since my last go-around with him has cast a black ball every time my name has been submitted for casting. I say to them, and in complete serenity, "The Devil rest you, merry gentlemen and to hell with you."

Actually, barring the inevitable pockets of resistance due to inherited hates and corporation files—like elephants, corporation men never forget an injury, either real or fancied—my career has been amazingly tranquil for the last fifteen years.

The most powerful of my former enemies are no longer around to harass me. Too, Hollywood has undergone a revolution of sorts. The major studios no longer control distribution. Since the government anti-trust action divorcing them from the theaters, they no longer enjoy an iron-clad monopoly. Consequently the creative field is open to competitive production.

The industry has entered into an era of package deals and independent production. It is a situation which, although chaotic and unnecessarily messy because of the infestation of fast-buck purveyors of sex, horror and gimmick shockers, is developing a handful of talented young producers and directors who possess a kind of imaginative magic which promises to supply the answers to those of us who dream of doing worth while things in the drama.

Happily this new breed's interest in talent is creative rather than destructive, making it no longer necessary for me to maintain twenty-four-hour alert . . .

From time to time during my career, young hopefuls have called upon me for help and guidance. I have encouraged a few and probably enraged many. For what they are worth, I offer a few words of gratuitous advice to any youngster about to plunge into show business . . .

Acting, whether one chooses to call it a profession, a secondary art form or a refuge of sorts for those who have no trade, truly offers a most precarious method of earning a living.

Let the glamour-struck tyro remember that only the successful are publicized and they are comparatively few. Thousands that you never hear about fall by the wayside.

Ponder that well.

Then, if you decide upon acting as a career you must be prepared to travel a long and treacherous road. It takes a lot of patience to become great at anything, but acting requires much more. You must have courage, perseverance, stamina and the ability to shrug off the rebuffs, discouragements and the real hardships you are bound to encounter during many years of hard training.

You must study, work hard and grab at every opportunity, remembering at all times that you are but one of thousands engaged in a savage fight for survival in a highly competitive field where no holds are barred.

If you endure, if you last long enough to learn how to act and are extraordinarily personable, busting out all over with sex appeal, unbelievably talented or very, very lucky, then you may finally find yourself among the chosen few.

Cynical words? Not really. Blunt, perhaps, but honest and written by one who has been through the mill. More than half a century has passed since my high-flying debut at Oakland, California; more than fifty years of hard work, hard play and constant fighting, not only for survival but for what I believe in.

Make no mistake. I love show business, in my fashion; and with my head held high, my eyes to the sun and my thumb still pressed firmly to my nose, I'm still in there pitching. And despite the golems and a few power-mad tycoons I'm busy with new scripts, new productions and exciting new ventures.

"Protect yourself in the clinches," I always say.

Up the rebels . . .